The European Tour
Yearbook 2012

OFFICIAL PUBLICATION

Turf Equipment and Irrigation Solutions

The leader in golf.

visit www.toro.com/golf

ST ANDREWS LINKS
SUPPLIER

EUROPEAN TOUR
OFFICIAL SUPPLIER

EGCOA
EUROPEAN GOLF COURSE OWNERS ASSOCIATION
PREFERRED SUPPLIER

TORO. Count on it.

CONTENTS

Severiano Ballesteros was the inspiration behind The European Tour. We continue to mourn his loss, but were blessed to have lived in his era. Seve encouraged others to reach for the stars and, in 2011, European Tour Members enjoyed a second successive season of phenomenal achievement by again winning three Major Championships and also dominating the World Number One position. All this and more is chronicled in our European Tour Yearbook; we hope you enjoy this very special publication.

George O'Grady CBE
Chief Executive, The European Tour

ACKNOWLEDGEMENTS

Executive Editor
Mitchell Platts
Deputy Executive Editor
Scott Crockett
Production Editor
Frances Jennings
Editorial Consultant
Chris Plumridge
Picture Editors
Andrew Redington, Rob Harborne

Art Direction
Tim Leney, Andrew Wright
TC Communications Ltd
Print Managed by
Peter Dane
Mark Baldwin
The Print House Ltd

The European Tour Yearbook 2012
is published by The European Tour, Wentworth
Drive, Virginia Water, Surrey GU25 4LX.
© The European Tour.

Six of the Best

You can dig intensely into scholastic history but in European golfing terms, this phrase only came to the fore for the first time in 2011. Put elementarily, Charl Schwartzel (Masters Tournament), Rory McIlroy (US Open) and Darren Clarke (The Open Championship) followed Graeme McDowell (US Open), Louis Oosthuizen (The Open Championship) and Martin Kaymer (US PGA Championship) into golfing folklore and, by so doing, completed six successive victories by European Tour Members in the Major Championships.

European Tour Members have long been at the forefront of educating the world to the finer aspects of a game that is fascinating, exhilarating, exasperating and, most importantly, played everywhere by people of all ages. In 2011, The Race to Dubai on The European Tour International Schedule visited 29 destinations where 52 tournaments were played on a plethora of magnificent courses, all offering challenges unique in character.

The Major Championships, of course, remain the Holy Grail of the Royal and Ancient game, but the Official World Golf Ranking has, since its introduction 25 years ago, provided tangible evidence of the most authoritative and talented hands in the kingdom of the sport.

Therefore irrefutable proof of the worldwide dominance of European golf was borne out by the examination papers submitted by Luke Donald, Martin Kaymer and Lee Westwood. In 2011 they were indisputably the Head Boys who dominated the Number One berth.

Westwood started the year on that noble perch, Kaymer succeeded him; Westwood then repossessed the prized position before Donald claimed control. He stayed there for 30 weeks and will start 2012 as the Number One golfer in the world.

This, then, was a season so sublime, so engagingly structured and so unquestionably European, that even the most parsimonious of schoolmasters would have found difficulty in not only awarding a gold star to all of these golfers, but also admitting that the class of 2011 had, perhaps, excelled even the supreme achievements of those of 2010.

What is beyond contradiction, however, is that The European Tour ended its first 40 years with the two greatest seasons in its history.

EUROPEAN TOUR MEMBERS' DOMINANCE OF THE OFFICIAL WORLD GOLF RANKING
(From October 2010 to December 2011)

WESTWOOD 31.10.10 – 20.02.11 (17 weeks) and 24.04.11 – 29.05.11 (5 weeks), 22 weeks in total.

KAYMER 20.02.11- 24.04.11, 9 weeks in total.

DONALD 29.05.11 onwards, 31 weeks in total.

NB: Donald will start 2012 as World Number One.

All this, too, without The Ryder Cup being on the agenda in 2011.

Not that it is far from anyone's thoughts with the new European captain José María Olazábal already immersed in concentration as he ponders his strategy ahead of the defence of the trophy at Medinah Country Club on the outskirts of Chicago in September. The much respected Davis Love III will lead the United States team, providing another enthralling week when the world will focus on a sport which continues to prosper.

Rory McIlroy, of course, continued to showcase his own stupendous skills by eclipsing one record after another en route to winning the US Open at Congressional Country Club. Furthermore, in 2011, we unearthed additional confirmation of the fountain of youth spawning dynamic challengers, all determined to follow in his footsteps.

Matteo Manassero

The joy that Matteo Manassero evoked by winning in 2010 was magnified when, before his 18th birthday, he gained a second European Tour title in Malaysia. Then along came Tom Lewis to caress fame at The Open Championship – his opening 65 was the lowest score by an amateur in 151 years of the event – and to consummate it by winning on The European Tour International Schedule in Portugal on only his third professional appearance.

Nevertheless, in reviewing The 2011 European Tour International Schedule we must start with the Joburg Open in January. It was where Charl Schwartzel launched his year with a successful title defence, helped greatly by a second round 61. Confidence is key to a golfer's spirit, and Schwartzel underscored that at the Masters Tournament. Never before had European Tour Members held all four Major Championships at the same time, but Schwartzel changed all that with an electrifying four-birdie finish to his final round at Augusta National. The European Tour 'Grand Slam' was in the bag, but there was more, much more, to acclaim.

Next it was Rory McIlroy's turn to make capital on the outskirts of Washington DC in June. Twelve months earlier his fellow Northern Irishman Graeme McDowell had ended a 40 year wait by becoming the first British winner of the US Open since Tony Jacklin in 1970. Now McIlroy was saluted as he won his first Major with a record score and by an astonishing eight shot margin. Records tumbled during four rounds of breath-taking golf which inspired youngsters in every corner of the globe to scurry to their local course in search of imitating the new kid on the block. There is nothing quite like a 22 year old with a spring in his step and a smile on his face to energise an expectant audience.

L-R: Rory McIlroy, Darren Clarke and Charl Schwartzel

Then again, there is nothing like a sportsman adored for his talent and tenacity and admired for his ability to overcome adversity to bring not just one nation, but the whole world together. Darren Clarke achieved that amid scenes of glorious jubilation and celebration at Royal St George's in July, moving everyone to the edge of their seats as they cheered him every step of the way to Open Championship immortality. Clarke, who won the Iberdrola Open in Mallorca in May, was, at 42 years and 337 days, the oldest Open Champion since Roberto de Vicenzo in 1967. Even teetotallers and tobacco antagonists alike could not fail to be smitten as he celebrated with his trademark pint of Guinness and a huge Cuban cigar.

Luke Donald

Six of the best might have become 'The Magnificent Seven' in August but American Keegan Bradley thwarted that magic number by winning the US PGA Championship. Nevertheless, Clarke had notched the 43rd Major Championship triumph by a European Tour Member since Seve Ballesteros so proudly won in 1979 The Open Championship at Royal Lytham and St Annes where the Claret Jug will next be presented in 2012.

That, of course, will be another poignant reminder of the loss to the world of golf in 2011 of Seve, the inspiration behind The European Tour, for it was on those famous Lancashire links that the dashing

José María Olazábal and Davis Love III

Spaniard won two of his three Open Championships.

Lee Westwood, whose own tribute to Ballesteros included the words; "We have lost an inspiration, a genius, a role model, a hero and a friend," linked the two greatest years in the history of The European Tour by closing 2010 as the Number One player in the Official World Golf Ranking and starting 2011 in that position.

He remained at Number One for 17 weeks in total before Martin Kaymer ascended to the summit in late February. Westwood regained the honour for five weeks, consolidated by his win in the Ballantine's Championship in Korea, before Luke Donald grasped the baton with his win in the BMW PGA Championship, The European Tour's flagship event, where he beat Westwood in a play-off on a dramatic afternoon on the West Course at Wentworth Club.

In any momentous year there are defining moments and for Donald, this was one. He had followed in the footsteps of a roll call of champions who had held the coveted Number One position – Bernhard Langer, Seve Ballesteros, Greg Norman, Sir Nick Faldo, Ian Woosnam, Fred Couples, Nick Price, Tom Lehman, Tiger Woods, Ernie Els,

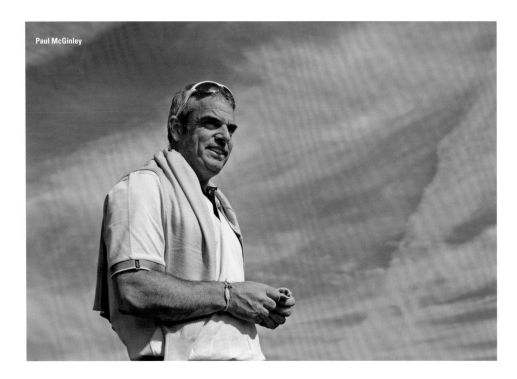
Paul McGinley

David Duval, Vijay Singh, Lee Westwood and Martin Kaymer.

Donald launched his annus mirabilis in the resounding manner of a true champion. He won the World Golf Championships – Accenture Match Play Championship, overcoming Kaymer in the final. His win in the BMW PGA Championship three months later catapulted him to the top of the world and he consolidated that by capturing the Barclays Scottish Open at

Castle Stuart Golf Links in July. By now he was also heading The Race to Dubai which he would secure at the season-ending Dubai World Championship where he became the first player in history to officially finish the leading money winner on both The European Tour and the US PGA Tour in the same season. He earned a record €5,323,400 for finishing first on The Race to Dubai and $6,683,214 for being top of the US PGA Tour money list after winning the season-ending tournament in Florida with a closing 64.

European Tour Members have enjoyed halcyon days in the past in terms of the World Rankings – Ian Woosnam, José María Olazábal, Sir Nick Faldo, Seve Ballesteros and Bernhard Langer held the top five positions on March 1, 1992 – but there would be a truly landmark moment on May 18, 2011, when Members held six of the top seven places with Westwood, Kaymer and Donald first, second and third while McDowell, McIlroy and Paul Casey occupied fifth, sixth and seventh.

The global influence of The European Tour is well recognised. In total no fewer than 38 countries have hosted competition on The European Tour International Schedule and players from no fewer than 35 countries have become Tour champions. The year of 1971

Tom Lewis

Alex Noren and Sergio Garcia

marked the birth of The European Tour and by the end of the 40th season there had been no fewer than 398 champions.

If Belgium had good reason to celebrate Volvo China Open champion Nicolas Colsaerts becoming their country's first winner since Phillipe Toussaint in 1974, then Denmark could equally hail the resurgence of Thomas Björn who, like Donald, won three times. The popular Chairman of The European Tour Tournament Committee captured the Commercialbank Qatar Masters presented by Dolphin Energy, the Johnnie Walker Championship at Gleneagles and the Omega European Masters, and set a special record by becoming the oldest player in Tour history – at 40 years and 198 days –to achieve back-to-back wins in the latter two events.

In winning the Masters Tournament, Schwartzel gained the 98th win by players

from South Africa before Thomas Aitken made it 99 in the Open de España and Garth Mulroy brought up the 100 with a win in the Alfred Dunhill Championship appropriately enough in South Africa in November. Donald, however, led English players to 14 wins in total, thus reinforcing their position as the provider of most victories (271) by one country.

Spain, for whom Pablo Martin, Alvaro Quiros and Pablo Larrazábal were champions in the first half of the year, remained in second place with 163 wins following the wondrous and welcome return to form later in the season of Sergio Garcia with back-to-back victories in the Castelló Masters and the Andalucia Masters, two weeks prior to Gonzalo Fernandez-Castaño winning the Barclays Singapore Open and Quiros triumphing in the Dubai World Championship presented by DP World.

Thomas Björn

However, if one country had bragging rights in 2011 it was surely Northern Ireland with McIlroy and Clarke's summer of Major success being bookended by Michael Hoey's wins in the Madeira Islands Open and the Alfred Dunhill Links Championship. Clarke and Hoey were two of nine players to each win two titles on The 2011 Race to Dubai – Simon Dyson, Alex Noren, Garcia, Kaymer, McIlroy, Quiros and Schwartzel being the others.

In terms of longevity Paul McGinley, who led Great Britain and Ireland to victory in the Vivendi Seve Trophy against Jean Van de Velde's Continental Europe, and Phillip Price both made their 500th appearances, while Thomas Aitken, Keegan Bradley, Nicolas Colsaerts, Oliver Fisher, Tom Lewis, Joost Luiten, Garth Mulroy, Lee Slattery, Robert Rock, Nick Watney and Matthew Zions were all first time winners on The 2011 European Tour International Schedule, setting a target for the graduates from the 2011 European Challenge Tour led by England's Tommy Fleetwood.

Michael Hoey

Intriguingly, four French players were among the 20 graduates in a year when France was announced as the Host Nation for The 2018 Ryder Cup. In fact Benjamin Hebert earned automatic elevation to The European Tour by winning three times – a feat matched by England's Sam Little – while Edouard Dubois, who triumphed twice, Julien Quesne and Charles-Edouard Russo subsequently followed.

The European Senior Tour visited no fewer than 16 destinations while Peter Fowler's renowned work ethic was richly rewarded as he pipped England's Barry Lane in the tussle for the John Jacobs Trophy awarded to the winner of the Senior Tour Order of Merit.

Elsewhere, Carl Mason won twice in Spain – the country where he secured his first European Tour win in 1994 – to claim a record 25 European Senior Tour titles.

All these spectacular achievements and much more are chronicled chapter by chapter in this, the 24th edition of the Official Yearbook which celebrates and rejoices the global landscape on which Members of The European Tour continue to ply their trade. They do so with such formidable skill that newcomers the world over are so captivated by the game, they cannot resist the challenge of following in the footsteps of giants.

Mitchell Platts

Simon Dyson

The Quiet Man

Small moments viewed by few sometimes lead to momentous days watched by many. So it was for Luke Campbell Donald in the spring of 2011 and the week of the BMW PGA Championship at Wentworth Club.

Before the golf began, however, there was The European Tour Players' Awards Dinner to attend. Black-tied and glittering, it is a dinner for winners and so Donald was among the most honoured of guests that evening at the Sofitel Hotel which all but embraces the runway at Heathrow's Terminal Five.

Already he had won the World Golf Championships – Accenture Match Play Championship and this wonderful triumph in the Arizona desert, along with a flurry of other top ten finishes, had elevated him to Number Two in the Official World Golf Ranking. Sitting on an adjoining table that evening in May was the only golfer ahead of him, Lee Westwood.

Part-way through the dinner Westwood ambled over to say hello. On the way he took off his tie. Donald raised a quizzical

eyebrow at his compatriot's sartorial decision and asked politely if it was okay to remove ties? Westwood smiled and said: "When you're Number One, you can do what you want!"

It was a typical, brisk piece of Westwood humour. The Worksop man was in good spirits that night and enjoying his position among his peers. Everyone laughed out loud, including Donald.

Five days later the two men were close again, this time in a play-off for the BMW PGA Championship itself. For The European Tour it was a dream scenario, the two highest-ranked golfers duelling face-to-face for the flagship title. Delicious spice was added by the fact that whoever won would be the top ranked player in the world. High stakes indeed.

Perfection in Bespoke Silver

THOMAS LYTE

This handcrafted sterling silver putter, inspired by an antique golf club, was presented to the Celtic Manor Resort by Colin Montgomerie on behalf of the European Team at the Ryder Cup in 2010.

Discover more at thomaslyte.com

Donald's wedge shot to the reconstructed 18th green of the West Course was inspired, his pitch thudding into the turf a few feet from the flag and obediently staying there. Westwood's own effort looked almost as good until the spin kicked in and his ball zipped back off the green and into the water. Game over, title won, and Luke was Number One.

Now here we are, several months later, and Donald is still Number One in the world. He is also, of course, the first player in history to officially top the money lists on both sides of the Atlantic in the same season. The manner of his play during the Dubai World

With wife Diane, daughter Elle and new arrival Sophia Ann

Championship, where his European coronation was confirmed, neatly summed up his whole season – determined, committed and, ultimately, vibrantly resourceful. Rory McIlroy, the player he beat to The Race to Dubai title, paid his rival a glowing tribute. "Luke deserves to be number one in Europe, number one in America and number one in the world. He has played great golf this year."

It is an extraordinary set of achievements for a player whose slight physical stature flies in the face of the current wisdom that the bigger you are, the better you are likely to be at golf.

Walter Hagen once suggested that if you showed him "a man with big hands, big feet and little in the way of brains," then he would show you a champion golfer. It remains an intriguing comment from the great man but the happy fact is that Donald fails the Hagen test on all counts.

He is five feet nine inches tall, with hands and feet to match, and he clearly has a more than adept brain. One good enough to take him, as an amateur, on a scholarship to Northwestern University in Illinois where he studied art and developed the skills as a painter that he still uses to relax, even if the time he used to devote to the canvas is now more limited as he works at being a good husband and father.

Success in life, as in golf, is often decided by how you perform in the moments that matter.

Moments like holing the winning putt in a Major Championship or donating that extra euro that could help vulnerable children to get the love, care and support they need to fulfill their potential, can all make a difference.

In 2011 Genworth's Putts4Charity, in partnership with the Tour Players Foundation reached a milestone of over €850,000 raised since 2007, for children in need. Moments like these don't come around every day, so we made it count.

For more information on Putts4Charity and the charities we support, visit
www.genworth.com/putts4charity

Daniel Josefsson from Genworth presents a cheque to Henrik Stenson for helping us reach the €750,000 milestone at the Nordea Scandinavian Masters in 2011

Total Funds Raised Since 2007

€ 750,000.00

Home is now Chicago and a vividly contrasting environment to a childhood spent in the heart of the Home Counties and an English education that was completed at the Royal Grammar School in High Wycombe. Although his father Colin hailed from Stranraer in Scotland, Donald was always quintessentially English.

His understated approach to life, his quiet determination to succeed and his instinctive good manners appeal to those who like to picture their Englishmen stepping out of the pages of a Graham Greene novel. Never, however, underestimate the steely ambition of the quiet man. Just because Donald does not shout does not mean he is anxious not to be heard.

"Yes, I'm sure people see me as quiet and someone who keeps things to himself a little bit," he said. "I might be quiet but there's a lot of fire inside me and hopefully people see that sometimes. As a golfer I guess I'm classified as an old-fashioned player because I like to shape the ball. A lot of the guys hit it forty yards past me so I have to rely on all parts of my game firing if I'm going to win. There are other ways to make birdies other than bombing 350 yard drives. I pride myself on a good short game. I work very hard at it."

Truth is, he always has worked very hard. A stellar amateur career – during which he became the NCAA individual champion, breaking Tiger Woods' scoring record along the way, as well as starring in consecutive Walker Cup victories – has been inevitably followed by a professional journey that has brought him a plethora of plaudits and, to date, around €30 million in official prize money alone.

There has, however, been some criticism, most notably a couple of years ago when an American journalist wrote in a British newspaper about a player that he considered was suffering from "the Luke Donald disease," a malaise that meant he was happy to coast along picking up big cheques without ever winning.

"Yes, that upset me," he admitted. "It was a poor article by a journalist who had

The winning 2001 Walker Cup team

never met me. Fair enough if you want to criticise that I haven't won enough – I'm the first to criticise myself on that score – but to say it's down to not having the desire or the work ethic, or that I don't really care about winning, was ridiculous. He should have come and watched me practice. If he'd seen me work he might have written that article differently."

It is a fair riposte to an unfair criticism but then Donald is equally sanguine when tackled about the absence of a Major Championship on his curriculum vitae. The fact is that his performance in these anointed weeks has not reflected either his ability or his standing in the game.

"I probably should have won a Major by now," he told one inquisitor. "I haven't had too many great chances but I'm getting closer and would love to win one. I've always wanted to win one whether I am World Number One or number 100 and that will never change."

Donald admitted that Padraig Harrington's three Major haul in 2007 and 2008 opened his eyes to high possibilities and he remains inspired by the Irishman's success.

Sir Nick Faldo, however, remains his template as a professional. The Englishman was dominating the game when Donald was winning the Beaconsfield Club championship as a 15 year old and it was

Faldo's swing that the teenager coveted. David Howell, a Ryder Cup team-mate, believes Donald's fixation with his idol can still be seen now. "It's the rhythm," said Howell. "Nick had a rhythm to die for and Luke's is the same. I've always thought that, always seen the similarity."

Still, the happy fact is that at 34, Donald is entering what should be his peak years. The other happy fact is that 34 still remains the median age for any golfer to win his first Major Championship. Barring further injury – he was forced out of the game for six months in 2008 by a wrist problem – there should be at least several more years for him to enjoy as a genuine contender when golf's biggest weeks occur.

Whether he wins one remains to be seen, as does the fact of whether or not we should so coldly judge a professional golfer's place in the game by the number of big ones he wins. What we can be sure of, however, is that Donald, far from under-achieving, has in fact reached out to caress more than he could have dreamt of when he turned professional a decade ago.

He accepts that his present ranking means there are greater expectations placed on his shoulders and he admits that nobody places these more carefully than he does himself. His present goal, he insists, is: "To keep going through the processes of trying to improve and do what I can do to become a better player and a better person."

More than anything, Donald also knows that what we are mostly talking about is only a game and a diversion from the reality of much that is life itself. He was cruelly reminded of this thought when, in November, as he waited with wife Diane for the arrival of their second daughter to join big sister Elle, news came through from England that his father had unexpectedly passed away.

As messages of sympathy from around the globe hit his phone and computer screen, he replied swiftly on Twitter. "It's a difficult time and your support means a lot to me. With death there is pain and loss but out of that comes light and appreciation. Appreciate what you have. I miss you Dad."

Four days later, Sophia Ann Donald arrived in the world. One day this little girl will be old enough to be very proud indeed of her own dad and his achievements in 2011.

Bill Elliott
Golf Monthly

LUKE DONALD - FACTS AND ACHIEVEMENTS

Became the first player to officially finish Number One in Europe and America in the same season.

Became just the second player, after Greg Norman, to be Number One on The European Tour (1982) and the US PGA Tour (1986, 1990 and 1995).

Played a combined total of 24 events on The European and US PGA Tour in 2011 and was placed in the top ten 18 times. From those 18, he was victorious four times and was a runner-up on a further three occasions.

After winning the BMW PGA Championship at Wentworth Club in May, when he defeated Lee Westwood in a play-off, he went to the top of the Official World Golf Ranking.

Became just the third Englishman, after Sir Nick Faldo and Lee Westwood, to be the World's Number One player.

At the end of 2011 he had been top of the Official World Golf Ranking for 31 consecutive weeks.

Since The European Tour's first season in 1972, he became the fifth Englishman to finish Number One in Europe. He follows: Peter Oosterhuis (1972-74), Sir Nick Faldo (1983, 1992), Lee Westwood (2000, 2009) and Justin Rose (2007).

THE 2011 RACE TO DUBAI FINAL STANDINGS

			€
1	**LUKE DONALD**		**5,323,400**
2	Rory McIlroy		4,002,168
3	Martin Kaymer		3,489,033
4	Charl Schwartzel		2,929,829
5	Lee Westwood		2,439,601
6	Alvaro Quiros		2,259,242
7	Anders Hansen		2,074,366
8	Sergio Garcia		1,962,723
9	Thomas Björn		1,814,115
10	Simon Dyson		1,694,779
11	Darren Clarke		1,590,415
12	Miguel Angel Jiménez		1,570,454
13	Peter Hanson		1,500,590
14	Alexander Noren		1,427,643
15	Louis Oosthuizen		1,409,126

Severiano Ballesteros Sota

An appreciation by Mitchell Platts

"You didn't have to like golf to love Seve"

Seve, the farmer's son who enraptured the world of golf from the moment he refused to surrender at Royal Birkdale in 1976, lost the one fight that not even his prodigious courage would allow him to beat.

Severiano Ballesteros Sota, of Spain, died on May 7, 2011, following a valiant battle with the cancer diagnosed as a malignant brain tumour after he lost consciousness in Madrid Airport on October 5, 2008. He underwent four operations at the La Paz Hospital in Madrid to remove the tumour and reduce the swelling in his skull as well as chemotherapy.

A superlative career offered a CV no other European golfer can match with five Major Championships, 50 European Tour wins, 38 other titles worldwide and, of course, a remarkable Ryder Cup record crowned by his winning performance as Captain in 1997 at Club de Golf Valderrama in Spain. That career was cut short by an arthritic back, but his death at 54 years old sadly brought a premature end to a life which embroidered the game and enriched us all.

Ballesteros blended skill, spirit and sheer will power as, playing with his heart, he fiercely contested every tournament in which he teed-up. Millions and millions globally were drawn to him by his passion and genius. His legacy can be measured not only by the titles he captured, but the way in which he won them. He threw caution and technique to the wind. You didn't have to like golf to love Seve.

Ballesteros, who on March 22, 1974, at the age of 16 years 11 months and 12 days, became the youngest accredited professional tournament player in the history of Spanish golf, made his European Tour full debut that year in, appropriately, the Open de España - coincidentally the tournament which brought the last of his European Tour wins in 1995 - and then in 1976 he moved centre-stage at The 105th Open Championship at Royal Birkdale.

There, at the age of 19, he led for three days. The week before he had been bailing hay at home in Pedreña, Northern Spain, where at the age of seven he struck his first shots on the beach with a cut-down three iron using stones as ammunition. Now he was living in a little house in Southport, on the cusp of a glittering career. His caddie was local, a policeman called Dick, and the weather was more Spanish than English. The country was in the grip of a heatwave.

The seaside crowd and those watching on TV were mesmerised by the young Spanish lad belting the ball as hard as he could. Ballesteros executed the pragmatism of youth – the shortest distance between two points being a straight line to the flag!

By the final day a nation was willing Ballesteros to hold off the might of America. He led by three with 17 holes to play but by the turn Johnny Miller had surged ahead. The title

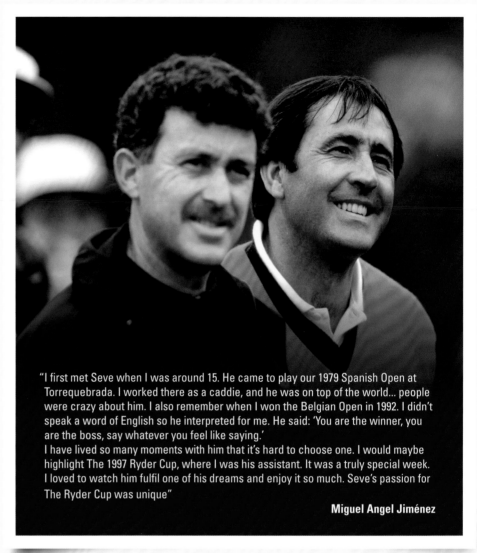

"I first met Seve when I was around 15. He came to play our 1979 Spanish Open at Torrequebrada. I worked there as a caddie, and he was on top of the world... people were crazy about him. I also remember when I won the Belgian Open in 1992. I didn't speak a word of English so he interpreted for me. He said: 'You are the winner, you are the boss, say whatever you feel like saying.'
I have lived so many moments with him that it's hard to choose one. I would maybe highlight The 1997 Ryder Cup, where I was his assistant. It was a truly special week. I loved to watch him fulfil one of his dreams and enjoy it so much. Seve's passion for The Ryder Cup was unique"

Miguel Angel Jiménez

belonged to the Californian; but Ballesteros refused to submit. He produced a blistering birdie-birdie-eagle-birdie finish – five under in four holes – and secured a tie for second with Jack Nicklaus with a deft, cheeky pitch and run between bunkers at the 18th with which everyone present knew they had seen the embryonic flourish of a true superstar.

In many respects it was hardly a surprise that Ballesteros should erupt on the scene in Southport. The course sits amongst the dunes on the Lancashire coast adjacent to the Irish Sea. Pedreña, where Ballesteros was born on April 9, 1957 in a two-storey stone farmhouse that overlooked the Real Club de Golf de Pedreña, is a fishing village near Santander influenced by the Bay of Biscay. There Ballesteros grew up, honed his game on the beach and later at the club built in 1929 at the request of King Alfonso XIII, and began to believe like all great players in a sense of destiny. It was inevitable that he would become a champion.

What increased his confidence was the loving encouragement he received from his father, Baldomero, himself a local hero as a five time winning oarsman in the Pedreña boat in the celebrated annual Regata de Traineras, and his mother, Carmen. They were a close family, especially on a Sunday, when Ballesteros would help his father in the cow shed while his mother prepared lunch.

I recall a breakfast with Seve at the Ritz in London when, with tears in his eyes, he spoke warmly of his parents – his father had now died - and three brothers. He said: "The biggest influence on my life was my parents and probably the surroundings because our house was right there on the golf course (Real Club de Golf de Pedreña). My uncle, Ramon Sota, was also a professional golfer and he was very good.

"My father was always optimistic; he always believed in me. The house had belonged to my mother's uncle. When we were growing

up Baldomero, my eldest brother, had one bedroom, Manuel had another and I shared with Vicente. We were a happy family. We kept cows which my father looked after. He also fished, some for us to eat and some to sell, and he caddied. It seemed that he and my mother were always working."

Later the tears turned to smiles when he recalled being drunk at the age of 12. He said: "I came home and my father and mother had gone fishing. My lunch had been left and there was a bottle of wine. I had four glasses. It did not go unnoticed when I returned to school; I was sent back home!"

Ballesteros swiftly gave up alcohol and school. His enjoyment at school was limited to playing with his friends and running. He won the regional championship for 1500m by 25 or 30m. He always craved to be a champion. His dreams never concerned money; quite simply he wanted to be the best.

Nevertheless it was challenging to learn the game. He said: "It was tough for me to begin with because I wasn't allowed on the golf course. And like any child, when someone stops you from doing something, then you want it more badly. I would sneak on the course in the evening, practise on the second hole. I would also play that second hole from our house by hitting the ball from out of the backyard over on to the green. Then I would run down the hill, grab the balls and run uphill again. This I did thousands of times."

Seve's upbringing unquestionably instilled the desire to succeed. Blessed with wonderful imagination, his ability to envisage and execute a shot took your breath away. You almost hoped that Ballesteros would stray from the straight and narrow because then you would be witness to a shot of such scintillating brilliance that even his playing partners would shake their heads in amazed acknowledgement.

That brilliance secured for him his first Open Championship at Royal Lytham & St Annes in 1979. He was the only player to finish under par for the week and claimed the famous Claret Jug by three shots from Ben Crenshaw and Jack Nicklaus. He would win The Open Championship again in 1984 at St Andrews and back at Royal Lytham & St Annes in 1988 and, of course, became in 1980 the first European to win the Masters Tournament and won again at Augusta National in 1983.

In 1979 Ballesteros and his compatriot Antonio Garrido created more history when they stepped onto the first tee at The Greenbrier in White Sulphur Springs, West Virginia, and became the first continental players in a now European Ryder Cup Team. This launched a revolution that would transform the biennial match with the United States and trigger a golfing explosion across the continent of Europe. In essence the

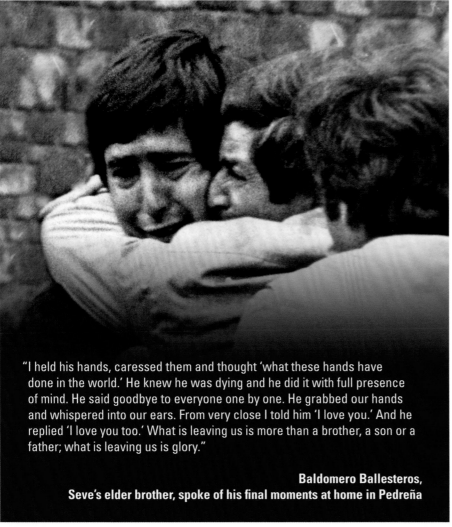

"I held his hands, caressed them and thought 'what these hands have done in the world.' He knew he was dying and he did it with full presence of mind. He said goodbye to everyone one by one. He grabbed our hands and whispered into our ears. From very close I told him 'I love you.' And he replied 'I love you too.' What is leaving us is more than a brother, a son or a father; what is leaving us is glory."

**Baldomero Ballesteros,
Seve's elder brother, spoke of his final moments at home in Pedreña**

"Unfortunately, we lost a great man and a dear friend when he died. He lived life to the full. I never saw any other player with his heart and determination on a golf course.
My first memory of Seve goes back to 1983. I was an amateur, and he called me to play in a charity event. It was a big surprise and I was very excited. It's hard to choose one of the many moments that I lived with him, but surely the most cherished are Ryder Cup moments, particular the 1997 edition.
He was a pioneer. He opened doors. He changed the image of golf and made it totally exciting. He could hit the most amazing shots from unbelievable places. He was a true genius.
What impressed me most about Seve was his strength, his fighting spirit and the passion he put into everything he did. I saw him for the last time the Saturday after the Masters. He was not well, but his head was clear. We talked about many things… so many common memories, and particularly about The Ryder Cup.
When cancer struck he had two goals - to never give up and to try to help as many people as possible and that's why he started the Seve Ballesteros Foundation which on the Olé Seve Day at Wentworth, only two weeks after he passed away, raised £725,905 for Cancer Research UK
The best tribute we can pay to Seve is to go on playing for him, although no tribute will ever do justice to everything he did for golf and to everything he gave us."

José María Olazábal

Seve Ballesteros
FOUNDATION
www.seveballesterosfoundation.org

Ballesteros factor meant that The European Tour, European golf, world golf would never be the same.

Ballesteros always wore his heart on his sleeve but such was his unique ability to blend consummate skill with unquenchable spirit and sheer will power that The Ryder Cup provided the perfect stage for his swashbuckling style. Even in the team's slender defeat in 1983 at PGA National Golf Club in Palm Beach Gardens, Florida, he produced another of those "shots heard round the world." It came at the 18th against Fuzzy Zoeller – a wood that exited the fairway bunker where the lip was at its lowest, flew high with a slice and landed as softly as you like 18 feet from the hole.

Zoeller still talks about that shot 28 years later. He said: "It is still the greatest shot I have ever seen – not just in The Ryder Cup but anywhere. I still don't believe it was possible but Seve saw what no-one else would have seen."

In all Ballesteros, having guided Spain to World Cup victories in 1976 and 1977 and later the Continent of Europe to success in the inaugural Seve Trophy, made eight Ryder Cup appearances as a player – winning 20 points from 37 matches – and he formed with José María Olazábal the greatest Ryder Cup partnership of all time with 11 wins and two halves from 15 matches. Then came that special moment in 1997 when Seve, a real Captain Marvel of a leader, led Europe to victory at Valderrama and was presented with the Cup by the Infanta Maria, daughter of King Juan Carlos.

What followed, of course, was the realisation for Ballesteros that his arthritic condition would not allow him to resurrect a career that had brought him and his millions of admirers so much pleasure and enabled him to become the Number One golfer in the world.

Yet even though he had come to terms with this by announcing his competitive retirement he was then forced to use every ounce of the guts and determination that brought him fame on the fairways to battle the wretched disease that would blight the last two years or more of his life.

Now we mourn the loss of Severiano Ballesteros Sota who captured all our hearts and whose legacy is not simply to be found in the record books but also in the knowledge that he leaves the game far, far better than he found it.

"Seve's unique legacy must be the inspiration he has given to so many to watch, support, and play golf, and finally to fight a cruel illness with equal flair, passion, and fierce determination. We have all been so blessed to live in his era. He was the inspiration behind The European Tour."

George O'Grady CBE, Chief Executive of The European Tour

"Seve was one of the brightest lights of our game and was an inspiration to millions. His iconic celebration here at St Andrews, on the 18th green in 1984, ranks as one of sport's greatest moments. The game has lost one of the greats."

Peter Dawson, Chief Executive of The R&A

"Seve was up there with the greatest names of world golf and will leave a lasting legacy and impression on the game like Bobby Jones, the Great Triumverate, Sam Snead and Ben Hogan."

Philip Weaver, Chairman of the PGA of Great Britain and Ireland

"He was wonderful to watch. He brought delight and joy to many people who watched and played golf. He tweaked a few tails along the way and bloodied a few noses but that's what helped make him what he was. He was a fighter, feisty, skilful, cheeky, lovable, he was everything."

Peter Alliss, the voice of BBC Golf

"He was brilliant and talented. A genius and a gentleman. Everything you could wish for in a sportsman and someone to idolise. He was fantastic to watch. Although I came on the scene towards the end of his career I could only imagine what he must have been like at his peak. A man you would definitely prefer to watch than to face as an opponent."

Thomas Björn - Chairman , The European Tour Tournament Committee

"For golf, he was the greatest show on earth. I was a fan and so fortunate that I had a front-row seat."

Sir Nick Faldo

"I remember looking at Seve in the team room at The 1991 Ryder Cup and thinking to myself that he seemed physically smaller than when I saw him on the golf course or on television. Any other week other than The Ryder Cup, he didn't know me very well. But that one week he cared so much that he went out of his way to make me feel like I was a friend of his. I only realised in retrospect that it wasn't that he looked smaller – it was that he made me feel bigger."

David Feherty

"He inspired me so much throughout my career and I admired him above all for his fighting spirit - never more so than in the manner in which he battled this terrible illness. It is the most enormous loss to the world of sport to lose this great man although he will be remembered and loved forever."

Sergio Garcia

"Nobody in the game has ever had the same charisma. When he smiled the whole world smiled with him…he lived his life in a very emotional way and that's what made him so enduring."

Paul McGinley

"There are very few legends in the world, Seve is one of them. I never saw such a talent to swing a golf club, and we may never see it again. We have lost one of the great icons of the game, it is a great loss for Spain, for Europe and for the world. But he has left us with so many wonderful lasting memories and his contributions to European golf are unquantifiable."

Colin Montgomerie OBE

"He meant so much to European golf. He had his battles with the European and the US Tours but he showed the rest of the world that we had some great players in Europe. When we saw that Seve could win Majors and tournaments all over the world, it gave us the belief that we could do the same thing. I was blessed to live at the same time as him and see one of the greatest golfers ever in action so many times."

Bernhard Langer

"We have lost somebody who meant so much to everyone in golf. To me, he was the best player and the most inspiring player in the world. I met him for the first time when I was four years old and he was my idol ever since then. He inspired me then and he will continue to inspire me throughout my career."

Matteo Manassero

"Golf has lost a great champion and a great friend. We have also lost a great entertainer and ambassador for our sport. It was his creativity, his imagination, and his desire to compete that made him so popular not only in Europe but throughout American galleries, too. We can only imagine how difficult this battle has been for him and his family the last few years, but I know Seve faced it with the same grit, fight and spirit he approached his golf career."

Jack Nicklaus

"Without Seve Ballesteros, where would we all be today? What would be the state of European golf and the interest in the sport around the world were it not for the charismatic Spaniard? There was never a golfer like him and very few whose influence was so widespread. Seve had it all, the looks, the charm, the style and, of course, a remarkable talent."

Sam Torrance OBE

"It is a sad day. We have lost an inspiration, a genius, a role model, a hero and a friend. Seve gave his all for golf and what the game and The European Tour particularly owes him is immense. We would not be playing where and for what we are today without him having graced the world's fairways. He was iconic."

Lee Westwood

Players from Barcelona and Espanyol observe a minute's silence before a match at the Nou Camp on May 8, 2011

Staging a golfing exhibition at the Nou Camp stadium, home of Barcelona.

"Severiano represented a beginning and an end in the history of Spanish sport: his example paved the way for the extraordinary success our sport is currently enjoying. He was the mirror which Spanish athletes who have reached the pinnacle of world sport looked into. Severiano was loved and respected for his great charisma and strength, which he showed until the very end of his life."

José Luis Rodriguez Zapatero, Spanish Prime Minister

"Seve discovered golf for the Spanish people and made all of us feel very proud of his victories. I had the privilege to cover his career since the very beginning. There was nothing like following Seve on a golf course. His fierceness, his desire, his way to play and his determination were unique. His image will be in our minds forever."

Núria Pastor (La Vanguardia)

"Seve brought a passion to golf that it never had before and has not enjoyed since. He made this stuffy old game seem sexy and exciting. He was the godfather of the modern European Tour, moving the interest from golf lovers to general sports fans and non-sports fans alike."

Bill Elliott (Golf Monthly)

"Seve made me understand the greatness of this sport through shots I could not understand at the beginning, but which later I realised were unrepeatable in other hands. Even in his decline, when his back was hurting, he always gave us one of his magic shots."

Isabel Trillo (Spanish Association Golf Writer)

"Seve Ballesteros at the highest of his powers might just have represented the zenith in the 500-year history of the Royal and Ancient game."

Derek Lawrenson (The Daily Mail)

"He changed the history of golf not only in Europe but also in the United States. There has been no other individual figure with so much influence in the development of his sport. He brought life and oxygen to an ancient sport. He was a wild and courageous man and a proud spirit. His soul was the soul of somebody who knew he was special and unique."

Carlos Arribas (El País)

"Passion, charisma, tenacity, spirit of fight, humanity, sense of humour...the list is very long. Seve was an unbelievable person and this is, for me, the saddest moment of my career. However, I've been a very privileged man to know him, to have meals and dinners with him, night chats with him and a drink, to watch soccer matches with him...to have a relationship with one of the world best athletes. God bless Seve, ADEMÁS DE CAMPEÓN, AMIGO."

Raul Andreu (Mundo Deportivo and Solo Golf Y Viajes)

"I started working with Seve at the 1974 Spanish Open. I had the privilege of spending 28 years of my life very close to Seve, not the legend or the golfer, but my friend. I shared many moments with him; victories, defeats, fights, joy, frustration. I sat next to him at hundreds of press conferences, many very interesting, others amusing, a few very tense. I was very pleased when he married Carmen Botín, an excellent person who left her life behind and gave him everything. I remember how happy he was when their children were born, he was a very proud daddy, especially when little Carmen called him 'Papote.' Seve, you thanked me many times for being your friend and for taking care of you. Be sure that from now on, I will always be there for Javier, Miguel and Carmen."

María Acacia López-Bachiller (European Tour Spanish Press Officer)

L-R: Baldomero, Severiano, Manuel and Vicente Ballesteros at Royal Lytham & St Annes in 1979

"Seve Ballesteros, the gallant warrior from Pedreña, Spain, was the ultimate competitor. We were fortunate to have had him choose golf. Seve played with a rare combination of talent and heart, and his intensity endeared him to his teammates in The Ryder Cup, a competition that elevated his talent and leadership. As long as the pipes may play to call teams together for The Ryder Cup, they will play for Seve."

Allen Wronowski, President of the PGA of America

"Severiano Ballesteros has always been a model of talent, determination and perseverance. His loss fills us with sadness and leaves a great void. It is our sacred duty to acknowledge his feats and to pass on to future generations his outstanding legacy."

Gonzaga Escauriaza, President of the Royal Spanish Golf Federation

"For more than 30 years, Seve had a large impact on the game and inspired many players with his creativity and flair on and off the golf course."

Tim Finchem, Commissioner of the PGA Tour

"Seve Ballesteros was a man of incredible skill, charisma and courage as a sportsman, and the dignified way that he fought against the disease was characteristic of the man and was an inspiration to us all. He was a 'once in a generation athlete' in his sport, and his influence on the game will live long after him."

Jacques Rogge, President of the International Olympic Committee

Seve's children, Carmen, Javier and Miguel lead the funeral procession in Pedreña

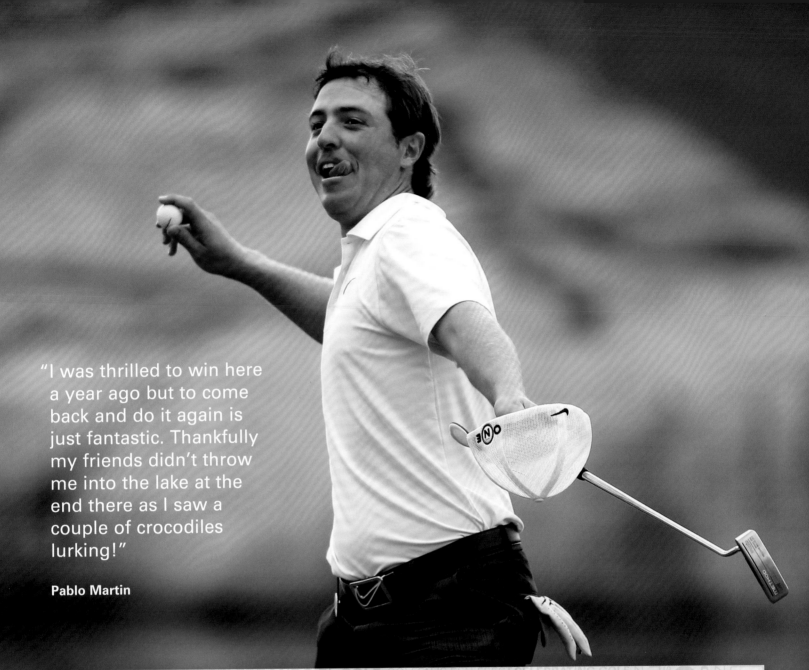

"I was thrilled to win here a year ago but to come back and do it again is just fantastic. Thankfully my friends didn't throw me into the lake at the end there as I saw a couple of crocodiles lurking!"

Pablo Martin

ALFRED DUNHILL CHAMPIONSHIP
Leopard Creek Country Club
Malelane, South Africa
December 9-12, 2010

1	**PABLO MARTIN**	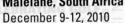	**69**	**70**	**68**	**70**	**277**	**-11**
2	Anthony Michael		66	69	71	73	279	-9
	Thorbjørn Olesen		71	68	74	66	279	-9
	Charl Schwartzel		70	70	69	70	279	-9
5	Thomas Aiken		72	72	67	70	281	-7
6	Robert Dinwiddie		69	72	71	70	282	-6
	Alex Haindl		71	66	72	73	282	-6
8	David Drysdale		70	70	72	71	283	-5
	Robert Rock		67	70	75	71	283	-5
10	James Kingston		69	71	77	67	284	-4
	Jbe' Kruger		72	69	71	72	284	-4
	Dawie Van Der Walt		67	70	70	77	284	-4

Gaynor Rupert, wife of Johann Rupert, Executive Chairman and CEO Richemont and Pablo Martin

Total Prize Fund €1,000,000   **First Prize** €158,500

Lee Slattery gets The 2011 Race to Dubai underway

Thorbjørn Olesen

Anthony Michael

From Seven to Heaven

There must be something about the start of a new European Tour season that appeals to golfers from Spain because, for the third year in a row, the honours in the opening event went to a player from that country.

Sergio Garcia triumphed at the HSBC Champions in 2009 but for the past two years it has been Pablo Martin who has reigned supreme in the Alfred Dunhill Championship at the spectacular Leopard Creek.

Twelve months ago the 24 year old held off the challenge of host country favourite Charl Schwartzel to triumph by a shot and, going into the final round this year, both players were again in the mix. However it was Martin who made the early move, a tap-in birdie at the first followed by an eagle three at the second laying the foundations for a five shot lead turning for home.

Victory seemed inevitable until a triple bogey seven at the 17th gave the chasing pack hope. But Martin, who finished in the top ten in both the Genworth Statistics Driving Accuracy and Putts per Green categories for the week, used both to good effect on the par five 18th, a fine drive leading to a two putt birdie four and an 11 under par total of 277 which was good enough for a two shot victory over Schwartzel once again, another South African Anthony Michael and 2010 Challenge Tour graduate Thorbjørn Olesen of Denmark.

Charl Schwartzel

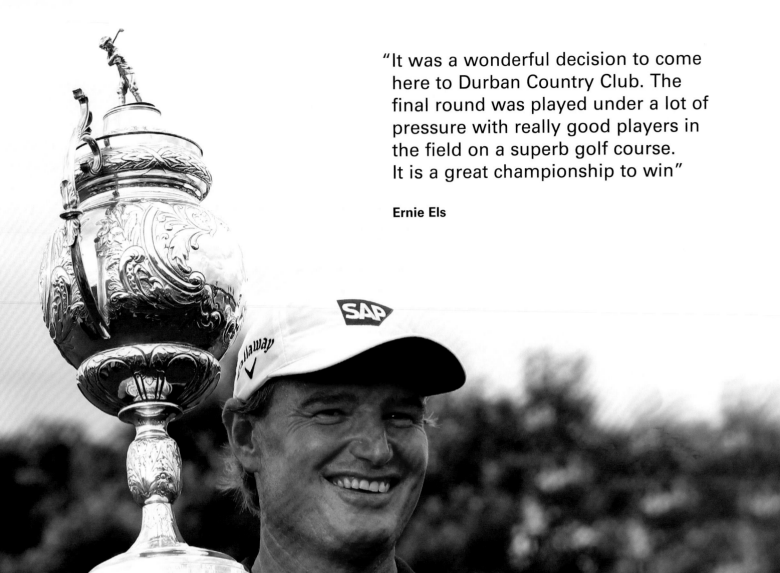

"It was a wonderful decision to come here to Durban Country Club. The final round was played under a lot of pressure with really good players in the field on a superb golf course. It is a great championship to win"

Ernie Els

SOUTH AFRICAN OPEN CHAMPIONSHIP
Durban Country Club
Durban, South Africa
December 16-19, 2010

1	**ERNIE ELS**		65	65	64	63	**257**	**-25**
2	Retief Goosen		64	68	63	63	258	-24
3	Louis Oosthuizen		67	67	64	63	261	-21
4	Charl Schwartzel		65	69	66	64	264	-18
5	Robert Rock		69	69	64	64	266	-16
	Romain Wattel		67	66	68	65	266	-16
7	Alex Cejka		64	72	66	65	267	-15
	Victor Riu		68	68	65	66	267	-15
9	Tim Clark		70	67	65	66	268	-14
	Robert Dinwiddie		71	69	63	65	268	-14
	Thorbjørn Olesen		68	69	65	66	268	-14

Dr Z L Mkhize, Premier of KwaZulu-Natal and Ernie Els

Total Prize Fund €1,006,182   **First Prize €158,500**

Louis Oosthuizen

Romain Wattel

Robert Rock

Centenary Celebrations

In a year when the South African Open Championship celebrated its 100th playing, it was perhaps fitting that Ernie Els was the man to get his hands on the famous silver trophy for the fifth time.

Arguably the greatest South African golfer of the modern era edged out compatriot Retief Goosen by a shot after a thrilling final day at Durban Country Club, a victory which took Els alongside George Fotheringham in the list of all time winners of the event, the only men ahead of them being Sid Brews with eight wins, Bobby Locke with nine and Gary Player with his record of 13 triumphs.

The final day saw the last two rounds contested after rain earlier in the week had washed out almost all of Thursday's play. It also made the fourth green unplayable meaning that instead of 36 holes, only 34 were played on Sunday, with the par being adjusted from 72 to 69.

Els, who carded a third round 64 in the morning, followed up with another excellent display in the afternoon as five birdies and an eagle helped him to a final round 63 and a winning total of 25 under par 257.

He by no means cruised to victory however, as Goosen rallied late on with four birdies in his last five holes. But the charge proved too late for the champion of 1995 and 2005, and despite emulating Els' 63, he fell just one shot shy with reigning Open Champion Louis Oosthuizen third, four shots behind Els.

Retief Goosen

"You always want to perform well when you play at home and I'm delighted to have done that. I will never forget what I achieved in 2010 and hopefully this can be the start of another great year for me"

Louis Oosthuizen

AFRICA OPEN
East London Golf Club
East London, Eastern Cape, South Africa
January 6-9, 2011

1	**LOUIS OOSTHUIZEN**		70	67	69	70	**276**	**-16**
2	Manuel Quiros		71	68	68	69	276	-16
	Chris Wood		72	69	67	68	276	-16
4	Steven O'Hara		72	71	68	66	277	-15
	Charl Schwartzel		69	70	68	70	277	-15
	Jaco Van Zyl		67	70	70	70	277	-15
7	Robert Dinwiddie		69	74	66	69	278	-14
8	Markus Brier		70	66	70	73	279	-13
	Branden Grace		67	69	72	71	279	-13
	Eirik Tage Johansen		71	71	70	67	279	-13
	Jbe' Kruger		68	72	67	72	279	-13
	Shaun Norris		70	73	70	66	279	-13
	Miles Tunnicliff		67	69	72	71	279	-13

L-R Councillor Luleka Simon, Louis Oosthuizen and Councillor Thembisa Nondala

Total Prize Fund €1,001,700   **First Prize** €158,500

Markus Brier

Manuel Quiros

Steven O'Hara

Major Achievement

Having won a Major Championship, especially one as prestigious as The Open at St Andrews, the pressure is always intense on a player to push on from there, prove his worth, and win again. For Louis Oosthuizen, however, the burden of expectation was even greater due to the fact he had to show he had also recovered from injury.

Stepping in a pothole while hunting in his native South Africa left the 28 year old with damaged ankle ligaments which saw him miss most of September and October on The 2010 European Tour International Schedule as well as having to play with his left foot strapped up on his return last season.

But, refreshed after a winter break, a fully fit Oosthuizen held his nerve to get the better of Manuel Quiros and Chris Wood at the first hole of a sudden-death play-off to capture the Africa Open title at East London.

A fine eagle three on the 15th in the final round enabled the South African to tie with the Spaniard and the Englishman – who finished with three consecutive birdies – on 16 under par 276, sending the trio back to the 18th tee to battle for the €158,500 first prize.

A pulled drive into the left rough did not make Oosthuizen favourite but he showed the class which saw him win by seven shots at St Andrews, to fire a superb recovery shot to eight feet from where he holed out for a winning birdie three.

Chris Wood

"I've been working really hard on my pitch shots and bunker play lately and I'm pleased that it paid off. I love playing on home soil and I think you can see from my record that I really love this tournament"

Charl Schwartzel

Open 2011

JOBURG OPEN
Royal Johannesburg and Kensington Golf Club
(East and West Courses)
Johannesburg, South Africa
January 13-16, 2011

#							Total	
1	**CHARL SCHWARTZEL**		68	61	69	67	265	-19
2	Garth Mulroy		65	64	69	71	269	-15
3	Thomas Aiken		64	66	68	72	270	-14
4	Jamie Elson		65	64	71	71	271	-13
5	Jean-Baptiste Gonnet		67	66	67	72	272	-12
6	Scott Jamieson		70	66	72	65	273	-11
7	George Coetzee		70	65	70	69	274	-10
	Oscar Floren		68	68	66	72	274	-10
	James Kingston		68	62	73	71	274	-10
	Tjaart Van Der Walt		69	68	70	67	274	-10
	Allan Versfeld		66	66	70	72	274	-10

Councillor Amos Masondo, the Executive Mayor of Johannesburg and Charl Schwartzel

Total Prize Fund €1,302,210   **First Prize** €206,050

Jamie Elson

Garth Mulroy

Jean-Baptiste Gonnet

Thomas Aiken

Charl the Second

It is a fair bet that if all European Tour events were co-sanctioned with the Sunshine Tour in South Africa, Charl Schwartzel would be Number One in The Race to Dubai every year because, quite simply, his record is outstanding.

In the 26 events he has contested, the 26 year old has won four times, made 23 cuts, and been in the top ten on a dozen occasions in total. However, if only the Joburg Open was contested, he would surely be World Number One.

The 26 year old won for the second year in succession in his home town, racking up a combined total of 42 under par for his two victories; 23 under par in 2010 and a 19 under par total of 265 this year which proved four shots too good for his nearest

challenger, fellow countryman Garth Mulroy, and five clear of another South African, Thomas Aiken.

The trio began the final day in a share of the lead but it was Schwartzel who quickly stole a march with birdies at the first and third. Mulroy and Aiken battled hard but, despite some erratic form from the tee, Schwartzel's unerringly accurate rescue play around the greens ensured the chasing pack could not close the gap.

Fittingly, another up and down birdie at the last sealed his victory and guaranteed he became only the third South African, after Ernie Els and Trevor Immelman, to make a successful defence of a European Tour title.

ABU DHABI HSBC GOLF CHAMPIONSHIP
Abu Dhabi Golf Club
Abu Dhabi, UAE
January 20–23, 2011

1	MARTIN KAYMER		67	65	66	66	264	-24
2	Rory McIlroy		71	67	65	69	272	-16
3	Retief Goosen		70	71	69	64	274	-14
	Graeme McDowell		66	70	71	67	274	-14
5	David Lynn		69	68	67	72	276	-12
	Gareth Maybin		71	67	69	69	276	-12
7	Rafael Cabrera-Bello		71	73	67	66	277	-11
8	Ricardo Gonzalez		72	68	71	67	278	-10
	Francesco Molinari		71	72	69	66	278	-10
	Charl Schwartzel		64	71	71	72	278	-10

His Highness Sheikh Hazza Bin Zayed Al Nahyan, National Security Advisor, Vice Chairman of the Executive Council, and Chairman of the Abu Dhabi Sports Council and Martin Kaymer

Total Prize Fund €2,006,391   **First Prize** €334,398

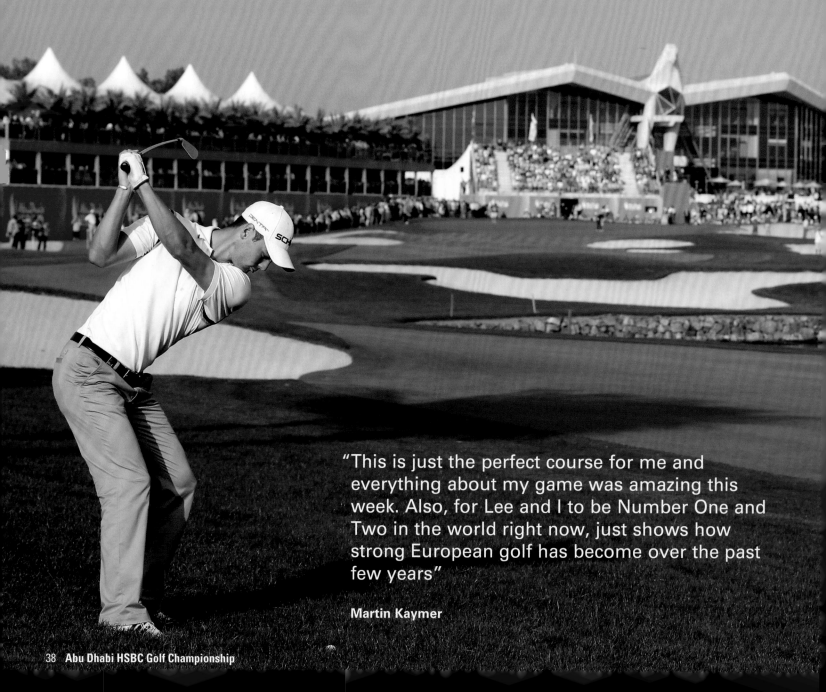

"This is just the perfect course for me and everything about my game was amazing this week. Also, for Lee and I to be Number One and Two in the world right now, just shows how strong European golf has become over the past few years"

Martin Kaymer

L-R: José María Olazábal, Martin Kaymer, Phil Mickelson, Graeme McDowell, Louis Oosthuizen, Lee Westwood and Paul Casey

David Lynn

At a press conference in Abu Dhabi, Spain's José María Olazábal was unveiled as European captain for The 2012 Ryder Cup at Medinah Country Club in Chicago, Illinois

Rory McIlroy

Abu Dhabi HSBC GOLF CHAMPIONSHIP
17th tee 483 yds Par 4

HSBC
The world's local bank

Formidable Force

There are presumably many ways to celebrate your 100th appearance on The European Tour, but to become the third youngest player in history to win an event for the third time on your way to moving to Number Two on the Official World Golf Ranking, must rank as one of the best.

Three time Major Champion Padraig Harrington described Martin Kaymer as "the most formidable player in the world when leading" and it is hard to argue with the Irishman after the German turned a five shot third round lead into an eight shot winning margin over a shell-shocked chasing pack led by runner-up Rory McIlroy and third placed duo of Retief Goosen and Graeme McDowell who found themselves ten shots in arrears. In the end, Kaymer dropped only one shot in 72 holes and his 24 under par total of 264 was the lowest, by three shots, in the tournament's history.

As well as being a personal triumph for the winner of The 2010 Race to Dubai – who became the quickest person in history to earn over €10 million in European Tour Official Career Earnings – the victory was also a milestone for Europe as Kaymer moved behind World Number One Lee Westwood in the rankings, the first time since 1993 that European golfers had occupied the top two spots.

Incredibly, Kaymer's triumph was also the third successful defence of a title in five events on The 2011 European Tour International Schedule, following Pablo Martin in the Alfred Dunhill Championship and Charl Schwartzel in the Joburg Open.

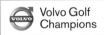

VOLVO GOLF CHAMPIONS
The Royal Golf Club
Kingdom of Bahrain, Bahrain
January 27–30, 2011

1	**PAUL CASEY**		67	67	66	68	268	**-20**
2	Peter Hanson		66	67	67	69	269	-19
	Miguel Angel Jiménez		68	65	69	67	269	-19
4	Stephen Gallacher		70	64	69	67	270	-18
5	Robert Karlsson		69	67	69	66	271	-17
6	Johan Edfors		64	71	68	69	272	-16
	Noh Seung-yul		69	68	70	65	272	-16
8	Darren Clarke		69	65	67	73	274	-14
	Edoardo Molinari		68	65	71	70	274	-14
	Alexander Noren		67	70	67	70	274	-14
	Alvaro Quiros		67	69	71	67	274	-14
	Richie Ramsay		72	68	67	67	274	-14

His Highness Shaikh Nasser Bin Hamad Al Khalifa, Chairman of the Supreme Council for Youth and Sport and President of the Bahrain Olympic Committee, Paul Casey and Per Ericsson, President of Volvo Event Management Golf

Total Prize Fund €1,705,097   **First Prize** €283,330

"It feels fantastic – the most important thing to me is winning and coming through to triumph like that was huge. I really do feel that my game is moving in the right direction"

Paul Casey

Devilish Triumph

However good a player you are – and unquestionably Paul Casey is a very good golfer – doubts start to creep into your mind about your ability the longer you remain outside the winners' circle. Which is why the Englishman was so delighted to end a 20 month trophy drought with victory in the inaugural Volvo Golf Champions in Bahrain.

Having shared the lead with Peter Hanson going into the final round over the Colin Montgomerie-designed Royal Golf Club, it was appropriate that the Englishman and the Swede continued to share the limelight as the tournament moved into its 72nd hole, both players one shot clear of Spain's Miguel Angel Jiménez who watched matters unfold from the nearby recorder's hut.

Neither player's approach to the 18th was ideal, Casey through the back of the green in the rough while Hanson found sand to the right of the putting surface, from where he escaped to ten feet. When he subsequently missed his par putt to join Jiménez on 19 under par 269, Casey had to make his eight foot par putt to avoid a three man play-off. The fist pump in the air seconds later signalled the ball had dropped below ground.

It was Casey's 11th European Tour triumph and the sixth destination in which he has tasted glory. It also proved he was not a man of superstition as, undaunted, he kept the Room 666 he had been given in the Ritz-Carlton despite constant jibes on the range to give it up.

Stephen Gallacher

Miguel Angel Jiménez

Peter Hanson

Robert Karlsson

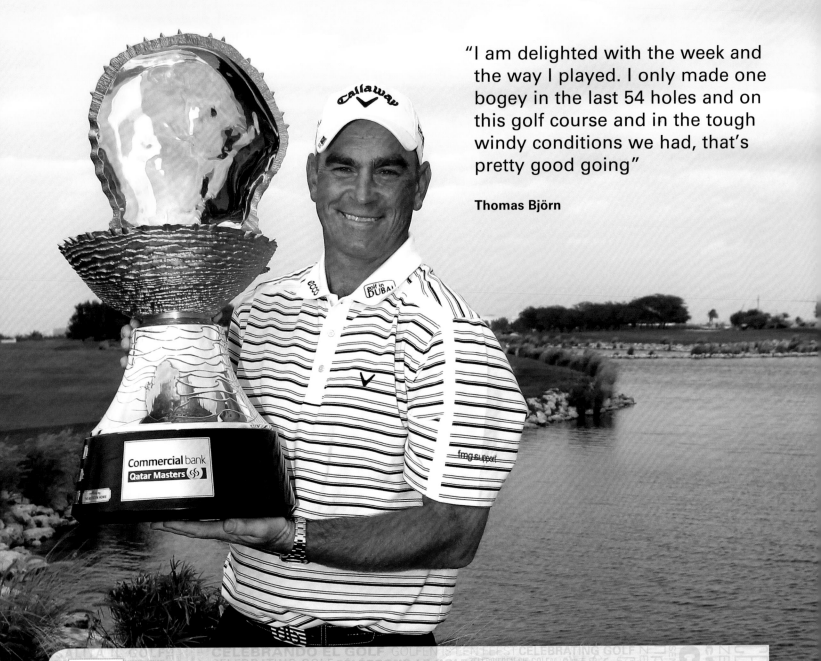

"I am delighted with the week and the way I played. I only made one bogey in the last 54 holes and on this golf course and in the tough windy conditions we had, that's pretty good going"

Thomas Björn

COMMERCIALBANK QATAR MASTERS presented by Dolphin Energy
Doha Golf Club
Doha, Qatar
February 3–6, 2011

1	**THOMAS BJÖRN**		74	65	66	69	274	-14
2	Alvaro Quiros		75	69	66	68	278	-10
3	Markus Brier		71	66	69	73	279	-9
	Rafael Cabrera-Bello		77	68	66	68	279	-9
5	David Howell		75	69	68	68	280	-8
6	Thomas Aiken		71	69	69	73	282	-6
	Søren Hansen		74	71	68	69	282	-6
	Robert Karlsson		70	69	69	74	282	-6
9	Victor Dubuisson		74	68	71	70	283	-5
	Richard Finch		70	69	71	73	283	-5
	Sergio Garcia		73	73	69	68	283	-5

L-R: Andy Stevens, Group CEO of Commercialbank, Thomas Björn and Hassan Al Nuaimi, President Qatar Golf Association

Total Prize Fund €1,835,034   First Prize €303,114

Thomas Aiken

Markus Brier

Commercial bank
Qatar Masters

Alvaro Quiros

For more information, please log onto www.qatar-masters.com

Rafael Cabrera-Bello

Søren Hansen

David Howell

The Björn Supremacy

It is a measure of how well respected within the game he is that when Thomas Björn speaks, people listen. Often it relates to his sterling work as Chairman of The European Tour Tournament Committee but often it is about his own game.

Therefore, during The Celtic Manor Wales Open last summer, when the Dane told the media he felt his game was coming back to the level he wanted it to be, copious notes were taken, all of which were dug out from notebooks the following week when he ended a four year winless streak with victory in Portugal.

His eventual finish of 56th in The Race to Dubai – his best since 2007 – hinted of more to come in 2011 and he duly delivered with his 11th European Tour title

in Qatar, finishing four shots clear of the strongest field in the tournament's 14 year history, a gathering which featured eight of the top 20 on the Official World Golf Ranking and 97 European Tour champions.

One shot clear of Markus Brier going into the final round, as the Austrian's challenge faltered it was left to Alvaro Quiros to prove the biggest threat. The Spaniard moved to within a shot with four holes to go but that simply served to ignite Björn who birdied the 15th, 16th and 18th holes to ease to victory.

Brier rallied over the back nine to share third with another Spaniard Rafael Cabrera-Bello, while David Howell of England took fifth after matching weekend rounds of 68.

Robert Karlsson

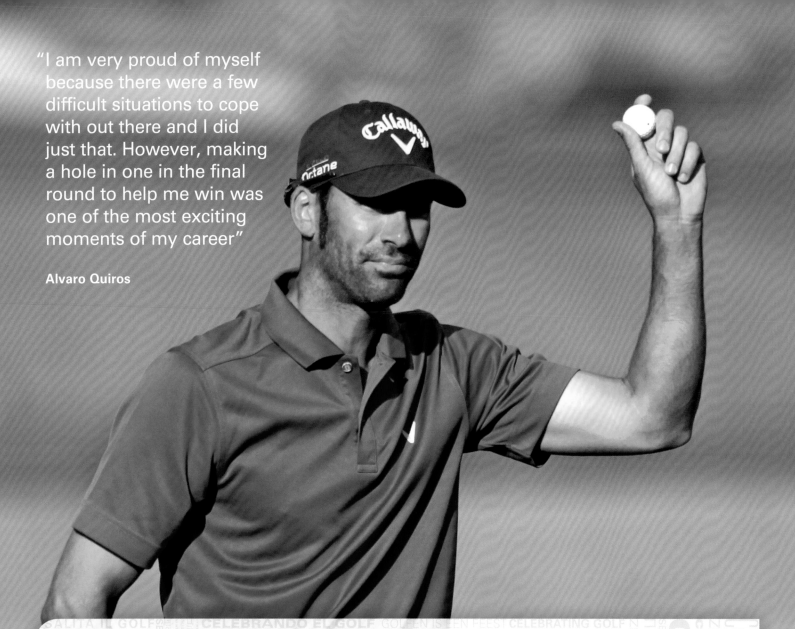

"I am very proud of myself because there were a few difficult situations to cope with out there and I did just that. However, making a hole in one in the final round to help me win was one of the most exciting moments of my career"

Alvaro Quiros

OMEGA DUBAI DESERT CLASSIC

Emirates Golf Club (Majlis Course)
Dubai, UAE
February 10-13, 2011

1	**ALVARO QUIROS**	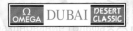	73	68	68	68	**277**	**-11**
2	Anders Hansen		69	68	71	70	278	-10
	James Kingston		72	72	67	67	278	-10
4	Jean-Baptiste Gonnet		68	69	72	70	279	-9
	Scott Strange		72	72	67	68	279	-9
	Alvaro Velasco		74	70	65	70	279	-9
7	Thomas Aiken		67	67	74	72	280	-8
	Fredrik Andersson Hed		69	71	69	71	280	-8
9	Peter Hanson		69	69	73	70	281	-7
10	Bradley Dredge		70	72	71	69	282	-6
	Ross Fisher		73	69	70	70	282	-6
	Stephen Gallacher		70	69	71	72	282	-6
	Rory McIlroy		65	68	75	74	282	-6
	Chris Wood		71	72	70	69	282	-6

Alvaro Quiros and His Highness Shaikh Maktoum bin Mohamed bin Rashid Al Maktoum, Deputy Ruler of Dubai

Total Prize Fund €1,808,148   **First Prize** €301,353

Anders Hansen

James Kingston

Alvaro Velasco

Glorious Hotchpotch

There are many ways to compile a final round capable of winning a golf tournament. Many people will cast their minds back to Muirfield in 1987 when Nick Faldo strung together 18 consecutive pars to capture The Open Championship, and those who did will have surely enjoyed the completely opposite end of the spectrum provided by Alvaro Quiros during his victory in the Omega Dubai Desert Classic.

Quite simply, the 27 year old Spaniard's final round had a bit of everything; four birdies, one bogey, a triple bogey seven, an eagle two and a hole in one – a glorious hotchpotch of figures which added up to his third consecutive 68, an 11 under par total of 277 and a one shot victory over Anders Hansen of Denmark and South Africa's James Kingston.

The hole in one came at the 161 yard 11th courtesy of a three quarter wedge and meant he became only the third player in European Tour history to have a hole in one in the final round and go on to win – following Thongchai Jaidee (2004 Carlsberg Malaysian Open) and Miguel Angel Jiménez (2008 BMW PGA Championship).

Following his triple bogey seven at the eighth hole, a birdie at the testing ninth followed by the ace itself got his title challenge completely back on track and although Hansen and Kingston threatened over the closing stages, Quiros held his nerve to grab his fifth European Tour title in his 100th Tour appearance. It also saw him move to the top of The 2011 Race to Dubai.

Jean-Baptiste Gonnet

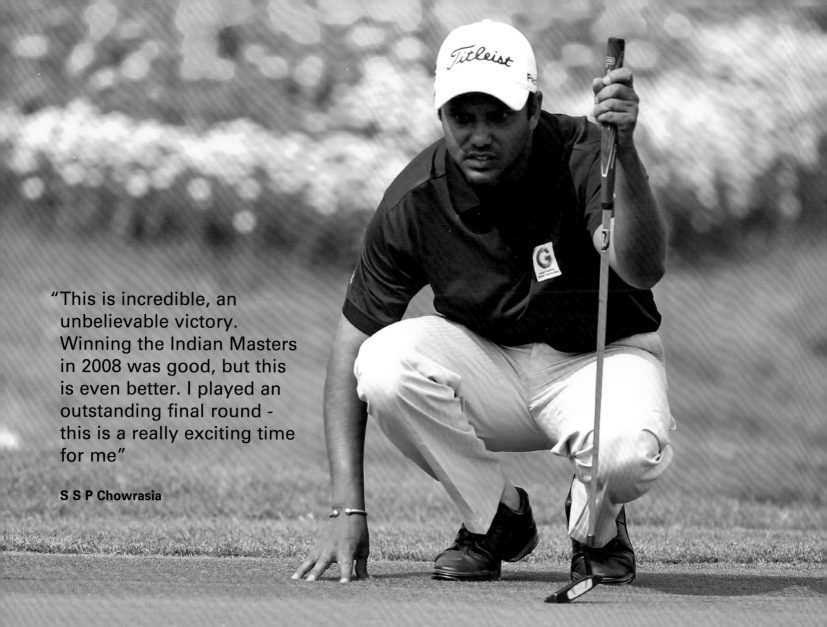

"This is incredible, an unbelievable victory. Winning the Indian Masters in 2008 was good, but this is even better. I played an outstanding final round - this is a really exciting time for me"

S S P Chowrasia

AVANTHA MASTERS
DLF Golf and Country Club
New Delhi, India
February 17–20, 2011

1	S S P CHOWRASIA		70	69	67	67	273	-15
2	Robert Coles		70	67	67	70	274	-14
3	Grégory Havret		72	67	68	68	275	-13
4	Robert-Jan Derksen		66	73	68	69	276	-12
5	Pablo Larrazábal		69	70	66	72	277	-11
	Sujjan Singh		69	69	68	71	277	-11
7	Mark F Haastrup		71	66	68	73	278	-10
	Chinnarat Phadungsil		70	68	71	69	278	-10
9	Shiv Kapur		72	65	72	70	279	-9
	Angelo Que		71	68	68	72	279	-9

L-R: Mr R H Khwaja, Union Secretary of Tourism for the Government of India, S S P Chowrasia and Mr Gautam Thapar, Chairman and Chief Executive Officer, Avantha Group and President of the PGTI

Total Prize Fund €1,829,535   **First Prize** €300,000

Smooth Silky Putter

S S P Chowrasia has always been good on the greens. Indeed, while his initials actually stand for Shiv Sankar Prasad, they could just as easily stand for Smooth Silky Putter.

On The European Tour in 2008, he topped the Average Putts per Round category of the Genworth Statistics for the entire season. Therefore, it came as no surprise to anyone at the DLF Golf and Country Club that it was his performance on the New Delhi club's greens which paved the way to victory in the Avantha Masters – his second European Tour title in his home country following his Indian Masters triumph three years ago.

In his final round 67, his total of 25 putts was the lowest of the entire field as was his average putt figure of 1.462. Those impressive statistics helped the 32 year old from Calcutta to be second overall for the entire week in the Putts per Greens in Regulation Category with 1.604 as well as fourth overall for the week in the Putts per Round Category with an average of 26.8 over the four days.

He was challenged for the title over the final stages, specifically when a double bogey five at the short 16th opened the door to the chasing pack and, in particular, Robert Coles.

Coles, however, was unable to apply the pressure and Chowrasia delighted his home fans by completing the eighth Indian victory on The European Tour International Schedule.

Pablo Larrazábal

Robert Coles

Sujjan Singh

Robert-Jan Derksen

"I can't describe this feeling – I'm close to tears. I've put in a lot of hard work so this victory means a lot not just for me, but for a lot of people. It's also a nice first birthday present for my daughter Elle"

Luke Donald

WGC - ACCENTURE MATCH PLAY CHAMPIONSHIP
Ritz-Carlton Golf Club
Dove Mountain, Marana, Arizona, USA
February 23–27, 2011

CHAMPION	**LUKE DONALD**
Runner-Up	Martin Kaymer
Third	Matt Kuchar
Fourth	Bubba Watson

Semi-Finals: Luke Donald beat Matt Kuchar 6 and 5
Martin Kaymer beat Bubba Watson 1 hole
Final: Donald beat Kaymer 3 and 2
Consolation Match: Kuchar beat Watson 2 and 1

Total Prize Fund €6,240,960   **First Prize** €1,027,923

William Green, Chairman of Accenture and Luke Donald

Matt Kuchar

Miguel Angel Jiménez

Matteo Manassero

Martin Kaymer

New World Order

If ever any tournament emphasised the current strength of European golf perfectly, then it was the World Golf Championships – Accenture Match Play Championship.

For the second year in succession the final featured two European golfers – England's Luke Donald and Germany's Martin Kaymer stepping into the limelight occupied 12 months ago by Donald's fellow Englishmen Ian Poulter and Paul Casey – but there was far more to be acclaimed for the continent in the bigger picture.

By virtue of making the final itself, Kaymer moved ahead of Lee Westwood as World Number One while Donald's eventual 3 and 2 triumph saw him move to Number Three, behind Westwood but ahead of fourth placed Graeme McDowell. It was the first time since 1992 that European golfers had occupied the top four places in a new world order.

Kaymer wanted to crown his ascent with overall victory but it was never likely in a week when Donald comfortably dealt with everyone who appeared before him. His dominance was such that he was never behind in any of his six matches and did not have to play the Dove Mountain course's 18th hole the entire week. The 33 year old added guile and finesse around the putting surfaces to his usual staple diet of unerringly finding fairways and greens, making him unbeatable.

Three down early on in the final, Kaymer battled level by the turn but fell behind again when Donald claimed the 11th and 12th. When the Englishman won the 15th, he was three up with three to play and a hole later the title was his, a victory which also saw him move top of The Race to Dubai.

"I'm not sure about this tournament owing me one as such, but I did feel I had something for this course and I think I settled the score, I could not have asked for a better ending"

Nick Watney

WGC - CADILLAC CHAMPIONSHIP
Doral Golf Resort and Spa
Doral, Florida, USA
March 10–13, 2011

1	**NICK WATNEY**		**67**	**70**	**68**	**67**	**272**	**-16**
2	Dustin Johnson		69	69	65	71	274	-14
3	Anders Hansen		71	69	68	67	275	-13
	Francesco Molinari		68	68	70	69	275	-13
5	Matt Kuchar		68	69	68	71	276	-12
6	Luke Donald		67	72	66	72	277	-11
	Adam Scott		68	70	68	71	277	-11
8	Rickie Fowler		71	73	68	66	278	-10
9	Hunter Mahan		64	71	71	73	279	-9
10	Jonathan Byrd		70	74	68	68	280	-8
	Padraig Harrington		68	71	68	73	280	-8
	Martin Laird		67	70	70	73	280	-8
	Rory McIlroy		68	69	69	74	280	-8
	Tiger Woods		70	74	70	66	280	-8

Don Butler, Vice President of Marketing for Cadillac and Nick Watney

Total Prize Fund €5,984,757 **First Prize** €999,572

Francesco Molinari

Dustin Johnson

Anders Hansen

Luke Donald

In Good Nick

Nick Watney not only put American golf back on the world map with his victory in the World Golf Championships – Cadillac Championship, he also banished his own unhappy memories of the tournament at Doral back in 2009.

Then, having gone into the final round tied for the lead with Phil Mickelson, the 29 year old Californian failed to take advantage of several opportunities which presented themselves during a rollercoaster Sunday afternoon, leaving the experienced left hander to win by a shot. This time, however, the outcome was very different.

A solid first three days saw Watney go into the final round in a share of second place, two shots adrift of his fellow American Dustin Johnson. But while

Johnson could only find one birdie in the first 12 holes, Watney bagged six to turn the contest on its head. One shot clear coming down the last, a closing birdie three on the demanding 467 yard 18th was the icing on the cake for the three time winner on the US PGA Tour.

Leading Europeans were Denmark's Anders Hansen and Italy's Francesco Molinari who closed with 67 and 69 respectively to share third place, three shots adrift of Watney, while England's Luke Donald, winner of the WGC – Accenture Match Play Championship in Arizona two weeks previously, shared sixth place with Australia's Adam Scott to help cement his place at the top of The Race to Dubai.

SICILIAN OPEN
Donnafugata Golf Resort and Spa (Parkland Course)
Sicily, Italy
March 17–20, 2011

1	**RAPHAËL JACQUELIN**		66	69	69	68	272	-12
2	Anthony Wall		66	67	72	68	273	-11
3	José Manuel Lara		65	75	68	69	277	-7
	Joel Sjöholm		70	68	70	69	277	-7
5	Nicolas Colsaerts		71	71	69	68	279	-5
	Carlos Del Moral		68	70	71	70	279	-5
	Simon Dyson		71	70	67	71	279	-5
	Jamie Elson		69	69	69	72	279	-5
	Oscar Floren		69	68	71	71	279	-5
	Lorenzo Gagli		72	69	69	69	279	-5
	Scott Jamieson		71	70	68	70	279	-5
	Peter Whiteford		74	68	66	71	279	-5

L-R: Patrick Buteaux, Special Events Manager Omega, Marco De Rossi, CEO Donnafugata Resort, Raphaël Jacquelin, Salvatore Leonardi, FIG Regional Delegate, Antonio Belcuore, General Manager project Sicilian Open

Total Prize Fund €1,005,982   **First Prize** €166,660

"I stayed patient but it was a good fight with Anthony, he put a lot of pressure on me. I enjoyed the tussle but there can only be one winner – I'm glad it was me"

Raphaël Jacquelin

Worth the Wait

When you have waited almost four years to notch your third title on The European Tour International Schedule, holding on for one more day is not too much to ask. So it was for Raphaël Jacquelin who wrapped up victory in the inaugural Sicilian Open on the Monday morning.

The Frenchman had last tasted success in the BMW Asian Open in April 2007 but a two and half hour delay for a thunderstorm on the Italian island on Sunday meant his next title celebrations were put on hold.

When play did resume some 14 hours later the 36 year old succeeded in holding off the brave challenge of Englishman Anthony Wall to notch the first French victory of the 2011 season and indeed the first French triumph

on The European Tour since Grégory Bourdy won the UBS Hong Kong Open in November 2009.

Wall had been the pacesetter at halfway but Jacquelin's third round 69, in response to the Englishman's one over par 72, saw him grab pole position going into the final day which became a two horse race as the pair entered the home straight.

Having resumed play at 7.00 am on the Monday morning, Wall immediately drew level with a birdie three at the 13th but saw his chance of victory evaporate when he found the water at the 17th en route to a double bogey six. He bravely birdied the 18th, but Jacquelin's two regulation pars were good enough for victory.

Joel Sjöholm

Anthony Wall

Lorenzo Gagli

Carlos Del Moral

José Manuel Lara

SicilianOpen

2

PAR 4
425 M
463 YARDS

"This has been a long time coming. I've always prided myself on being a good putter but in the past few years the ball has just not gone in the hole. This week, it did"

Paul Lawrie

OPEN DE ANDALUCIA DE GOLF BY TURKISH AIRLINES
Parador de Málaga Golf (Old Course)
Málaga, Spain
March 24–27, 2011

1	**PAUL LAWRIE**		66	67	65	70	268	-12
2	Johan Edfors		65	71	65	68	269	-11
3	Felipe Aguilar		67	69	66	68	270	-10
4	Mark Foster		67	67	65	72	271	-9
	Jeppe Huldahl		66	66	72	67	271	-9
	Raphaël Jacquelin		68	69	65	69	271	-9
7	Christian Nilsson		68	69	67	68	272	-8
8	Florian Fritsch		66	68	69	70	273	-7
	José Manuel Lara		67	70	65	71	273	-7
	Hennie Otto		68	68	67	70	273	-7

Paul Lawrie and Luciano Alonso, Minister of Tourism, Trade and Sport for Junta de Andalucía

Total Prize Fund €1,001,500   **First Prize** €166,660

Felipe Aguilar

Raphaël Jacquelin and Johan Edfors

TURKISH
AIRLINES

FROM ISTANBUL TO MALAGA
STARTING ON 27ᵗʰ APRIL 2011

TURKISH
AIRLINES

Jeppe Huldahl

Mark Foster

En Andalucía todo sale bajo par

www.andalucia.org

Andalucía
TE QUIERE

Scotland the Brave

Scottish golf might not have had much reason to celebrate in recent years but Paul Lawrie helped put the smile back on the face of the nation which gave the game to the world with a battling victory in the Open de Andalucia de Golf by Turkish Airlines.

It was not only the 42 year old's first victory on The European Tour for nearly nine years, but also proved to be the first leg of a notable Scottish double on Sunday March 27 as, later that evening, Lawrie's fellow countryman Martin Laird won the Arnold Palmer Invitational at Bay Hill on the US PGA Tour – the first time in history two Scots have won on opposite sides of the Atlantic on the same day.

With six runners-up finishes to his name since his last victory in the 2002 Celtic Manor Wales Open, Lawrie must have feared it was going to be another near miss when, from one shot ahead overnight, he bogeyed the first two holes at the same time as his closest challenger, England's Mark Foster, birdied them.

But the winner of The 1999 Open Championship at Carnoustie kept his composure and, as Foster slipped back, he turned matters around – a scintillating stretch of four birdies in five holes from the turn helping him to a 12 under par total of 268, one shot too good for Sweden's Johan Edfors who took second and two ahead of third placed Felipe Aguilar of Chile.

TROPHÉE HASSAN II
Golf du Palais Royal and Golf de L'Océan
Agadir, Morocco
March 31–April 3, 2011

His Royal Highness Prince Moulay Rachid and David Horsey

Total Prize Fund €1,517,916   **First Prize** €250,000

1	**DAVID HORSEY**		67	71	67	69	274	-13
2	Rhys Davies		67	70	68	69	274	-13
	Jaco Van Zyl		68	73	65	68	274	-13
4	George Coetzee		67	71	69	69	276	-11
5	Oscar Floren		67	74	68	68	277	-10
	Jean-Baptiste Gonnet		71	68	71	67	277	-10
7	Mikko Ilonen		74	64	69	71	278	-9
	Richie Ramsay		70	74	66	68	278	-9
9	Tetsuji Hiratsuka		71	68	70	70	279	-8
	David Lynn		75	69	67	68	279	-8

"Getting my second European Tour win is very sweet indeed. I had a bit of luck out there but you need that at times in this game and the secret is taking advantage of it when you do get it. I managed to do that today"

David Horsey

Scott Kelly, Group Marketing Director of The European Tour (front centre) headed a delegation from the Trophée Hassan II who showed solidarity with the Japanese players in the field in the wake of their country's terrible earthquake. Agadir itself suffered 15,000 casualties during an earthquake in 1960

George Coetzee

Jaco Van Zyl

Rhys Davies

By a Neck

Sometimes, in professional golf, it is clear who is going to win a tournament as the leader strides down the final hole with a four or five shot lead. On occasion, however, it is simply impossible to pick a winner and the denouement of the Trophée Hassan II fell into the latter category.

With one hole to play, it looked like England's David Horsey – who had holed in one at the second – was the man poised to pick up his second European Tour title but, with a one shot lead over the field, he contrived to make double bogey six from the centre of the fairway.

Would it then be South African Jaco Van Zyl's opportunity to pick up his first Tour triumph? The 32

year old from Johannesburg needed a birdie three to pip Horsey but could only make par four. Surely then, it would be defending champion Rhys Davies who would win for the second year in succession? But, needing only to hole his four foot par putt for glory, inexplicably, one of the Tour's best putters ran the ball past the hole.

It meant a three-way play-off and on the first return to the 452 yard 18th Horsey showed his mettle with a brave eight footer for par to keep himself in the reckoning. It proved to be a crucial stroke for, on their second trip moments later and with Davies and Van Zyl repeating their par fours, the Englishman fired his approach to three feet and holed for a winning birdie three.

Drama and Dignity

"This is such a special feeling for me, I don't know where to start. It is obviously the highlight of my golfing career but I always thought if there was a chance that I would win a Major it would be this one – the course just suits my eye"

Charl Schwartzel

MASTERS TOURNAMENT
Augusta National Golf Club
Augusta, Georgia, USA
April 7-10, 2011

1	**CHARL SCHWARTZEL**		69	71	68	66	274	-14
2	Jason Day		72	64	72	68	276	-12
	Adam Scott		72	70	67	67	276	-12
4	Luke Donald		72	68	69	69	278	-10
	Geoff Ogilvy		69	69	73	67	278	-10
	Tiger Woods		71	66	74	67	278	-10
7	Angel Cabrera		71	70	67	71	279	-9
8	K J Choi		67	70	71	72	280	-8
	Bo Van Pelt		73	69	68	70	280	-8
10	Ryan Palmer		71	72	69	70	282	-6

Charl Schwartzel receives the Green Jacket from 2010 Masters Champion, Phil Mickelson

Total Prize Fund €5,660,915   **First Prize** €1,011,691

When a memorable 75th Masters Tournament had been consigned to the record books, the man who claimed the Green Jacket and the man who did not but who provided most of the headlines, did something you could not imagine happening in any other sport.

They travelled together for 20 long hours to another port, another tournament.

Photographs appeared on Twitter from the aeroplane, of Charl Schwartzel wearing the most coveted piece of clothing in golf and Rory McIlroy wearing a smile that was a testament to sportsmanship and dignity in defeat.

What drama this pair and, to be fair, plenty of others had provided in what was hailed in the aftermath as one of the finest endings the Masters Tournament had seen. Certainly, it could claim to have had everything, from a finish of sheer brilliance from Schwartzel to the heartbreaking sight of McIlroy close to tears as he became another victim of the fabled back nine at Augusta National.

Yet while these last two hours demonstrated that McIlroy was 21 after all, it would be a terrible oversight to dwell on them and forget the pure joy and exuberance he brought to this tournament over the first 63 holes.

Anyone who watches golf closely knows how good the Northern Irishman is but here he embraced a whole new audience and how they cheered from all corners of the globe as he moved to the brink of becoming the second youngest winner after Tiger Woods in 1997; and how they watched through the gaps in their fingers as he fell apart late on. The standing ovation he received from the patrons as he left the 18th green said everything about the indelible impression he had left.

Is he as nice as he seems? That was the question asked time and again the following week. Let Augusta's locker room attendant deliver the truth on that one. "Kind of sad it had to end up that way," he said. "He is as kind as can be."

As for the winner, the cognoscenti were all too aware that 26 year old Schwartzel was a coming man. Never mind the fact that he was without a top ten finish in a Major before this event. Four times a winner of the Sunshine Tour Order of Merit, six times a winner on The European Tour including a successful defence, in January, of the Joburg Open – all were indicative of a man who knew what to do when poised to triumph.

His victory completed a unique Grand Slam for The European Tour, with all four Major Championships residing in the hands of its members for the first time, following the victories for Graeme McDowell (US Open Championship), Schwartzel's great friend Louis Oosthuizen (The Open Championship) and Martin Kaymer (US PGA Championship) in 2010.

Schwartzel took up golf at the age of four, when his father instilled in him five fundamentals that he goes back to even to this day: grip, stance, posture, rhythm and balance. All were in perfect harmony during this tournament but he still would not have won without calling upon two other vital pieces of guidance.

Rory McIlroy

Angel Cabrera

Adam Scott

Jason Day

Tiger Woods

One came from Nick Price, after he had struggled to get the lightning pace of Augusta's greens last year. Every tournament you go to, practice the fastest putt on each green, the Zimbabwean master told him. Even if the putt is just five feet, learn how to hit them softly. "I can't tell you how much that helped," revealed Schwartzel.

The other came when that great patriarchal figure of South African golf, Johann Rupert, invited Jack Nicklaus to join them for lunch. After fighting the awe he felt, Schwartzel bucked up the courage to ask him for any tips on Augusta. By that stage, the great man was so taken he proceeded to give Schwartzel chapter and verse, with Rupert acting as stenographer.

Schwartzel was close enough to the lead over the first 54 holes but not that close he was expending energy on endless rounds of media work. McIlroy, by contrast, was in the spotlight every day. "You have no idea how tiring that can all be," said Justin Rose. "There seems to be more media work to do at Augusta than any other tournament."

PROQUIP

Ahead of the Game

COLLECTION

RYDER CUP 2012

MEDINAH 2012

Preferred Supplier to
The 2012 Ryder Cup European Team

www.proquipgolf.com

There certainly was for McIlroy, for people simply could not get enough of him. A brilliant 65 to be joint leader with the personable Spaniard Alvaro Quiros on day one was followed by a 69 for a two stroke advantage. That became four following a 70 on Saturday where he showed a remarkably mature head for one so young.

So to the amazing last day. So to a charge from Tiger Woods over the front nine that showcased all his remarkable gifts, as he went to the turn in just 31 shots. Still McIlroy was not fazed, as he reached the back nine with a one stroke lead. Then came a triple bogey seven at the tenth, and everything started to unravel.

Schwartzel had begun the day with a holed chip from off the green at the first, followed by a holed approach with a sand wedge at the third. Was fate lending a helping hand? Maybe. But what happened from the 15th onwards owed nothing to chance or to the gods of fortune, but everything to the wonderful gifts he possesses. By that stage there were no less than nine players within two strokes of the lead. Who would emerge from the peloton?

Fifty years after Gary Player became the first non American to win the Masters,

step forward his fellow countryman with a performance that must have made the former feel justifiably proud. By that stage Woods was in the clubhouse with a ten under par score of 278 he thought had a chance. So did Luke Donald, on the same mark after chipping in at the last. Soon, two Australians in Jason Day and Adam Scott, would raise the mark by two strokes with wonderful golf of their own, as they sought to end 74 years of hurt for their nation at this event.

It was hard to imagine at that stage that someone would beat that score by two more but that was the measure of Schwartzel's achievement as, quite remarkably, he birdied the last four holes. What could top that?

Well, for us old romantics, how about the fact the following day he shared a jet as well as tales of glory and stories of adventure with the other leading contributor to this great Masters, a young Ulsterman who - fingers and toes crossed - will get to wear green of his own one day?

Derek Lawrenson
Daily Mail

Honorary Starters Jack Nicklaus (left) and Arnold Palmer got the 2011 Masters Tournament underway

Fred Couples and Geoff Ogilvy

Augusta National Chairman Billy Payne presents the low amateur prize to Japan's Hideki Matsuyama

Luke Donald

"This is a great achievement and the perfect way to celebrate my 18th birthday. I never expected to have one victory on Tour before I was 18 and now I have two – I couldn't imagine anything better"

Matteo Manassero

MAYBANK MALAYSIAN OPEN
Kuala Lumpur Golf and Country Club (West Course)
Kuala Lumpur, Malaysia
April 14–17, 2011

1	MATTEO MANASSERO		66	71	67	68	272	-16
2	Grégory Bourdy		71	69	66	67	273	-15
3	Rory McIlroy		69	64	72	69	274	-14
4	Rafael Cabrera-Bello		69	70	69	67	275	-13
	Alexander Noren		64	69	71	71	275	-13
6	Felipe Aguilar		70	70	66	70	276	-12
7	Simon Dyson		70	64	76	68	278	-10
8	Siddikur Rahman		68	71	71	69	279	-9
9	Alejandro Cañizares		69	72	68	71	280	-8
	Martin Kaymer		70	71	67	72	280	-8

L-R: Datuk Seri Abdul Wahid Omar, President & CEO, Maybank, Matteo Manassero, Dato' Sri Mohd Najib bin Tun Abdul Razak, Prime Minister of Malaysia and Datuk Robin Loh, then President of the Malaysian Golf Association

Total Prize Fund €1,741,188   **First Prize** €288,466

Teenage Kicks

The presence in the field of three current Major Champions – Martin Kaymer, Louis Oosthuizen and Charl Schwartzel – was a fitting tribute to the 50th anniversary staging of the Maybank Malaysian Open, but the crowds departed marvelling at the talent of a young man who will surely challenge for similar titles in the near future.

Italian teenager Matteo Manassero is already in the record books as the youngest player to win on The European Tour and, two days before his 18th birthday, he assured himself of second place on that list as well with an impressively composed one shot victory, a triumph which once again belied his tender years.

The leaders had 27 holes to complete on the final day as a result of weather delays earlier in the week and when the last round began, Manassero shared pole position with Sweden's Alex Noren. Rory McIlroy, showing admirable courage in bouncing back from his disappointing final round in the Masters Tournament the previous week, flirted with the lead before a double bogey at the 12th halted his progress, while Frenchman Grégory Bourdy threatened before his own double bogey at the 11th set him back.

With Noren unable to add to his two birdies in the first three holes, the stage was set for Manassero and he did not disappoint. An eagle at the tenth followed by birdies at the 11th and 14th put him ahead and four solid pars to finish sealed the deal.

L-R: Martin Kaymer, Charl Schwartzel and Louis Oosthuizen

Alex Noren

Rory McIlroy

Grégory Bourdy

"I am enjoying every second of this. I'm dizzy and my head is all over the place. I've been waiting for this moment for a very long time and I did it in the best of ways so I'm really delighted"

Nicolas Colsaerts

VOLVO CHINA OPEN
Luxehills International Country Club
Chengdu, China
April 21–24, 2011

1	**NICOLAS COLSAERTS**		65	67	66	66	264	-24
2	Søren Kjeldsen		65	71	66	66	268	-20
	Peter Lawrie		68	64	68	68	268	-20
	Danny Lee		66	68	69	65	268	-20
	Pablo Martin		70	68	67	63	268	-20
6	Christian Nilsson		70	65	70	64	269	-19
7	Jamie Donaldson		70	61	70	69	270	-18
	Grégory Havret		66	66	68	70	270	-18
	Danny Willett		70	66	69	65	270	-18
10	Richard Finch		69	67	71	64	271	-17
	Pablo Larrazábal		70	67	70	64	271	-17
	Gareth Maybin		65	67	72	67	271	-17
	Jeev Milkha Singh		66	66	71	68	271	-17
	Aaron Townsend		68	66	68	69	271	-17

Nicolas Colsaerts and Per Ericsson, President of Volvo Event Management Golf

Total Prize Fund €2,118,298   **First Prize** €350,946

Søren Kjeldsen

Great Expectations

The pressure of expectation can be a difficult burden to carry in golf and no-one knows that better than Nicolas Colsaerts.

The man from Brussels was eight years from arriving on the earth the last time a Belgian golfer won on The European Tour – in the guise of Phillipe Toussaint in the 1974 Benson and Hedges International Open at Fulford – but ever since he turned professional on his 18th birthday after having become the second youngest player to graduate from The European Tour Qualifying School, great things have been forecast for the 28 year old.

However, turning expectation into glory is not easy and Colsaerts struggled to make an impact. His personal nadir came at the end of the 2007 season when he lost his playing privileges and decided to take time out to re-evaluate not only his career but his life. He did that successfully and, having graduated from the Challenge Tour in 2009, he finished 67th on The 2010 Race to Dubai to indicate he was moving in the right direction.

Renowned as a big-hitter, the Belgian harnessed that power in addition to finesse around the greens to coast to victory in China. He began the final round with a one shot advantage and a fine closing 66, which featured three birdies in four holes from the 12th, saw him win comfortably by four shots from Søren Kjeldsen, Peter Lawrie, Danny Lee and Pablo Martin.

Danny Lee

Peter Lawrie

Christian Nilsson and Pablo Martin

"It was a little nerve-wracking watching the final few holes to see if anyone could catch me but this feels great. Professional golf is all about winning and to do it two weeks in a row is special"

Lee Westwood

BALLANTINE'S CHAMPIONSHIP
Blackstone Golf Club (West and North Courses)
Icheon, Seoul, South Korea
April 28–May 1, 2011

1	**LEE WESTWOOD**		72	68	69	67	276	-12
2	Miguel Angel Jiménez		70	67	69	71	277	-11
3	Sang-hyun Park		67	72	70	69	278	-10
4	Dustin Johnson		70	69	71	69	279	-9
5	Soon-sang Hong		69	72	70	69	280	-8
	Alexander Noren		70	69	67	74	280	-8
7	Jbe Kruger		73	70	69	69	281	-7
	James Morrison		69	69	72	71	281	-7
	Brett Rumford		71	63	73	74	281	-7
10	Dae-hyun Kim		71	69	71	71	282	-6
	Kyung-tae Kim		69	71	72	70	282	-6
	Joong-kyung Mo		71	70	72	69	282	-6

Paul Scanlon, Commercial Vice President, Ballantine's and Lee Westwood

Total Prize Fund €2,211,611   **First Prize** €367,500

WATCH FOR SNAKES

유해동물 주의

Sang-hyun Park

Dustin Johnson

Alex Noren

Class Act

The golfing CV of Lee Westwood is one of the most impressive in the sport. The 38 year old Englishman has achieved almost everything in the game but one thing which irked him was the fact he had not won a tournament as World Number One.

Having first attained the pinnacle of golf in October 2010, and having returned to the summit the week before travelling to South Korea following victory in the Indonesian Masters on the Asian Tour, Westwood arrived determined to deliver a performance and a victory commensurate with his status. He achieved both of those objectives in style.

Starting the final round three shots in arrears of leaders Rhys Davies, Miguel Angel Jiménez and Alex Noren, Westwood exuded class with a superb best of day 67 which gave him a winning total of 12 under par 276, one shot clear of Jiménez who narrowly missed out on forcing a play-off when his 15 foot birdie putt on the 72nd hole stayed above ground.

Host country favourite Sang-hyun Park thrilled the home fans with a 69 to take third place, one shot ahead of American Ryder Cup player Dustin Johnson who completed a truly international top four, but all eyes, at the end of the day, were on Westwood.

Rightly priding himself on being a global player, the victory represented the Englishman's 35th professional triumph worldwide, those wins now spread across an incredible array of 19 countries.

Miguel Angel Jiménez

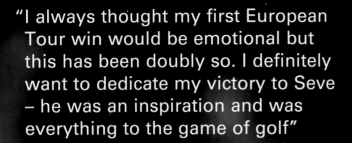

"I always thought my first European Tour win would be emotional but this has been doubly so. I definitely want to dedicate my victory to Seve – he was an inspiration and was everything to the game of golf"

Thomas Aiken

OPEN DE ESPAÑA
Real Club de Golf El Prat (Violet Course)
Terrassa, Barcelona, Spain
May 5–8, 2011

1	**THOMAS AIKEN**		68	68	72	70	278	-10
2	Anders Hansen		69	72	69	70	280	-8
3	Scott Jamieson		66	72	72	71	281	-7
	Pablo Larrazábal		67	70	73	71	281	-7
5	Simon Dyson		75	67	72	68	282	-6
	Grégory Havret		71	72	69	70	282	-6
	David Horsey		71	70	71	70	282	-6
	Paul Lawrie		72	71	72	67	282	-6
	Phillip Price		70	71	72	69	282	-6
	Romain Wattel		67	71	72	72	282	-6

Thomas Aiken and Gonzaga Escauriaza, Presidente de la Real Federación Española de Golf

Total Prize Fund €2,000,000   **First Prize** €333,330

Scott Jamieson

Pablo Larrazábal

Players, officials and their families observe a minute's silence to mark the passing of Severiano Ballesteros

Anders Hansen

Mark of Respect

The Open de España, rightly, belonged to Thomas Aiken who produced a stirring showing at Real Club de Golf El Prat to claim his maiden European Tour title. But the thoughts of everyone at the Barcelona venue, and indeed around the world, were for Seve Ballesteros who lost his fight for life in the early hours of Saturday morning.

There would never be a good time for the world to lose the charismatic Spaniard but perhaps there was a certain synchronicity that he left us during a week where the eyes of European golf were focused on his home country. Certainly, it was a point touched on by the new champion who, respectfully, dedicated his win to Ballesteros.

Coming into the tournament after a seven week lay-off, Aiken did not know what to expect but after consecutive rounds of 68 gave him the lead at the halfway stage, the 27 year old South African soon knew what he wanted.

A level par 72 on an emotionally charged Saturday, where every single player wore a black ribbon on their clothing as a mark of respect, kept Aiken's nose in front and he held his nerve coming down the stretch on Sunday to hold off the challenge of the eventual runner-up, the experienced Dane Anders Hansen, to win by two shots.

It was Aiken's first victory in his 104th event and marked the fifth time this season that a European Tour event had ended with a South African winner.

Reale

Open
de españa
2011

9
PAR 4
METROS 426
YARDAS 466

ESPAÑA I need Spain

ESPAÑA I need Spain

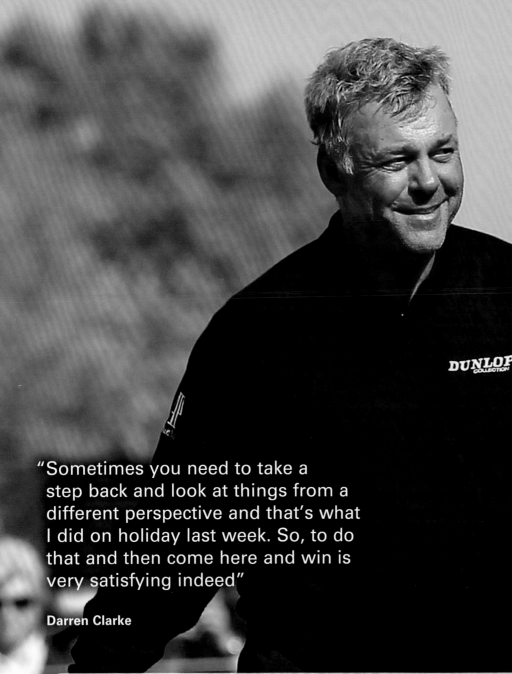

"Sometimes you need to take a step back and look at things from a different perspective and that's what I did on holiday last week. So, to do that and then come here and win is very satisfying indeed"

Darren Clarke

 IBERDROLA OPEN
Pula Golf Club
Son Servera, Mallorca, Spain
May 12–15, 2011

1	**DARREN CLARKE**		65	70	70	69	274	-6
2	David Lynn		68	68	71	70	277	-3
	Chris Wood		67	65	69	76	277	-3
4	Alastair Forsyth		68	72	68	70	278	-2
5	Paul Lawrie		68	69	72	70	279	-1
	Shane Lowry		72	70	63	74	279	-1
	José María Olazábal		71	69	66	73	279	-1
	Graeme Storm		71	71	67	70	279	-1
9	Thomas Aiken		70	72	66	72	280	0
	Grégory Bourdy		63	77	67	73	280	0
	Damien McGrane		68	74	68	70	280	0

Darren Clarke and Celia Jaume, representative of Iberdrola in the Balearic Islands

Total Prize Fund €1,000,000   **First Prize €166,660**

David Lynn

Shane Lowry

Alastair Forsyth

Chris Wood

Lucky Thirteen

It might represent the archetypal unlucky number for most people, but for Darren Clarke such a sentiment was far from his thoughts as he embraced his 13th European Tour International Schedule title in Mallorca.

The 42 year old Northern Irishman used all the experience gained from his 20 years as a Tour professional to come from four shots behind at the start of the final round to eventually overhaul his International Sports Management stablemate Chris Wood, who appeared on course for his maiden triumph.

Clarke, who like the previous week's winner Thomas Aiken was playing in his first event back following a holiday in the Bahamas, had reduced the young Englishman's advantage to one shot within three holes but a double bogey at the 11th after a trip into a water

hazard looked to have cost him the chance of his first victory since his KLM Open win in the Netherlands in 2008.

But Wood encountered his own problems on the back nine which opened the door for Clarke and he did not need a second invitation, finishing in style with a final round 69, which equalled the best score of the day, for a six under par total of 274 and a three shot winning margin over Wood and his fellow Englishman David Lynn who had moved through the field with a closing 70.

The victory moved the Northern Irishman to 35th in The Race to Dubai and back into the top 90 on the Official World Golf Ranking. Important certainly, but for Clarke, the only figure which mattered was the fact he was once again, number one on a Sunday.

"It was very tough out there, I had to dig deep at times, but I'm delighted with the win. I thought I had a good chance this week and when I saw the wind on the final day, I knew I did"

Michael Hoey

MADEIRA ISLANDS OPEN
Porto Santo Golfe
Madeira, Portugal
May 19–22, 2011

1	**MICHAEL HOEY**		72	68	67	71	278	-10
2	Jamie Elson		71	68	68	73	280	-8
	Chris Gane		67	72	70	71	280	-8
4	Federico Colombo		70	73	72	67	282	-6
	José-Filipe Lima		70	75	69	68	282	-6
	Lloyd Saltman		68	73	71	70	282	-6
7	Markus Brier		74	69	72	68	283	-5
	Magnus A Carlsson		71	71	72	69	283	-5
	Colm Moriarty		72	70	71	70	283	-5
10	Alastair Forsyth		71	69	69	75	284	-4
	Sebi Garcia		74	69	70	71	284	-4
	Branden Grace		74	69	71	70	284	-4
	Ricardo Santos		72	73	66	73	284	-4
	Lee Slattery		72	70	70	72	284	-4
	Tom Whitehouse		74	70	72	68	284	-4

João Cuna e Silva, Vice-President of Madeira's Regional Government and Michael Hoey

Total Prize Fund €702,097   **First Prize** €116,660

Chris Gane

Federico Colombo

madeira islands
TURISMO DE PORTUGAL

José-Filipe Lima

Shooting the Breeze

The phrase horses for courses could well have been designed to describe Michael Hoey's success story for, two years after picking up his maiden European Tour title at the windswept Estoril Open de Portugal, the Northern Irishman once again conquered the breeze in Portugal to claim the Madeira Islands Open.

Having grown up on the majestic links courses of the Province and having honed his game to such an extent in the wind that he went on to win The Amateur Championship in 2001 and be part of the winning Great Britain and Ireland Walker Cup team later that year, Hoey was always going to start favourite in the blustery final round.

He began the day tied with Englishman Jamie Elson but used his experience to par the first seven holes before moving ahead with a birdie at the eighth. With another Englishman, Chris Gane, closing in at the top of the leaderboard, Hoey gave the left hander a glimmer of hope with a dropped shot at the 13th but recovered admirably with a birdie at the next to re-establish his superiority and he pushed on to close with a 71 for a ten under par total of 278 and a two shot winning margin over Elson and Gane.

Earlier in the final round another Englishman, Simon Wakefield, broke the Porto Santo Golfe course record with a magnificent 63 which, for a moment, threatened to be the Tour's first official 59 before he double bogeyed the final hole.

Jamie Elson

"I don't know what it is about match play but I just love it. I've tried to work it out but I think I just get more adrenalin and get more 'up' for it. Can we have 20 match play events a year please"

Ian Poulter

Volvo World Match Play Championship

VOLVO WORLD MATCH PLAY CHAMPIONSHIP
Finca Cortesin Golf Club
Caseras, Andalucía, Spain
May 19-22, 2011

CHAMPION	**IAN POULTER**	
Runner-Up	Luke Donald	
Third	Nicolas Colsaerts	
	Martin Kaymer	

Semi-Finals: Ian Poulter beat Nicolas Colsaerts at 19th
Luke Donald beat Martin Kaymer 5 and 3
Final: Poulter beat Donald 2 and 1

Total Prize Fund €3,400,000*   First Prize €800,000*
* Capped for The Race to Dubai €2,571,390 / €566,660

Per Ericsson, President of Volvo Event Management Golf and Ian Poulter

www.volvoworldmatchplay.com

471 yds 431 mtrs
Par 4
1

Volvo World
Match Play
Championship

Nicolas Colsaerts

Luke Donald

Players gather for a welcome dinner prior to the Championship

Happy Birthday, Son

He delighted one Luke while disappointing another, but when the dust had settled at Finca Cortesin there was one man left with the biggest smile of them all: Ian Poulter.

In the first all English final of the Volvo World Match Play Championship since the illustrious competition began at Wentworth Club back in 1964, Poulter saw off compatriot Luke Donald 2 and 1 in the 18 hole showdown; in the process denying Donald the opportunity to oust Lee Westwood from the Number One position on the Official World Golf Ranking.

One Luke disappointed certainly but another, in the shape of Poulter's son Luke, was more than ecstatic as his daddy lifted the €800,000 first prize on the day of his seventh birthday.

Given the fact the finalist were joint top points scorers for Europe in last year's Ryder Cup and were also the last two winners of the WGC-Accenture Match Play title, their appearance in the final should not have come as a surprise.

Having come through the group stages, Poulter then ousted his Ryder Cup team-mates Francesco Molinari and Westwood along with rising Belgian star Nicolas Colsaerts in the semi-final while Donald disposed of Johan Edfors as well as Major champions Charl Schwartzel and Martin Kaymer.

Donald held sway early on in the final but a 40 foot putt on the 12th saw Poulter level. He moved ahead two holes later and never looked back, capturing the title on his first appearance.

Martin Kaymer

Top of the World

"It doesn't get much better than the Number One and Two in the world playing off for that honour as well as the flagship title on The European Tour. History was made today and I was delighted to be a part of it"

Luke Donald

BMW PGA CHAMPIONSHIP
Wentworth Club (West Course)
Surrey, England
May 26-29, 2011

1	**LUKE DONALD**		64	72	72	70	278	-6
2	Lee Westwood		72	69	69	68	278	-6
3	Simon Dyson		71	68	72	69	280	-4
4	Marcus Fraser		70	72	73	67	282	-2
	Raphaël Jacquelin		72	70	69	71	282	-2
	Shane Lowry		74	72	69	67	282	-2
7	Jamie Donaldson		71	71	72	69	283	-1
	Johan Edfors		66	75	71	71	283	-1
	David Horsey		70	68	74	71	283	-1
	Matteo Manassero		66	70	72	75	283	-1
	Colin Montgomerie		69	75	71	68	283	-1
	Peter Whiteford		71	69	73	70	283	-1

L-R: Tim Abbott, Managing Director, BMW UK, Luke Donald and Ian Robertson, Member of the Board of Management, BMW AG

Total Prize Fund €4,500,000   **First Prize** €750,000

A fleet of silver BMW cars ferried a startling array of golfing talent to a night of nights that heralded an historic week for The European Tour. Best bib and tucker had been donned that Tuesday evening in the luxury of Heathrow's Sofitel Hotel to celebrate the Players' Awards Dinner and an unprecedented year of success. Little did the guests realise that, what was to come, would be even better.

Never before had the two best golfers on the planet contested a play-off, not only for the Tour's flagship BMW PGA Championship title but also for the right to the World Number One position. But that was what precisely unfolded on a memorable Sunday afternoon at Wentworth Club where Luke Donald narrowly and dramatically edged Lee Westwood for both accolades.

But more of that later. The Players' Awards Dinner was not simply playing host to the game's leading protagonists. The most prestigious prizes in the game were also there; The Open Championship's Claret Jug, the silver trophies that accompany the US Open and the US PGA Championship and, of course, the pot of gold that is The Ryder Cup. There was also special dispensation for Charl Schwartzel to ignore the function's black tie rule so he could don his recently acquired Masters Tournament Green Jacket.

In his keynote speech European Tour Chief Executive George O'Grady revelled in a past year of golfing glory for his organisation's members. As well as celebrating Ryder Cup success, he prompted us to recall the inspired performances that brought victories for Graeme McDowell at the US Open, Louis Oosthuizen at The Open, Martin Kaymer at the US PGA and Schwartzel's triumph at Augusta as well as saluting the consistency that had taken Westwood to the top of the Official World Golf Ranking.

Inevitably there was also a more sombre note to be sounded because this was the biggest gathering of the golfing family since the untimely death of Severiano Ballesteros three weeks earlier. It was a most appropriate time to remember the man whose genius, charisma and will to win were so influential in popularising the sport.

Raphaël Jacquelin

Colin Montgomerie

Lee Westwood

Appropriately Seve's brother Manuel, sons Javier and Miguel, and nephew Ivan were present to share in the evening. They watched with us a film that superbly portrayed the great man's brilliance after Ryder Cup captain José María Olazábal had emotionally and eloquently addressed guests with his own unique stories of partnering Seve in the biennial contest against the United States.

Olazábal had been one of 26 professionals who had signalled the start of this extraordinary week by playing in the Olé Seve Charity Pro-Am over the West Course to raise money for the Seve Ballesteros Foundation.

Seve had set up the organisation to help fight brain cancer, the disease to which he succumbed at the age of 54. The Foundation works in partnership with Cancer Research UK and the Pro-Am and auction that followed raised £618,168. By the end of the week, as a result of further events and collections, the figure had risen to an impressive £725,905.

Seve, the ultimate Ryder Cup warrior, would have loved that Tuesday evening. How he would have wanted to be among the dozen players and skipper Colin Montgomerie who were asked on stage to reflect on the continent's thrilling victory at Celtic Manor. They did so in a lively and good humoured chat with American interviewer Steve Sands of The Golf Channel.

It was asking an awful lot for the serious business of the week to live up to that glittering night, but the BMW PGA Championship succeeded with ease. Never before had the championship boasted a stronger field with the four Major

Marcus Fraser

Shane Lowry

Simon Dyson

JOY IS MAKING THE CUT.

Staying at the top of your game is about consistently performing. With the BMW 6 Series Convertible you can enjoy the ultimate performance. Immerse yourself in elegance, exclusivity and uncompromising sportiness. To experience the perfect drive contact your local BMW Dealer or visit **bmw.co.uk/6seriesconvertible**

JOY IS THE BMW 6 SERIES CONVERTIBLE.

Official fuel economy figures for the BMW 6 Series Convertible range: Urban 18.2 – 41.5 mpg (15.5 – 6.8 ltr/100 km). Extra Urban 35.8 – 57.6 mpg

(7.9 – 4.9 ltr/100 km). Combined 26.4 – 50.4 mpg (10.7 – 5.6 ltr/100 km). CO_2 emissions 249 – 148 g/km.

L-R: Anthony Scanlon, Executive Director of the International Golf Federation, George O'Grady, Chief Executive of The European Tour, and Matteo Manassero met a group of Special Olympics Athletes during their tour of the BMW PGA Championship

Francesco Molinari and Rory McIlroy had fun with the fans in the Tented Village during Cotter's Questions

Champions and 11 of Europe's victorious Ryder Cup team on show. Only the injured Padraig Harrington was missing.

In Westwood, Donald and Kaymer, the field also boasted the top three players in the world and by the time Thursday arrived spectators flocked to the West Course in their thousands to catch a glimpse of the game's genuine elite. They were rewarded with four days of thrilling golf that climaxed in an unprecedented shoot-out.

Westwood was top of the pile but knew his position was vulnerable if the man lying second was to beat him. That was Donald, who signalled his intent with a blistering first round 64 that had fellow professionals gasping in disbelief that such a score was possible on a course toughened by breezy conditions.

Attendance records were smashed as 25,472 people watched Friday's second round. It was impossible to accommodate another single vehicle on the Wentworth estate as car parks filled to capacity. By the end of the week, a record 93,404 spectators had been packed in.

Fans took part in a myriad of activities in a tented village that, thanks to the standard of its facilities, took on the feel of a Major Championship. On the course, Donald was plugging away at the top of the leaderboard while the Italian youngster Matteo Manassero was announcing himself to the vast crowds in Seve-like style.

Indeed it was all things Seve on that Friday as the players dressed in the Spaniard's trademark navy blue as a visual tribute to the great man. For the rest of the week it was almost as though he was looking down on proceedings as the tournament built to the most fitting climax imaginable.

Westwood had manfully eaten away at Donald's advantage and with three holes to go in the final round the man from Worksop led by two shots. Then, crucially, he bogeyed the 16th while Donald, playing in the group behind, birdied the same hole to draw level.

With the early evening sunshine glistening on the BMW hospitality pavilion beside the home green, both players had birdie putts

THE PLAYERS' AWARDS

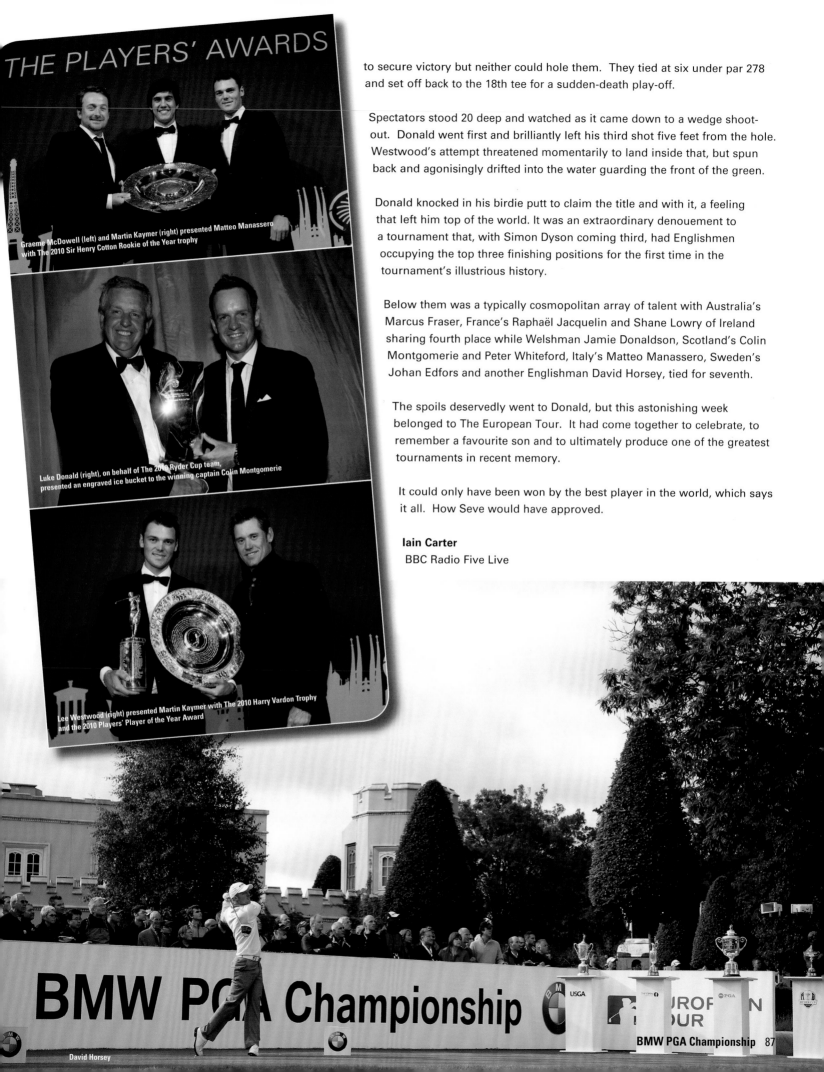

Graeme McDowell (left) and Martin Kaymer (right) presented Matteo Manassero with The 2010 Sir Henry Cotton Rookie of the Year trophy

Luke Donald (right), on behalf of The 2010 Ryder Cup team, presented an engraved ice bucket to the winning captain Colin Montgomerie

Lee Westwood (right) presented Martin Kaymer with The 2010 Harry Vardon Trophy and the 2010 Players' Player of the Year Award

David Horsey

to secure victory but neither could hole them. They tied at six under par 278 and set off back to the 18th tee for a sudden-death play-off.

Spectators stood 20 deep and watched as it came down to a wedge shoot-out. Donald went first and brilliantly left his third shot five feet from the hole. Westwood's attempt threatened momentarily to land inside that, but spun back and agonisingly drifted into the water guarding the front of the green.

Donald knocked in his birdie putt to claim the title and with it, a feeling that left him top of the world. It was an extraordinary denouement to a tournament that, with Simon Dyson coming third, had Englishmen occupying the top three finishing positions for the first time in the tournament's illustrious history.

Below them was a typically cosmopolitan array of talent with Australia's Marcus Fraser, France's Raphaël Jacquelin and Shane Lowry of Ireland sharing fourth place while Welshman Jamie Donaldson, Scotland's Colin Montgomerie and Peter Whiteford, Italy's Matteo Manassero, Sweden's Johan Edfors and another Englishman David Horsey, tied for seventh.

The spoils deservedly went to Donald, but this astonishing week belonged to The European Tour. It had come together to celebrate, to remember a favourite son and to ultimately produce one of the greatest tournaments in recent memory.

It could only have been won by the best player in the world, which says it all. How Seve would have approved.

Iain Carter
BBC Radio Five Live

"This proves to me that I can still win which is the most important thing. Having won two years ago and then doing nothing really last year, you do begin to doubt, but this has removed all of that"

Alex Noren

SAAB WALES OPEN
The Celtic Manor Resort (Twenty Ten Course)
City of Newport, Wales
June 2–5, 2011

1	**ALEXANDER NOREN**		**67**	**67**	**71**	**70**	**275**	**-9**
2	Grégory Bourdy		67	73	70	67	277	-7
	Anders Hansen		70	70	66	71	277	-7
4	Johan Edfors		68	71	70	69	278	-6
	Ricardo Gonzalez		71	67	73	67	278	-6
	Peter Hanson		65	72	69	72	278	-6
	Pablo Larrazábal		70	70	71	67	278	-6
8	Magnus A Carlsson		71	70	69	70	280	-4
	Jamie Donaldson		68	68	71	73	280	-4
	Joel Sjöholm		72	69	71	68	280	-4
	Peter Whiteford		70	70	73	67	280	-4

L-R: Sir Terry Matthews, Chairman of The Celtic Manor Resort, Alex Noren and Charles Toosey, Managing Director of Saab Great Britain Ltd

Total Prize Fund €2,040,689   First Prize €344,358

Jamie Donaldson

Grégory Bourdy

Anders Hansen

SAAB
WALES OPEN

17

211 yds - 193 mtrs
PAR 3

ROLEX

RACE TO DUBAI

Graeme McDowell

Peter Hanson

Johan Edfors

Ice Cold is Alex

There are many different ways to win a golf tournament. Sometimes it is a moment of magic which sparks the run to the finishing line, sometimes it can simply be solid play which succeeds, and Alex Noren has now exhibited both ends of that particular spectrum in his two European Tour victories.

His first, in the 2009 Omega European Masters in Switzerland, was ignited by a sensational holed bunker shot for an eagle two, four holes from home, which gave him the impetus to go on and beat Welshman Bradley Dredge.

The second came in Dredge's home country as a supremely consistent display saw him fend off the challenge spearheaded by Frenchman Grégory Bourdy and Anders Hansen of Denmark to stride to victory in the Saab Wales Open.

Played on The Twenty Ten Course which seven months earlier had seen the sensational denouement of The Ryder Cup, it appeared written in the stars that defending champion and Ryder Cup hero Graeme McDowell, one behind Noren at halfway, would go on to triumph.

However, a third round 81 from the Northern Irishman ended his hopes leaving Noren as the man to catch. Several tried but a final round 70 from the Swede which contained just two birdies and one bogey did the business by two shots.

It completed a dream week for the 28 year old from Stockholm who, on the Monday, came through the 36 hole qualifying tournament at Walton Heath to book his place in the US Open Championship for the first time.

BMW Golfsport
bmw-golfsport.com

The Ultimate Driving Machine

BMW Italian Open 2011
presented by CartaSi

BMW ITALIAN OPEN presented by CartaSi
Royal Park I Roveri (Robert Trent Jones Snr Course)
Turin, Italy
June 9–12, 2011

EUROPEAN TOUR RACE TO DUBAI 2011

1	**ROBERT ROCK**		64	68	68	67	267	-21
2	Gary Boyd		69	65	68	66	268	-20
	Thorbjørn Olesen		65	71	70	62	268	-20
4	Peter Whiteford		68	67	68	66	269	-19
5	Joost Luiten		66	67	69	68	270	-18
6	Niclas Fasth		69	69	64	69	271	-17
	Michael Jonzon		69	68	69	65	271	-17
8	Jbe Kruger		69	66	67	70	272	-16
	Matteo Manassero		66	68	70	68	272	-16
	Francesco Molinari		66	68	68	70	272	-16

BMW Italian Open

presented by

Robert Rock and Franz Jung, President BMW Italia

Total Prize Fund €1,504,497   First Prize €250,000

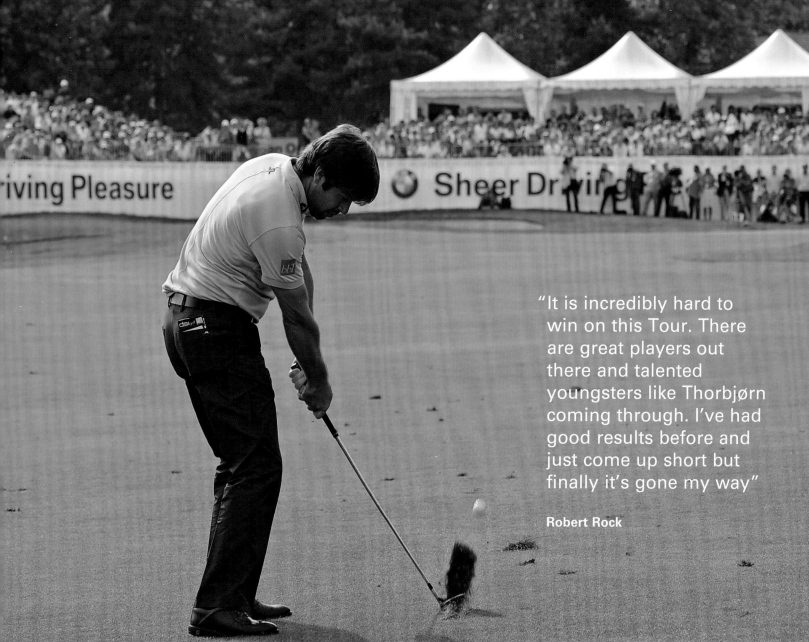

"It is incredibly hard to win on this Tour. There are great players out there and talented youngsters like Thorbjørn coming through. I've had good results before and just come up short but finally it's gone my way"

Robert Rock

Thorbjørn Olesen

Gary Boyd

Peter Whiteford

Joost Luiten

Rock Steady

He might well have a surname which is manna from heaven for sub editors in newspapers or magazines - the only problem for Robert Rock was the fact that in 208 prior appearances on The European Tour he had been unable to produce the victory which would allow the creative juices of the page makers to flow.

He had endured three runners-up finishes in 2009, including in this very tournament at Royal Park I Roveri, but all that was forgotten with a bold display on an enthralling afternoon which saw the Englishman finally emerge with his hands on the trophy. A closing 67 gave him a wire-to-wire victory but it was far from straightforward on a day when the Turin golf course offered up plenty of birdie opportunities.

One man who needed no second invitation to take advantage of the chances was young Dane Thorbjørn Olesen who started his final round a full two hours before Rock but who set the clubhouse target of 20 under par 268 with a stunning ten under par 62 that included five birdies and an eagle in a remarkable outward half of 29.

It was an overall score matched by England's Gary Boyd, leaving Rock knowing what he had to do to win. One ahead with two to play, Rock looked in trouble after a poor drive on the 17th but a great escape saw him save par and another regulation figure at the 18th was sufficient for victory.

SAINT-OMER OPEN presented by Neuflize OBC
Aa Saint Omer Golf Club
Lumbres, France
June 16–19, 2011

1	**MATTHEW ZIONS**		68	72	67	69	276	-8
2	Daniel Denison		69	74	67	73	283	-1
	Peter Gustafsson		73	71	70	69	283	-1
	Craig Lee		69	68	74	72	283	-1
5	Jorge Campillo		76	66	70	72	284	0
	Lorenzo Gagli		73	68	72	71	284	0
	Anders Schmidt Hansen		70	72	71	71	284	0
	Andrea Perrino		68	69	75	72	284	0
	Marco Ruiz		70	70	74	70	284	0
	Lee Slattery		73	68	73	70	284	0
	Andrew Tampion		69	71	74	70	284	0

Matthew Zions and Emmanuel Debavelaere, Directeur centre de gestion patrimoniale, Banque Neuflize OBC Lille

Total Prize Fund €606,237   **First Prize €100,000**

"This feels like I'm dreaming. Over the last four holes I was wondering when I could start thinking about winning because I didn't want to tempt fate. But when I did, I had a lump in my throat"

Matt Zions

Peter Gustafsson

Danny Denison

Lorenzo Gagli

Aussie Rules

Matt Zions carved his own niche in European Tour history with a record breaking seven shot maiden victory in the SAINT-OMER OPEN presented by Neuflize OBC.

The previous biggest winning margin in the dual ranking tournament between The European Tour and the Challenge Tour had been Christian Nilsson's six shot triumph in 2009 but the Australian's weekend rounds of 67-69 helped him romp out of sight of the rest of the field on eight under par 276.

The 32 year old started the final day three shots clear of a trio of players and was never seriously troubled as he became the 37th different Australian golfer to win on The European Tour as well as also, significantly, extending Australia's run

of consecutive winning years on The European Tour to 28, dating back to the 1984 season.

England's Danny Denison, one of the trio who started the day closest to Zions, carded a final round 73 which was good enough for a share of second place on one under par 283 with Sweden's Peter Gustafsson and Craig Lee of Scotland who signed off with rounds of 69 and 72 respectively.

It continued the encouraging rehabilitation of Denison, the 26 year old from Leeds, who suffered a badly broken leg in a car accident during the MAN NÖ Open on the European Challenge Tour in July 2007.

Craig Lee

Soaring into History

"To win my first Major early in my career, especially after what happened in the last few months, feels really special and I look forward to putting myself in the picture for many more. It's also great to follow my friend Graeme McDowell onto this trophy"

Rory McIlroy

It was a shot for the ages … in every respect. The key moment of Rory McIlroy's coronation on Sunday at the US Open Championship occurred on the tenth tee at Congressional Country Club.

It was captured in the pages of newspapers and magazines worldwide, a photograph almost biblical in tone – thousands of people falling silent on the vast terraced banks and bleachers which overlooked this treacherous par three.

Time was frozen as McIlroy played a towering six iron which soared into history. It was the shot of the championship and of 22 year old Rory's life.

The ball arced across the lake and over the flag, touching down on the putting surface just 15 feet beyond the hole. It bit into the short grass and, roared on by the multitude, rolled back down the slope and mere inches past the cup.

McIlroy had almost aced the last great test of his championship. Just 69 days, 23 hours and 42 minutes after his Masters Tournament meltdown had begun on the tenth tee at Augusta National, he now knew for sure the moment of redemption had come.

The tap in birdie moved him to 17 under, the lowest anyone has ever gone against par at the US Open. McIlroy would complete the 72 holes in 268 strokes and 16 below par, in both cases beating the tournament record by four.

Eight ahead of his closest challenger, Jason Day of Australia, McIlroy blitzed the opposition and humbled a formidable golf course as he ambled to the most outrageous victory by a first-time winner at the Majors since Tiger Woods overwhelmed Augusta in 1997.

'Golf's New Era', was emblazoned across the cover of Sports Illustrated and that is precisely how it seemed after four days in which 'Wee Mac' grew into a phenomenon.

McIlroy ripped up the record books as he became the youngest player to win the US Open since Bobby Jones in 1923. Yet the true glory of this success transcends statistics and extends well beyond his mesmeric swing.

Congressional witnessed a wonderful triumph of a young, resilient mind over sporting misadventure. If McIlroy's dignity in those dark hours immediately after the Masters had been impressive, his rapid recovery from that potentially crushing experience was utterly astonishing.

Jason Day

Y E Yang

McIlroy surprised even his closest friends with his calm that Sunday night in Augusta as he began the forensic examination of his meltdown. Over the next week or so, he picked his way through the wreckage and formally identified his errors.

Next began the process of sifting the advice he was offered from every imaginable quarter. McIlroy had touched a chord at the Masters and the entire world, it seemed, wanted to reach out and help. Expert counsel came from the great and the good, like Jack Nicklaus, Dave Stockton and many others.

McIlroy had been on unfamiliar ground as he took a four stroke lead into the final round in Georgia and this uncertainty showed. So Nicklaus advised him to set himself small, interim targets in every round and always to be aggressive in trying to achieve them.

Former England cricket captain Michael Vaughan, noting that McIlroy's body language had been poor on Sunday at the Masters, urged him to walk with his head up at all times. Fitness coach Stephen McGregor

advised him to open up and talk with his caddie, JP Fitzgerald, and everyone else within earshot on the golf course. Crucially, short game guru Stockton, a two-time winner of the US PGA Championship and former US Ryder Cup captain, helped McIlroy restore the natural flow in his putting stroke.

According to Michael Bannon, McIlroy's coach since childhood, Stockton did a great job. "He brought Rory's putting back into his natural way of playing the game," he said. "He cleared out a lot of the clutter; gave him a few simple things like see the line and hit it, and came up with a couple of technical tips. That was it."

Yet McIlroy deserves most credit for the adroit way in which he mixed and matched a myriad of advice, melding it to his advantage. This lad might have left school at 15 to pursue his sporting dream but he is an incredibly quick learner and

Sergio Garcia

THE #1 BALL FOR YOUR GAME.

A lot goes into your game, and that's why we put so much into your golf ball. The Titleist Pro V1® with our innovative ZG process core technology delivers exceptional distance, penetrating ball flight, Drop-and-Stop™ control and soft feel, while the Titleist Pro V1x™ provides low long game spin for exceptionally long distance and Drop-and-Stop control. Titleist is the ball of choice for players across the worldwide professional tours, and Pro V1 and Pro V1x are the #1 performing golf balls for all golfers. Visit your local golf shop to experience the #1 ball for your game.

The Pro V1 and Pro V1x.

Lee Westwood

Kevin Chappell

Robert Garrigus

Peter Hanson

is clearly blessed with the resilience and mental agility to excel in the university of life.

Almost as significant in the healing process was McIlroy's first field trip as sporting ambassador for UNICEF Ireland to earthquake-torn Haiti the week before the US Open. He found perspective amid the rubble and in the smiling eyes of the schoolchildren he met.

If cruel fate had been against McIlroy in Georgia, Mother Nature did her best to make amends in Maryland, defying the best intentions of the USGA to have Congressional playing hard and running fast by damping down the course each night and early morning with rain.

McIlroy plainly revelled in the conditions. From the off, he lived up to his pledge to be "more cocky" on the golf course, surging into the lead with a bogey free 65 on Thursday and following-up with a second round 66.

The highlight that Friday was an eagle with his pitching wedge from the fairway at the eighth, which established McIlroy as the fastest (by 13 holes) ever to reach double figures under par at the US Open. Furthermore, despite a double bogey at the 18th, he still set the lowest 36 hole total in the championship (131) and equalled the biggest halfway lead (six strokes).

His third round 68 contributed to a record 54 hole total of 199, while he also became the first man in history to reach 14 under par at the US Open as he took an eight stroke lead into Sunday.

Padraig Harrington put the feelings of many into words when he said: "What age is he, just 22? If you're talking about someone to beat Jack's record of 18 Majors, there's your man". To which McIlroy famously responded with a shake of the head: "Oh, Paddy, Paddy, Paddy!" Sometimes it seemed as if Rory was the coolest man at Congressional.

On Sunday evening, McIlroy etched his name directly under that of another proud son of Ulster, Graeme McDowell, on the trophy, and in the process thrilled the watching world with a spark of genius he clearly shares with other Northern Ireland sporting greats George Best and Alex Higgins.

Yet amid the hype, McIlroy merely glowed with quiet satisfaction, saying: "This was a chance to prove to myself and to everyone else that what happened at Augusta wasn't me and that I wouldn't let that define how I played for the rest of my career."

Most of all, it was surely the first of many for The Celtic Tiger.

Karl MacGinty
Irish Independent

Charl Schwartzel and Louis Oosthuizen

"Sergio was one of my heroes when I was growing up so to win like this is just a dream. It is also very emotional after losing my grandfather last week – this win is definitely for him"

Pablo Larrazábal

BMW Golfsport
bmw-golfsport.com

The Ultimate Driving Machine

BMW INTERNATIONAL OPEN
Golfclub München Eichenried
Munich, Germany
June 23–26, 2011

1	**PABLO LARRAZÁBAL**		68	67	69	68	**272**	**-16**
2	Sergio Garcia		69	71	64	68	272	-16
3	George Coetzee		67	67	70	70	274	-14
	Mark Foster		68	68	66	72	274	-14
	Retief Goosen		68	69	67	70	274	-14
	Scott Jamieson		69	69	72	64	274	-14
	Joost Luiten		70	69	68	67	274	-14
8	Robert Coles		72	67	65	71	275	-13
9	Ross Fisher		71	70	68	67	276	-12
	Lee Slattery		67	72	66	71	276	-12
	Henrik Stenson		64	70	73	69	276	-12

BMW International Open

Pablo Larrazábal and Dr Friedrich Eichiner, Member of the Board of Management, BMW AG

Total Prize Fund €2,000,000   **First Prize** €333,330

Bernhard Langer and Dustin Johnson

Mark Foster

Henrik Stenson

BMW INTERNATIONAL OPEN 2011.

Sergio García

Precision.
Agility.
Strength and reach.

All attributes of a great golfer. Those are also the attributes of a great logistics company.

To learn more about what UPS does for The European Tour and what we can do for you, visit us at ups.com/golf.

WE ♡ LOGISTICS™

Scott Jamieson

George Coetzee

Retief Goosen

Two's Company

It is very rare that both players leave a play-off with a smile on their faces but that was precisely the situation which unfolded when Pablo Larrazábal finally beat compatriot Sergio Garcia on the fifth extra hole to win the BMW International Open.

Without question Larrazábal's joy was greater, his second European Tour triumph giving the 28 year old from Barcelona not only a cheque for €333,330, which moved him into the top ten on The Race to Dubai, but also a European Tour exemption until the end of the 2013 season.

But Garcia quietly acknowledged his own satisfaction as not only did the 31 year old continue to show an encouraging return to form, his performance also guaranteed him a place in The Open Championship at Royal St George's through the

cumulative money list which took in all European Tour events from the BMW PGA Championship at Wentworth Club through to Germany.

Larrazábal will be there, too, thanks to his victory, his only regret being that his beloved grandfather Manuel will not be there to witness it; the "captain of the family" as the new champion referred to him, having passed away the previous week.

However, if he was looking down on events in Munich, Manuel would have been proud of the way his grandson matched Garcia's 68 in the final round before halving the first four holes of the play-off – twice in birdie four on the 18th, the 12th and the 17th – before another birdie four at the 18th was good enough as Garcia's putt touched the right side of the hole but stayed above ground.

"Today was a dream. It was crazy with all my friends in the crowd and all the people cheering. The atmosphere was incredible and you can tell everyone in terms of The Ryder Cup – France is ready"

Thomas Levet

ALSTOM OPEN DE FRANCE
Le Golf National (Albatros Course)
Paris, France
June 30–July 3, 2011

1	**THOMAS LEVET**		70	70	67	70	**277**	**-7**
2	Mark Foster		68	68	68	74	278	-6
	Thorbjørn Olesen		66	71	71	70	278	-6
4	Martin Kaymer		71	69	67	73	280	-4
5	Simon Khan		70	70	70	71	281	-3
	Richie Ramsay		69	68	68	76	281	-3
7	James Morrison		66	66	72	78	282	-2
	Hennie Otto		69	71	71	71	282	-2
	Brendan Steele		74	70	67	71	282	-2
10	Anthony Wall		68	73	69	73	283	-1

Thomas Levet, Alstom Open de France Champion 2011

Total Prize Fund €3,000,000   **First Prize** €500,000

Richie Ramsay

Thorbjørn Olesen

L-R: Thomas Levet, Romain Wattel, Christian Cévaër, Grégory Bourdy and Julien Guerrier celebrate France being awarded The 2018 Ryder Cup

Mark Foster

FROGGIES LOVE GOLF TOO

Je t'aime

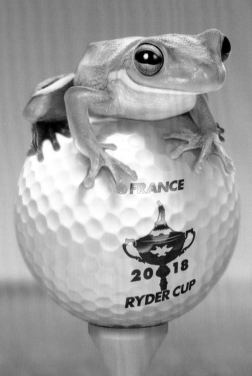

THANKS TO THE FRENCH BID PARTNERS

Vive la France

The Ryder Cup is a truly special occasion with a unique atmosphere. A mere six weeks after the decision was made to award The 2018 Ryder Cup to France, the crowds at Le Golf National gave some indication of what to expect as they cheered Thomas Levet home in the Alstom Open de France.

The 42 year old finished one shot clear of the impressive Thorbjørn Olesen and joint third round leader Mark Foster after holding his nerve over the notoriously difficult closing stretch to become only the second French champion in the event – since the birth of The European Tour in 1972 – following in the footsteps of 2004 and 2005 winner Jean-François Remesy.

While others faltered throughout an enthralling final day, Levet carded his third round of 70 over the week to claim his sixth victory on The European Tour International Schedule and his first since the 2009 Open de España at PGA Golf Catalunya. It not only helped move the Frenchman some 215 places up the Official World Golf Ranking to 137, it also propelled him into 16th place in The Race to Dubai.

Olesen, whose rookie season on The European Tour has been highly notable, followed up his tie for second in the BMW Italian Open in May with another joint runners-up slot and indeed the 21 year old could have forced a play-off but missed his par effort from three feet at the last, leaving him on 278 alongside Foster, who closed with a 74.

Simon Khan

Martin Kaymer

"There is always added pressure to perform when you go into a tournament as the World Number One but hopefully I have proved I can handle that. Another win is very nice – I can get used to this"

Luke Donald

BARCLAYS
SCOTTISH OPEN

BARCLAYS SCOTTISH OPEN
Castle Stuart Golf Links
Inverness, Scotland
July 7–10, 2011

1	**LUKE DONALD**		67	67	63	197	-19
2	Fredrik Andersson Hed		73	66	62	201	-15
3	Angel Cabrera		71	64	67	202	-14
	George Coetzee		66	69	67	202	-14
	Nicolas Colsaerts		69	66	67	202	-14
	Lorenzo Gagli		68	68	66	202	-14
	Scott Jamieson		67	66	69	202	-14
	Mark Tullo		65	71	66	202	-14
	Martin Wiegele		69	68	65	202	-14
10	Robert Coles		70	69	64	203	-13
	Jamie Donaldson		67	68	68	203	-13
	Peter Hanson		66	67	70	203	-13
	Matt Kuchar		70	66	67	203	-13

Luke Donald and Bob Diamond, CEO, Barclays PLC

Total Prize Fund €3,331,167   **First Prize €550,250**

Scott Jamieson

Nicolas Colsaerts

Angel Cabrera

Fredrik Andersson Hed

DEDICATION DRIVES SUCCESS.

Phil Mickelson uses his determination and focus to his advantage every time he steps up to the tee. At Barclays Capital, we bring that same level of dedication to our clients every day. We are proud to sponsor Phil as he personifies the game's values of integrity, commitment and success.

Earn Success Every Day

BARCLAYS CAPITAL

Martin Wiegele

The Right Honourable Alex Salmond MSP, First Minister of Scotland and Phil Mickelson

Mark Tullo

King of the Castle

It might not have been quite the home victory the crowds were hoping for but the knowledgeable Scottish galleries nevertheless appreciated the tartan trousers sported by Luke Donald on the final day as he continued a truly glorious 2011 season with victory in the Barclays Scottish Open.

With Scotland's First Minister Alex Salmond in attendance, the 33 year old Englishman closed with a flawless 63 on the magnificent Castle Stuart Golf Links to the east of Inverness for a 19 under par total of 197 and a four shot winning margin from Sweden's Fredrik Andersson Hed who stormed through the field with a superb final day 62.

The tournament had been cut to 54 holes after unprecedented downpours in the Inverness area

– double the average monthly amount of rainfall in a single day – washed out play altogether on the Saturday. However, it spoke volumes for the tenacity and teamwork of everyone connected with the championship that everything was back in place for Sunday's denouement that saw Donald card the lowest round of his European Tour career to firmly cement his place not only in pole position in The Race to Dubai, but also as Number One on the Official World Golf Ranking.

Seven players shared third place on 14 under par 202, among their number, two time Major Champion Angel Cabrera. But the happiest of this group was Scotland's own Scott Jamieson who claimed the final spot up for grabs in the following week's Open Championship at Royal St George's.

THE OPEN CHAMPIONSHIP

THE 140TH OPEN CHAMPIONSHIP
Royal St George's Golf Club
Sandwich, Kent, England
July 14-17, 2011

1	**DARREN CLARKE**		**68**	**68**	**69**	**70**	**275**	**-5**
2	Dustin Johnson		70	68	68	72	278	-2
	Phil Mickelson		70	69	71	68	278	-2
4	Thomas Björn		65	72	71	71	279	-1
5	Chad Campbell		69	68	74	69	280	0
	Rickie Fowler		70	70	68	72	280	0
	Anthony Kim		72	68	70	70	280	0
8	Raphaël Jacquelin		74	67	71	69	281	1
9	Simon Dyson		68	72	72	70	282	2
	Sergio Garcia		70	70	74	68	282	2
	Davis Love III		70	68	72	72	282	2

Darren Clarke and Edward Demery, Captain of Royal St George's Golf Club

Total Prize Fund €5,435,665   **First Prize** €999,540

Turning the Tide

"This is amazing. It has been a dream of mine ever since I was a kid to win The Open. I'm sure most kids who play golf dream about that but I've been able to do it. That feeling, I can tell you, is pretty incredible"

Darren Clarke

It is probably unlikely that when Darren Clarke fluttered his eyelids open on the final morning of The 2011 Open Championship, his first thought was one of William Shakespeare's more thrillingly perceptive lines.

"There is a tide in the affairs of men which, taken at the flood, leads on to fortune," is from a speech by Brutus to Cassius in Julius Caesar. If the Northern Irishman did not immediately recognise how apposite that summation of life was to his own position that day in a far-flung corner of Kent, he does now. Put simply, this was Clarke's moment.

If successful, he would not close the sad recent chapter of his life, rather begin a new and reviving one nobody would begrudge a man who had had to withstand the bitterest of blows in recent times with the loss of his wife.

It was this sad fact and his defiant reaction to it when, just a few weeks later he played for a triumphant European Ryder Cup team in Ireland, that parlayed Clarke from outstanding golfer and interesting character into the sort of bloke the public could identify with, even if he lived in an impossibly attractive house outside which he parked a succession of equally attractive motor vehicles.

No matter how successful Clarke was prior to this Open, irrespective of how much money he happily sprayed around, he was seen as one of the boys. A self-confessed 42-going-on-18 year old, his taste for a pint, his craving for a cigarette and his rejection of the gym made him instantly accessible to the men and women who patiently make their way to these great sporting occasions.

Yet while the hearts were always with him, the minds were focused elsewhere. Odds of 150/1 failed to seduce any customers for the bookmakers before the action began at Royal St George's. A poll of 58 experienced golf writers prior to the event did not throw up even one speculative punt on the Ulsterman. Clarke, as one intense writer put it, was on the "irrevocable slide to irrelevance."

Some slide, some irrelevance, some irrevocable misjudgement.

But then who, apart from the thin optimism hidden inside his own heart, could have seen this victory coming? Maybe his sons, Conor and Tyrone? Maybe his fiancée Alison? Maybe his parents or his sister? Maybe perhaps his manager and pal Andrew 'Chubby' Chandler? Even this group, however, must have realised they were clutching at the slimmest of hopeful straws as this Open got under way.

Yet there had been a hint for those who look for these things. In mid-May Clarke won the Iberdrola Open at the Pula Golf Club in Mallorca. The tournament may not carry the caché attached to the bigger weeks but for Darren Clarke it was immense. It was his 13th European Tour win and his first for three years. The slide had been halted. The big question was, however, could he push on from there?

We now know the answer. Victory on the island revived not just Clarke's curriculum vitae, it reassured him that, yes, it was worth carrying on. This was vital because just a few weeks earlier he had told Chandler that he had had enough of the messing about, that maybe it was time to throw the clubs into the garage for good and get on with something more meaningful.

Chandler's response had been swift and emphatic. 'Go away and forget it, relax with the family and then come back and get on with it because you've still got all the talent in the world,' is an accurate approximation of the International Sports Management boss' advice to his client. Mallorca marked his return to action. Mallorca marked a fresh start. Mallorca meant everything.

It is, however, rarely enough to have a reignited appetite for the game when it comes to The Open. The old jousting field requires a man to play towards the top of his game and then to enjoy some decent fortune given the vagaries of links golf and the unpredictability of links weather.

It is here that Clarke had his share of luck, missing the very worst of the weather during a Saturday third round that threatened and indeed destroyed the majority of players whose halfway scores meant they had to tee off earlier in the day. Even so, the Dungannon man's game was back on the money. Eternally recognised as one of the purist of ball strikers, Clarke was now in his element.

The long, lonely hours of practice in the gales back home on Royal Portrush's daunting links were never designed to win an Open but, with hindsight, this is exactly what those rounds of golf turned out to be. A wind? Some rain? In Kent? Easy for a man who has swung in the centre of so many stifling storms which blow in off the Atlantic to attack Ulster's ruggedly beautiful northern coastline.

Raphaël Jacquelin

Thomas Björn

Phil Mickelson

LIVE FOR

HIS GRIP REMAINS RELAXED; COMFORTABLE. A PICTURE OF CALM. DETERMINED BEST DESCRIBES HIS ASCENT TO THE TOP. METHODICAL WORKS TOO. AND THEN COMES HIS SWING. IT'S BEAUTIFUL, FLUID AND EFFORTLESS. CAMERAS FIRE. HEADLINES ARE WRITTEN. HIS ATTENTION, LIKE HIS RISE TO THE TOP, REMAINS STEADY.

MARTIN KAYMER

GREATNESS

OYSTER PERPETUAL DATEJUST II

ROLEX

His 69 that day was added to a 68-68 start and took him into Sunday embracing a one stroke lead over Dustin Johnson with a further ten players within five shots. Clearly it was not yet a done deal for a man whose emotions occasionally get the better of him. Indeed, when Phil Mickelson made up five shots over the front nine as he rode one of those spectacular golfing rollercoasters he sometimes finds, Clarke's supporters began to have their doubts.

Then the left-handed American missed a piffling putt on the 11th green and, horrified at his own error, he proceeded to retreat to the edges. Johnson, too, had his chance but his ambition was blunted by a wildly incoherent and nervous swing that sent his ball out of bounds at the 14th.

It all left a controlled and focused Clarke with a barrage of shots with which he could trundle home over the closing holes. And trundle he did, scrambling to save par before dropping a shot at the 17th but still reaching the final green embracing a healthy cushion. He dropped another shot there but still won by three shots before raising those hefty arms aloft to acknowledge his triumph.

It was precisely that moment that the 42 year old retreated and the teenager re-emerged, embarking on a three day hooley with friends, family and anyone else with the time, energy and inclination.

Four days later in London's Piccadilly where he picked up a sponsor's bonus cheque for £2 million, he looked exhausted, his face puffy, his eyes blurred. When this fact was mentioned to him, he agreed. "Yes," he said. "I am tired but I'm also very happy and content."

Northern Ireland's third Major Champion in 13 months was not alone in his contentment at that moment. Not by a very long way. As that fellow Shakespeare said, this time in Henry VI..."My crown is called content, a crown that kings seldom wear."

Bill Elliott
Golf Monthly

Tom Watson and Tom Lewis, winner of the Silver Medal as leading amateur

Dustin Johnson

Sergio Garcia

Simon Dyson

NORDEA MASTERS
Bro Hof Slott Golf Club (Stadium Course)
Stockholm, Sweden
July 21–24, 2011

1	**ALEXANDER NOREN**		67	66	63	77	273	-15
2	Richard Finch		69	72	70	69	280	-8
3	Niklas Lemke		68	72	70	73	283	-5
4	Scott Hend		69	70	71	74	284	-4
	Pablo Martin		69	72	69	74	284	-4
6	Dustin Johnson		73	71	67	74	285	-3
	Seung-yul Noh		73	68	69	75	285	-3
	Jeev Milkha Singh		70	71	69	75	285	-3
	Bubba Watson		71	67	69	78	285	-3
10	Jamie Donaldson		73	70	67	76	286	-2
	Tano Goya		71	70	70	75	286	-2
	John Parry		68	73	70	75	286	-2

Alex Noren and Christian Clausen, President and Group CEO of Nordea

Total Prize Fund €1,500,000   **First Prize** €250,000

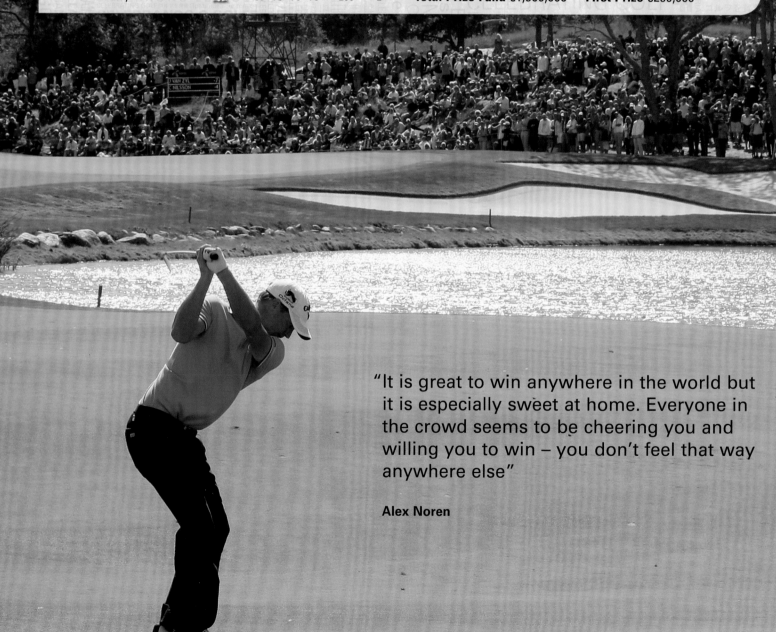

"It is great to win anywhere in the world but it is especially sweet at home. Everyone in the crowd seems to be cheering you and willing you to win – you don't feel that way anywhere else"

Alex Noren

Richard Finch

Niklas Lemke

Bubba Watson

Scott Hend

Pablo Martin

Swede Dreams

Alex Noren is certainly a player comfortable winning from the front as he proved with his success on home soil in the Nordea Masters at Bro Hof Slott – the third time he has triumphed on The European Tour International Schedule having taken a lead into the final day.

But while his win in the 2009 Omega European Masters and in June's Saab Wales Open saw him capitalise on third round leads of two and one shot respectively, this was an advantage of entirely different proportions.

A stunning course record 63 in the third round, allied to his opening salvos of 67-66, gave the 29 year old from Stockholm a 20 under par aggregate of 196 and a whopping 11 shot lead over his nearest pursuer, American Bubba Watson.

It was the joint second highest third round lead in European Tour history, tieing Ken Brown's 11 shot figure in the Glasgow Open at Haggs Castle in 1984, and only two shots adrift of the eye-watering 13 shot advantage Retief Goosen took into the final round of the Johnnie Walker Classic at Lake Karrinyup in 2002.

Both men went on to triumph and it was no surprise, therefore, that Noren followed suit although it was by no means plain sailing on a final day made tough by such treacherous winds that only one player – second placed Richard Finch – managed to break the par of 72.

The Englishman's 69 gave him an eight under par total of 280 while Noren closed with a 77 for a 15 under par total of 273.

"It's a shame you can't bottle how you feel sometimes because this is amazing, it really is. The golf I've played this week is probably the best I've ever played"

Simon Dyson

IRISH OPEN presented by Discover Ireland
Killarney Golf and Fishing Club (Killeen Course)
Killarney, Co. Kerry, Ireland
July 28–31, 2011

1	**SIMON DYSON**		70	65	67	67	269	-15
2	Richard Green		67	68	67	68	270	-14
3	Stephen Gallacher		71	66	67	68	272	-12
4	Bernd Wiesberger		67	69	71	66	273	-11
5	Ignacio Garrido		69	65	72	68	274	-10
	Søren Hansen		67	66	72	69	274	-10
	Alexandre Kaleka		65	75	66	68	274	-10
8	Lorenzo Gagli		68	69	73	65	275	-9
	David Howell		69	69	64	73	275	-9
	Peter Lawrie		70	66	70	69	275	-9

L-R: George O'Grady, Chief Executive of The European Tour, Simon Dyson and Taoiseach Enda Kenny

Total Prize Fund €1,500,000   First Prize €250,000

Rory McIlroy and Darren Clarke

Graeme McDowell

Padraig Harrington

Simple for Simon

They came in their tens of thousands to herald Ireland's four Major Champions but the huge galleries left the Irish Open marvelling at the supreme golfing talents of England's Simon Dyson who claimed his fifth victory on The European Tour International Schedule.

Without question, the crowds gave a hero's welcome to Darren Clarke, Padraig Harrington, Graeme McDowell and Rory McIlroy but their innate golfing knowledge allowed them to also appreciate Dyson's ability which saw him move from outside the top 40 after round one to tied fifth at the halfway stage, into a share of the lead at the end of the third round before eventually walking into the winners' circle on Sunday.

The win capped a wonderful July for Dyson, a fortnight after finishing ninth in The Open at Royal St George's, a tournament he got into despite being fifth reserve less than a week before the Championship begun.

However, it is widely recognised that every victory needs a bit of good fortune and Dyson's came thanks to a missed opportunity by Australian Richard Green. The left hander had shared pole position with David Howell and Dyson going into the final round and early birdies saw him lead on his own into the final stages.

But Dyson's birdies at the 16th and 17th moved him level and a play-off looked likely until Green three putted from 60 feet on the final green for a bogey five to confirm the Englishman's success.

Richard Green

Stephen Gallacher

IRISH OPEN
DISCOVER IRELAND

Golf Ireland
Time to play

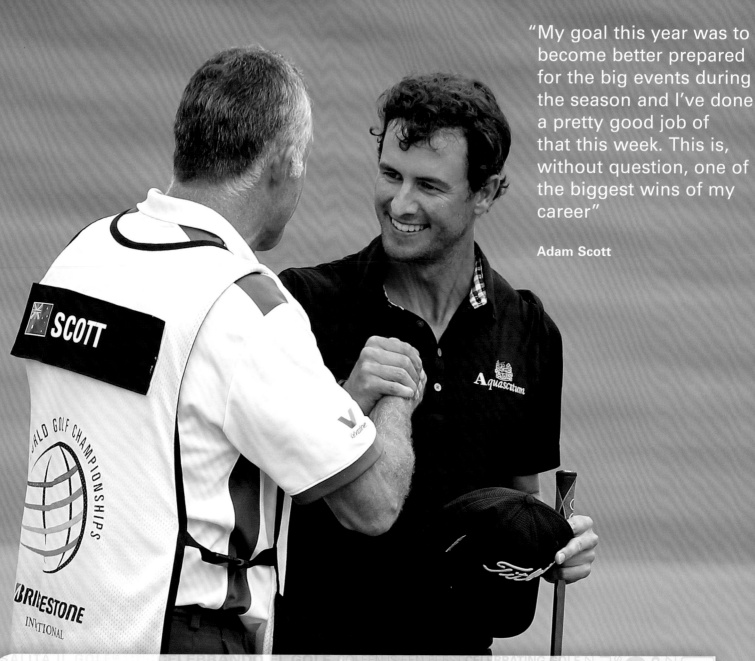

"My goal this year was to become better prepared for the big events during the season and I've done a pretty good job of that this week. This is, without question, one of the biggest wins of my career"

Adam Scott

WGC - BRIDGESTONE INVITATIONAL
Firestone Country Club (South Course)
Akron, Ohio, USA
August 4–7, 2011

1	**ADAM SCOTT**		62	70	66	65	263	-17
2	Luke Donald		68	69	64	66	267	-13
	Rickie Fowler		68	64	69	66	267	-13
4	Jason Day		63	70	66	69	268	-12
	Ryo Ishikawa		67	68	64	69	268	-12
6	Zach Johnson		70	68	64	68	270	-10
	Kyung-tae Kim		66	72	66	66	270	-10
	Rory McIlroy		68	68	67	67	270	-10
9	David Toms		68	68	68	67	271	-9
	Lee Westwood		67	71	68	65	271	-9

Kazuhisa Nishigai, SVP Member of the Board of Bridgestone Corporation and Adam Scott

Total Prize Fund €5,804,071   **First Prize** €972,148

Luke Donald

Ryo Ishikawa

Jason Day

Rickie Fowler

BRIDGESTONE
Your Journey, Our Passion

WORLD GOLF CHA...

Rory McIlroy

In the Bag

Rarely in the history of golf can so much interest have centred on the man carrying the bag of the winner rather than on the champion himself, but that was exactly the scenario which unfolded in the wake of Adam Scott's victory in the World Golf Championships – Bridgestone Invitational.

It was, however, unsurprising, given the fact the caddie in question was Steve Williams who had been at the side of Tiger Woods in his pomp, gathering 62 titles worldwide including seven victories at Firestone Country Club in a 12 year partnership.

But with that relationship at an end, Williams was ecstatic as his new boss produced a superb four shot victory whose foundation was laid with a sensational opening round of 62 and which

was closed out with impressive weekend figures of 66-65 for a 17 under par total of 263.

Yet, despite his eventual dominance, Scott – who claimed his eighth European Tour victory in total – had to battle hard in the final round. Twice he was caught on the front nine, firstly by his fellow Australian Jason Day and secondly by Japanese teenager Ryo Ishikawa, but responded both times to pull away.

Turning for home, birdies at the tenth, 12th and 14th gave Scott a comfortable cushion and a closing birdie at the final hole put the seal on his success. American Rickie Fowler and England's Luke Donald matched each other's closing 66s to leapfrog into a tie for second place with Day and Ishikawa sharing fourth.

Gone with the Wind

"This feels unbelievable and seems like a dream – one I'm afraid I'm going to wake up from in the next five minutes and it's not going to be true. It is a real honour to stand here as the PGA Champion"

Keegan Bradley

US PGA CHAMPIONSHIP
Atlanta Athletic Club (Highlands Course)
Johns Creek, Georgia, USA
August 11-14, 2011

1	**KEEGAN BRADLEY**		71	64	69	68	272	-8
2	Jason Dufner		70	65	68	69	272	-8
3	Anders Hansen		68	69	70	66	273	-7
4	Robert Karlsson		70	71	67	67	275	-5
	David Toms		72	71	65	67	275	-5
	Scott Verplank		67	69	69	70	275	-5
7	Adam Scott		69	69	70	68	276	-4
8	Luke Donald		70	71	68	68	277	-3
	Lee Westwood		71	68	70	68	277	-3
10	Kevin Na		72	69	70	67	278	-2
	D A Points		69	67	71	71	278	-2

Allen Wronowski, President of the PGA of America and Keegan Bradley

Total Prize Fund €5,645,086   **First Prize** €1,028,126

Somewhere in Vermont, the Sunday evening peace was shattered by a woman running up and down the street rattling wind chimes. To welcome the finale of a Major Championship season which never relented from dropping jaws, this surreal spectacle was entirely appropriate.

Except Mrs Bradley's revelry was more specific than the mere celebration of golf's enduring ability to enthral. Her son, Keegan, had just won the US PGA Championship – in the very first Major he had played.

Since Francis Ouimet shook the world order at the 1913 US Open, only Ben Curtis in The Open at Royal St George's in 2003, had achieved golf's ultimate debut. The Atlanta Athletic Club had never seen anything like it; the PGA of America had never seen anything like it; in fact, considering Bradley was using a long putter, golf had never seen anything like it. At last, the belly brigade had their champion.

And what a champion he was, coming back from a five stroke deficit with just three holes remaining to end America's record drought of six Majors without a victory. Those nail-biting scenes, as he tore into Jason Dufner's advantage before prevailing in a three-hole play-off, have inevitably monopolised the memory bank. Yet on a perfectly manicured layout in blazing sun, the 93rd edition of the US PGA Championship gripped the attention from the very off.

The first two rounds were perhaps most notable because of Rory McIlroy's failure

to miss a tree root on the first afternoon and Tiger Woods' failure to make the cut on the second. The latter struggled to shake off the rust as he slumped to 77-73 for a ten over par total of 150. Injuries to his Achilles and knee had forced him out of the US Open and The Open and he arrived in Georgia with victory on his mind. However, the 35 year old left contemplating his first finish outside the top one hundred in a decade and a half of Major outings.

McIlroy did progress to the weekend, but did not produce anything like the strength of challenge many expected. There was good reason for that though. On the third hole in his first round, the 22 year old smashed his seven iron against the root of a tree positioned a few inches ahead of his ball. It was a gamble which backfired. He bravely completed an opening round of 70, but a rush to a nearby medical centre revealed a sprain in his right wrist. It could have been worse, but it should have been better. "In hindsight I should have chipped out sideways," he said, before battling bravely to a share of 64th place.

Still, the US Open champion had plenty to take from his 2011 Major campaign. Yet for Luke Donald and Lee Westwood, there was only a sense of frustration in

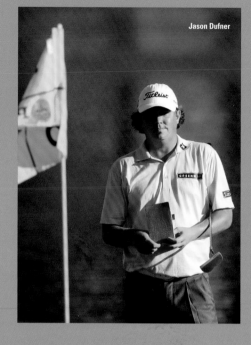

Jason Dufner

that realm to take into 2012. Of course, their year will be remembered for many other feats; both won multiple titles and, at different stages, both held the Number One position on the Official World Golf Ranking. But it says much about the scale of their ambition that they left Atlanta refusing to rest on any laurels.

A tie for eighth place for the pair was anything but a disaster, but Westwood was left bemoaning his putting after yet another stellar performance of ball striking, while Donald was to reflect on what might have been. Before he double-bogeyed the 15th in his final round he had been lurking menacingly. His hopes were sunk right there and then on that imposing par three.

But then, so many had been as the climax intensified. Steve Stricker had taken the lead into the second round and the multiple US PGA Tour winner seemed a good bet to stride on to victory. However the Atlanta Athletic Club gobbled him up, just as it did Brendan Steele. Like Bradley, this was the American's first Major and like his fellow countryman, he had dared to dream when holding a share of the 54 hole lead with Jason Dufner. A nervy final round 77, though, taught him the merciless side of Major competition.

Robert Karlsson

Rory McIlroy

Anders Hansen

The new DryJoys Tour golf shoes have been engineered to meet the demands of the world's top professionals. Featuring the latest outsole technology, DryJoys Tour shoes provide the stability and performance required to compete on the tour's demanding courses. Timeless styles, crafted from the finest premium leathers, offer understated contemporary fashion, while delivering unsurpassed comfort.

FJ
#1 SHOE IN GOLF

BUILT FOR THE TOUR THAT INSPIRED THEM.
DRYJOYS TOUR™

However, nobody was to learn that more painfully than his playing partner. Dufner, 34 years old and eleven years a professional without a victory, looked impervious to the pressure. Robert Karlsson arrived in his wing mirror in the final round when he eagled the 12th to get within one shot but the towering Swede disappeared when the bogeys came. Then Denmark's Anders Hansen, twice a winner of the BMW PGA Championship at Wentworth Club, threatened to pull off a remarkable PGA treble. As it transpired, his seven under par total of 273 was one short of making the play-off. Yet Hansen was not to know what was to befall Dufner.

Suddenly the nerves hit. Dufner was five clear with just four holes left but three bogeys from the 15th gave Bradley a sniff of a chance and it was one he accepted like a bloodhound. What a comeback this was after his own treble bogey on the 15th after chipping into the water – a ten footer for birdie on the 16th, a 40 footer for another gain on the 17th and a resolute par on the last. So much for many labelling this "the toughest stretch in golf."

But it did get Dufner who, to be fair, showed great resilience to par the last to ensure his place in the shootout. After birdieing the first play-off hole (the 16th), Bradley was always in front and when he tapped in to confirm victory on the 18th, a new American hero was born.

Over the next few hours, the game learned more about Bradley; how he was the nephew of Pat Bradley, the seven time LPGA Major winner; how he chose golf over skiing and how he worked with the mind guru Bob Rotella, just as the Open champion Darren Clarke had the previous month.

Yet what of his mother watching back home in Vermont? Where did those chimes come into it? It was a story which neatly encapsulated Bradley's golfing pedigree.

"When my Aunt Pat won her first tournament it was in Australia and so it was the middle of the night in America," he explained. "Well, my grandmother was freaking out because she wanted everyone to know. So she ran up and down the streets ringing a cowbell. It became sort of a family tradition after that whenever she won."

And so the custom lives on. "Now whenever I win, my mom runs up-and-down the street with wind chimes like a crazy woman!" Just like all of America now, she is simply crazy for Keegan.

Jamie Corrigan
The Independent

Luke Donald

Lee Westwood

"This just goes to show you that golf can be a funny game at times after the season I've had. Getting my first win is obviously very special and hopefully this will be the start of big things for me"

Oli Fisher

CZECH OPEN
Prosper Golf Resort (Old and New Courses)
Čeladná, Czech Republic
August 18–21, 2011

1	**OLIVER FISHER**		**71**	**67**	**68**	**69**	**275**	**-13**
2	Mikael Lundberg		68	68	72	69	277	-11
3	Fabrizio Zanotti		71	71	71	66	279	-9
4	Gary Boyd		71	67	70	72	280	-8
5	David Drysdale		69	72	69	71	281	-7
	Lorenzo Gagli		69	70	74	68	281	-7
	Steven O'Hara		70	71	65	75	281	-7
	Steve Webster		70	70	71	70	281	-7
9	Gaganjeet Bhullar		70	74	64	74	282	-6
	Tano Goya		73	66	72	71	282	-6
	Damien McGrane		67	71	72	72	282	-6

Václav Klaus, President of the Czech Republic and Oli Fisher

Total Prize Fund €1,500,000   **First Prize** €250,000

David Drysdale

Fabrizio Zanotti

Gary Boyd

Try, try again

There are many attributes you need to be a successful professional golfer and, without question, perseverance is one of them. Never was that better illustrated than by Oli Fisher in his two shot maiden European Tour triumph in the Czech Open.

The 22 year old Londoner arrived on the professional scene in a blaze of glory, having been the youngest amateur, at 16 years and 334 days, to play in the 2005 Walker Cup match before, the following year, becoming the youngest British player to gain his card at the European Tour Qualifying School Finals.

Great things were expected from the young man dubbed a star of the future by Sir Nick Faldo, but success proved elusive and he arrived in the Czech Republic for his 147th Tour event

having started the 2011 season with 19 missed cuts out of 20.

However, the end of July saw him complete two solid four round outings in the Nordea Masters and in the Irish Open presented by Discover Ireland, both of which gave him the impetus to move forward in Celadná to the extent where he ended the third round tied for the lead with Steven O'Hara.

While the Scot slipped back on the final day with a 75 to eventually finish in a tie for fifth place, Fisher pressed on, three birdies in a row from the seventh giving him the advantage. His back nine was a rollercoaster affair with three birdies and three bogeys, but it was enough to hold off the threat of the chasing Mikael Lundberg and Fabrizio Zanotti.

Mikael Lundberg

JOHNNIE WALKER CHAMPIONSHIP AT GLENEAGLES
The Gleneagles Hotel (PGA Centenary Course)
Perthshire, Scotland
August 25–28, 2011

L-R: Lord Macfarlane of Bearsden, Honorary Life President of Diageo Scotland, The Right Honourable Alex Salmond MSP, First Minister of Scotland, Thomas Björn and Ian Wright, Corporate Relations Director, Diageo

1	**THOMAS BJÖRN**		68	69	71	69	**277**	**-11**
2	George Coetzee		77	66	67	67	277	-11
	Mark Foster		66	71	68	72	277	-11
	Pablo Larrazábal		70	68	70	69	277	-11
	Bernd Wiesberger		69	71	68	69	277	-11
6	Stephen Gallacher		74	68	67	69	278	-10
	Joel Sjöholm		70	71	69	68	278	-10
8	Victor Dubuisson		69	70	73	67	279	-9
	Kenneth Ferrie		68	69	73	69	279	-9
	Ignacio Garrido		67	69	69	74	279	-9

Total Prize Fund €1,587,270   **First Prize** €266,629

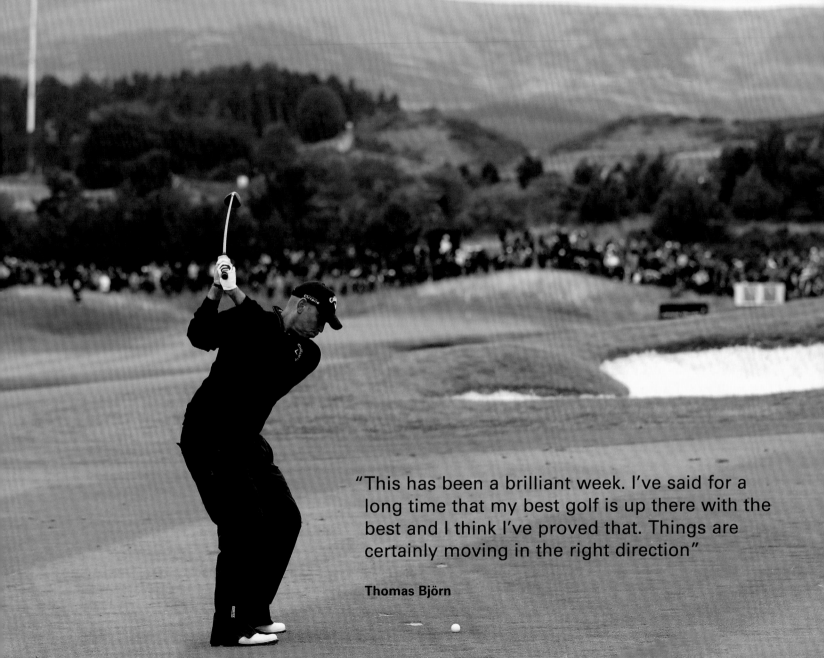

"This has been a brilliant week. I've said for a long time that my best golf is up there with the best and I think I've proved that. Things are certainly moving in the right direction"

Thomas Björn

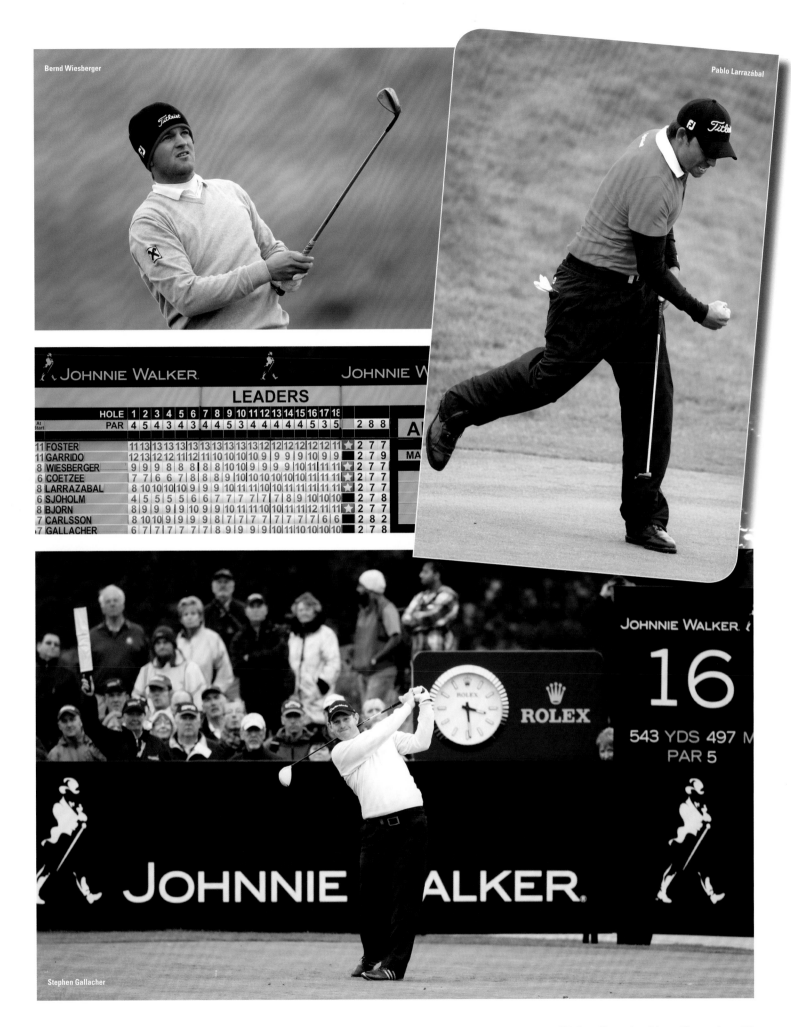

Bernd Wiesberger

Pablo Larrazábal

Stephen Gallacher

Scotland
The Home of Golf

**Castle Stuart Golf Links,
venue for the 2012 Scottish Open**

EventScotland, the national events agency, is proud to be working in partnership with The European Tour to enhance and develop the game in Scotland, the Home of Golf. We support a fantastic calendar of golf events every year and 2011 was no exception as we build up to hosting The 2014 Ryder Cup at Gleneagles.

To find out more about how EventScotland invests in golf, and about golf in Scotland visit **www.EventScotland.org/golf**

George Coetzee

Björn Again

The PGA Centenary Course will make its mark in golfing history in a couple of years' time when it plays host to The Ryder Cup, but it carved its own special niche in European Tour history following Thomas Björn's remarkable victory in the Johnnie Walker Championship at Gleneagles.

Only once in the 40 year history of The European Tour have five men contested a play-off – that coming in the 1992 BMW International Open in Munich when Paul Azinger beat Glen Day, Anders Fosbrand, Mark James and Bernhard Langer.

But fast forward 19 years and, once again, five men were required to move into extra holes; George Coetzee, Mark Foster, Pablo Larrazábal, Bernd Wiesberger and Björn after finishing the regulation 72 holes on 11 under par 277.

Of the quintet, Coetzee's closing 67 had been the most impressive while a play-off would not have been required at all had Foster made par five at the last for a 71 instead of a bogey six for a 72.

Into sudden-death, played continuously over the 533 yard 18th, Wiesberger dropped out at the first time of asking with a bogey six as did Larrazábal, second time round.

The remaining trio all produced birdie fours on the third occasion before Foster's hopes of his second Tour win disappeared on the fourth extra hole where, like the 72nd hole, he made bogey six.

It left only Björn and Coetzee standing but the Dane made sure of his 12th European Tour title, and his second of the 2011 season, at the fifth time of asking with a birdie four to the South African's five.

Mark Foster

"This really has been a quite amazing two weeks. I started hitting my wedges well last week and at the end here you actually think nothing can go wrong. Golf seems easy when it's like that"

Thomas Björn

OMEGA EUROPEAN MASTERS
Crans-sur-Sierre
Crans Montana, Switzerland
September 1–4, 2011

EUROPEAN TOUR
RACE TO DUBAI
2011

1	**THOMAS BJÖRN**		**68**	**68**	**66**	**62**	**264**	**-20**
2	Martin Kaymer		65	70	68	65	268	-16
3	Jamie Donaldson		68	66	65	70	269	-15
	Rory McIlroy		65	69	67	68	269	-15
	Jaco Van Zyl		67	68	70	64	269	-15
6	Fredrik Andersson Hed		70	70	66	64	270	-14
	David Lynn		68	68	69	65	270	-14
	Lee Westwood		67	69	64	70	270	-14
9	Alejandro Cañizares		66	71	70	64	271	-13
	Miguel Angel Jiménez		70	68	67	66	271	-13
	Alexander Noren		69	67	68	67	271	-13

Stephen Urquhart, President of Omega and Thomas Björn

Total Prize Fund €2,000,000   **First Prize** €333,330

Björn Three

Seven days previously, Thomas Björn had been Monarch of the Glen; now the rampaging Dane was King of the Mountains after a stunning victory in the Omega European Masters.

It was the first back-to-back victory on The European Tour since Charl Schwartzel won the Africa Open and the Joburg Open in 2010 and one which saw Björn, at 40 years and 198 days, become the oldest man in Tour history to achieve the feat.

Furthermore, it saw the Dane take his place alongside Luke Donald as a three time winner on Tour in 2011; move to seventh in The Race to Dubai; move to 28th from outside the top 50 on the Official World Golf Ranking; and move to the top of the Ryder Cup points table in this, the first counting event.

Just as at Gleneagles, Björn began the final round three strokes in arrears of the lead but while steely grit and determination saw him post a 69 in Scotland before coming through a five man, five hole play-off; in Switzerland it was sheer class that blew the opposition away.

Early in the final round it looked like reigning European Number One Martin Kaymer was the man to beat, two eagles and two birdies in his first eight holes giving the German the advantage. But his challenge stalled and ten par figures to finish gave Björn a chance that he grabbed with both hands.

The Dane stormed home, covering the final five holes in five under par to post the best round of his European Tour career – a superb nine under par 62 – for a four shot victory.

Rory McIlroy

Jaco Van Zyl

Jamie Donaldson

Martin Kaymer

KLM OPEN
Hilversumsche Golf Club
Hilversum, The Netherlands
September 8–11, 2011

1	**SIMON DYSON**		65	66	71	66	268	-12
2	David Lynn		67	66	68	68	269	-11
3	Rory McIlroy		70	65	68	67	270	-10
4	Gary Orr		68	66	66	71	271	-9
5	Lee Westwood		70	66	70	66	272	-8
6	Ross Fisher		66	74	67	66	273	-7
	David Horsey		69	69	66	69	273	-7
	James Kingston		66	68	66	73	273	-7
	José Manuel Lara		68	69	68	68	273	-7
	Joost Luiten		73	67	64	69	273	-7
	Paul McGinley		70	68	64	71	273	-7

Erik Varwijk, Managing Director KLM and Simon Dyson

Total Prize Fund €1,805,397   **First Prize** €300,000

"To be mentioned in the same breath as
Seve and Bernhard as three time winners
here is really something special, a dream
come true. To win any title once is tough,
so to win three times is fantastic"

Simon Dyson

Rory McIlroy

Lee Westwood

Joost Luiten

Gary Orr

David Lynn

Dutch Master

Simon Dyson not only continued his sensational form of 2011, he also rekindled his love affair with the Netherlands with a third victory in the KLM Open.

The 33 year old Englishman's previous two triumphs had come at Kennemer – in 2006 and 2009 – but this time round he proved he was the master of Hilversumsche, coping with both a challenging week's weather and the strongest field in the tournament's history; led by World Number Two Lee Westwood, Number Three Rory McIlroy and Number Four, the defending champion Martin Kaymer.

McIlroy and Westwood finished third and fifth respectively, the main challenger to Dyson being his fellow countryman David Lynn, himself a winner of the tournament in 2004.

Tightly bunched around the turn, Dyson made the crucial move with three birdies in a row from the 12th, a run which took him into the lead for the first time and when he added a further birdie at the last, he posted a total Lynn could not match.

It was Dyson's second win of 2011, following his success in the Irish Open presented by Discover Ireland, and his sixth European Tour title overall. It was also the seventh time he had finished in the top ten in 2011.

Furthermore, he joined a very exclusive group of players to have won the KLM Open on three occasions; the other two members of the club being none other than Bernhard Langer, who won in 1984, 1992 and 2001; and the late Seve Ballesteros who triumphed in 1976, 1980 and 1986.

vivendi seve trophy

VIVENDI SEVE TROPHY
Saint-Nom-la-Bretèche Golf Club (Seve 1 Course)
Paris, France
September 15–18, 2011

CONTINENTAL EUROPE	12½	GREAT BRITAIN AND IRELAND	15½
(Captain: Jean Van de Velde)		(Captain: Paul McGinley)	

Total Prize Fund €1,150,000
Per player winning Team €65,000
Per player losing Team €50,000

Jean-Bernard Lévy, CEO of Vivendi and Paul McGinley

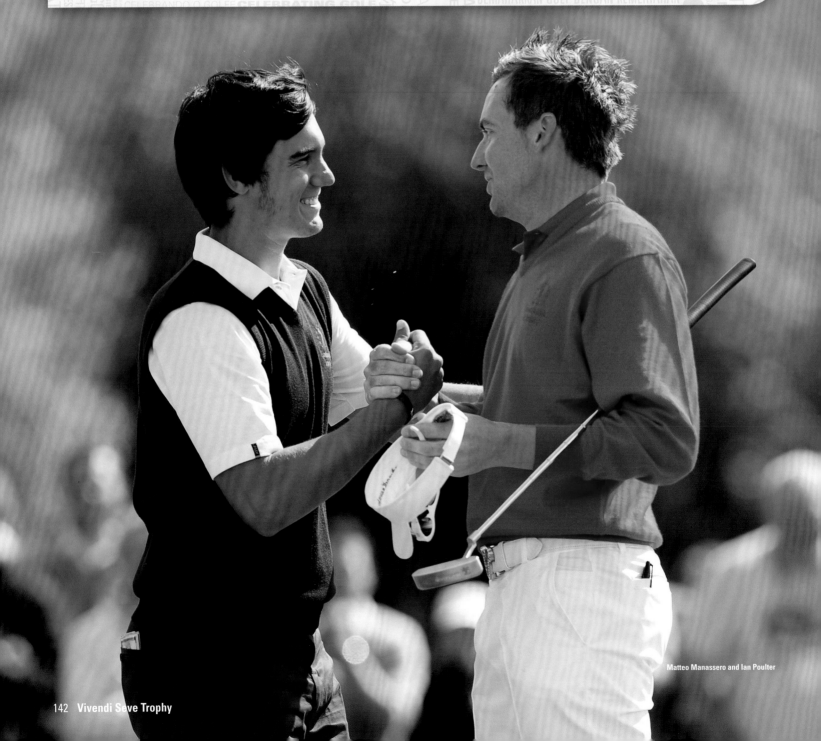

Matteo Manassero and Ian Poulter

Olé Seve

Severiano Ballesteros loved match play. The cut and thrust of head to head combat brought the best from him in both The Ryder Cup and in the World Match Play Championship at Wentworth Club which he won on five occasions.

So, in non-Ryder Cup years, the ultimate competitor dreamed up an event which would pit the best of Continental Europe's golfers against the best players from Great Britain and Ireland.

It all started at Sunningdale in 2000 where the Continental European team won by 13 ½ - 12 ½ with Seve, who sadly passed away in 2011 aged 54, gaining a crucial point in the singles against his opposing captain that week, Colin Montgomerie.

Today the Vivendi Seve Trophy has become a memorial to Europe's most talented and inspirational player, and those who took part at Saint-Nom-la-Bretèche were expressing their gratitude for what the Spanish golfing genius from Santander did for them and for European golf.

Despite GB&I having won the next five contests following on from Sunningdale, the Continental European team arrived in France the stronger on paper. They had eight of the top 20 in The Race to Dubai in

their line-up but GB&I could count on world number two Lee Westwood, reigning Open champion Darren Clarke and the man who has match play in his very golfing fibre, Ian Poulter. To balance matters, both sides had four players new to the competition.

Watched by José María Olazábal, on hand to run the rule over potential candidates for The Ryder Cup side he will captain in Chicago in 2012, GB&I quickly indicated their reluctance to surrender the trophy.

In Thursday's opening fourball series, they delighted captain Paul McGinley by collectively shooting 38 under par to take a 4-1 lead. Good friends Symon Dyson and Jamie Donaldson were nine under in beating Miguel Angel Jiménez – who as a tribute to Ballesteros had been allowed to hit the first shot – and Pablo Larrazábal. So too were Robert Rock and Poulter in beating two multiple winners on Tour this year; Thomas Björn and Alex Noren.

The Continental Europeans did better in the second series of fourball matches on Friday, winning three and a half points out of five –the highlight being Peter Hanson and Noren's 5 and 3 demolition of Poulter and Rock – to end the second day of competition only one point in arrears; 5 ½ - 4 ½.

Thomas Björn and Lee Westwood

Miguel Angel Jiménez

Mark Foster

Saturday saw the format change to greensomes in the morning and foursomes in the afternoon and also saw the momentum swing back to GB&I. Continental European team captain Jean Van de Velde's victory plan was seriously dented when his side picked up only one and a half points from the eight on offer. It meant GB&I required only three of the final day's ten singles to score a sixth successive victory.

Yet the beauty of match play golf is its uncertainty. Card and pencil form counts for little in head-to-head encounters and, as if to prove that very point, after six hours of singles action the overall result was still very much in doubt.

Continental Europe were quickly into their stride, with the exception of Björn who lost three of the first five holes to superb Westwood birdies. Not that that mattered. By the 17th, their match was all over and it was the great Dane who was celebrating, showing remarkable resilience to battle back and win 2 and 1.

Further victories quickly followed from Anders Hansen, Francesco Molinari, Noren and Jiménez, and when rookie Nicolas Colsaerts held another debutant David Horsey to a half, it was all square on the leaderboard with four games to go.

However, cometh the hour, cometh the man, and for GB&I those men were Mark Foster and Scott Jamieson who dispatched Raphaël Jacquelin and Larrazábal respectively on the final green.

It was left to Poulter to deliver the coup-de-grâce; three birdies in his final five holes proving decisive for yet another 18th green victory, this time against the talented teenager Matteo Manassero. Hanson and Ross Fisher, all square playing the last, sportingly called their match a half to crown GB&I's 15 ½ - 12 ½ victory.

The golf had been stunning and even if it was not the result Seve would have preferred, there is no question he would have loved every cut and thrust minute of it.

Renton Laidlaw

Jean Van de Velde

Scott Jamieson

Anders Hansen

VIVENDI SEVE TROPHY

Saint-Nom-la-Bretèche Golf Club (Seve 1 Course)
Paris, France
September 15–18, 2011

"I have some great characters on my team, there is no doubt about that, and they showed their character today. I'm proud of each and every one of them for the performance they produced against a very talented Continental side"

Paul McGinley

CONTINENTAL EUROPE (Captain: Jean Van de Velde)		GREAT BRITAIN AND IRELAND (Captain: Paul McGinley)	
Thursday: Fourballs			
M A Jiménez (ESP) & P Larrazábal (ESP)	0	S Dyson (ENG) & J Donaldson (WAL) (2 & 1)	1
P Hanson (SWE) & R Jacquelin (FRA)	0	R Fisher (ENG) & S Jamieson (SCO) (6 & 4)	1
A Hansen (DEN) & F Molinari (ITA) (1 hole)	1	L Westwood (ENG) & M Foster (ENG)	0
N Colsaerts (BEL) & M Manassero (ITA)	0	D Clarke (NIR) & D Horsey (ENG) (1 hole)	1
T Björn (DEN) & A Noren (SWE)	0	I Poulter (ENG) & R Rock (ENG) (5 & 3)	1
Session Score:	**1**		**4**
Match Position:	**1**		**4**
Friday: Fourballs			
T Björn & R Jacquelin (halved)	½	S Dyson & J Donaldson (halved)	½
P Hanson & A Noren (5 & 3)	1	I Poulter & R Rock	0
N Colsaerts & M Manassero (1 hole)	1	R Fisher & S Jamieson	0
A Hansen & F Molinari	0	L Westwood & M Foster (5 & 3)	1
M A Jiménez & P Larrazábal (3 & 2)	1	D Clarke & D Horsey	0
Session Score:	**3½**		**1½**
Match Position:	**4½**		**5½**
Saturday September 17: Morning Greensomes			
N Colsaerts & M Manassero	0	S Dyson & J Donaldson (2 & 1)	1
P Hanson & A Noren (halved)	½	D Clarke & D Horsey (halved)	½
T Björn & R Jacquelin	0	I Poulter & R Fisher (2 & 1)	1
M A Jiménez & P Larrazábal	0	L Westwood & S Jamieson (4 & 3)	1
Session Score:	**½**		**3½**
Match Position:	**5**		**9**
Saturday: Afternoon Foursomes			
F Molinari & M Manassero (halved)	½	R Rock & J Donaldson (halved)	½
T Björn & A Hansen (3 & 2)	1	R Fisher & M Foster	0
P Larrazábal & A Noren	0	S Dyson & I Poulter (3 & 1)	1
R Jacquelin & N Colsaerts	0	L Westwood & D Horsey (4 & 3)	1
Session Score:	**1½**		**2½**
Match Position:	**6½**		**11½**
Sunday September 18: Singles			
T Björn (2 & 1)	1	L Westwood	0
A Hansen (1 hole)	1	S Dyson	0
F Molinari (4 & 3)	1	J Donaldson	0
A Noren (4 & 3)	1	R Rock	0
M A Jiménez (4 & 2)	1	Darren Clarke	0
N Colsaerts (halved)	½	D Horsey (halved)	½
P Larrazábal	0	S Jamieson (1 hole)	1
Matteo Manassero	0	I Poulter (1 hole)	1
R Jacquelin	0	M Foster (1 hole)	1
P Hanson (halved)	½	R Fisher (halved)	½
Session Score:	**6**		**4**
CONTINENTAL EUROPE	**12½**	**GREAT BRITAIN & IRELAND**	**15½**

"This means the world to me and I feel amazing. I've been working hard and doing all the right things but just haven't had the results to back it up. So to now win here, makes it all worthwhile"

Kenneth Ferrie

AUSTRIAN GOLFOPEN presented by Lyoness
Diamond Country Club (Diamond Course)
Atzenbrugg, Austria
September 22–25, 2011

1	**KENNETH FERRIE**		72	70	67	67	276	-12
2	Simon Wakefield		73	66	70	67	276	-12
3	Joost Luiten		67	70	72	68	277	-11
4	Thomas Nørret		67	70	70	72	279	-9
5	Victor Dubuisson		72	71	67	70	280	-8
	Cesar Monasterio		72	72	70	66	280	-8
	Bernd Wiesberger		70	71	71	68	280	-8
8	Magnus A Carlsson		71	75	67	68	281	-7
	Christian Nilsson		71	70	70	70	281	-7
10	Robert Coles		72	65	72	73	282	-6
	Tommy Fleetwood		72	72	69	69	282	-6
	Tom Lewis		74	70	70	68	282	-6
	Gary Orr		69	71	72	70	282	-6

Christian Guzy, owner of the Diamond Country Club and Kenneth Ferrie

Total Prize Fund €1,007,470   **First Prize** €166,660

Diamond Standard

Kenneth Ferrie ended a six year title drought on The European Tour when he overcame his fellow countryman Simon Wakefield to win the Austrian GolfOpen presented by Lyoness after a thrilling final round at the Diamond Country Club.

The Englishman – who turned 33 three days after his triumph – had last held silverware in his hands after the Smurfit European Open in July 2005 and, understandably, harboured doubts about whether it was ever going to happen again.

Indeed, when the Tour exemption for that victory in Ireland ran out at the end of last season, Ferrie only kept his playing privileges for 2011 thanks to a gutsy performance in his final outing of the year in Hong Kong. But the Englishman has no worries on that score now.

Going into the final round in Austria it was Danish rookie Thomas Nørret who led, but a double bogey at the 13th saw him slip back to fourth, leaving Ferrie, Wakefield and Dutchman Joost Luiten to contest the spoils.

When Luiten three putted the 18th for bogey and, in the final match behind, Wakefield bogeyed the 17th, the advantage was with Ferrie but Wakefield bravely birdied the 18th to draw level with his compatriot and send the contest into extra holes.

Returning to the 18th, Wakefield could not repeat the feat and he overshot the green on his way to a bogey five. A superb approach from Ferrie saw him finish a mere six feet from the pin and when his birdie putt dropped below ground, the title was his.

Thomas Nørret

Joost Luiten

Bernd Wiesberger

Simon Wakefield

ALFRED DUNHILL
LINKS CHAMPIONSHIP

ALFRED DUNHILL LINKS CHAMPIONSHIP
Old Course St Andrews, Carnoustie and Kingsbarns Scotland
September 29–October 2, 2011

1	**MICHAEL HOEY**		66	66	66	68	266	-22
2	Rory McIlroy		70	67	66	65	268	-20
3	Graeme McDowell		67	67	67	69	270	-18
	George Murray		70	66	67	67	270	-18
5	Tommy Fleetwood		69	63	71	68	271	-17
	Louis Oosthuizen		66	67	69	69	271	-17
	Marc Warren		67	67	70	67	271	-17
8	Padraig Harrington		68	71	64	69	272	-16
9	Nicolas Colsaerts		70	67	69	67	273	-15
	Luke Donald		69	71	63	70	273	-15
	Jamie Donaldson		71	65	70	67	273	-15
	Simon Dyson		69	71	63	70	273	-15
	Peter Hanson		68	69	69	67	273	-15
	Joost Luiten		72	68	65	68	273	-15
	Charl Schwartzel		69	69	66	69	273	-15
	Jaco Van Zyl		67	67	69	70	273	-15

Michael Hoey and Sir Michael Bonallack, OBE, Championship Committee

Total Prize Fund €3,528,893   **First Prize** €588,149

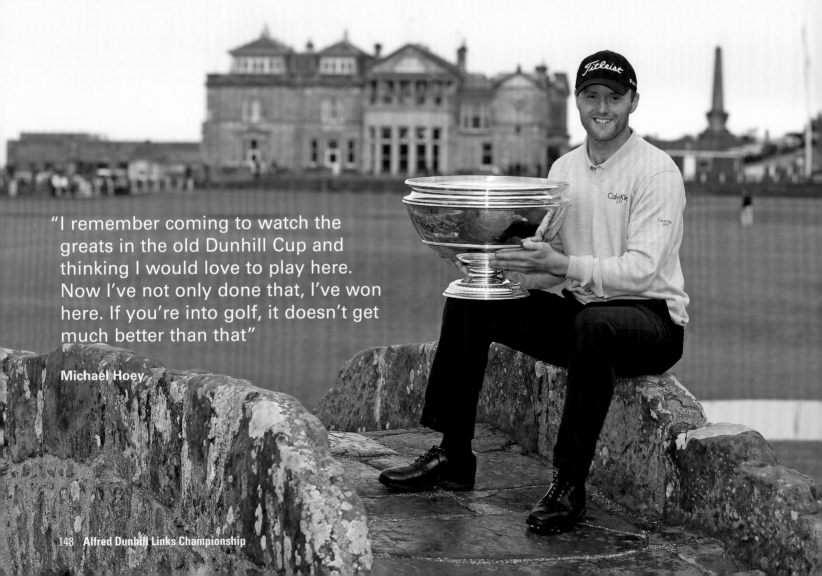

"I remember coming to watch the greats in the old Dunhill Cup and thinking I would love to play here. Now I've not only done that, I've won here. If you're into golf, it doesn't get much better than that"

Michael Hoey

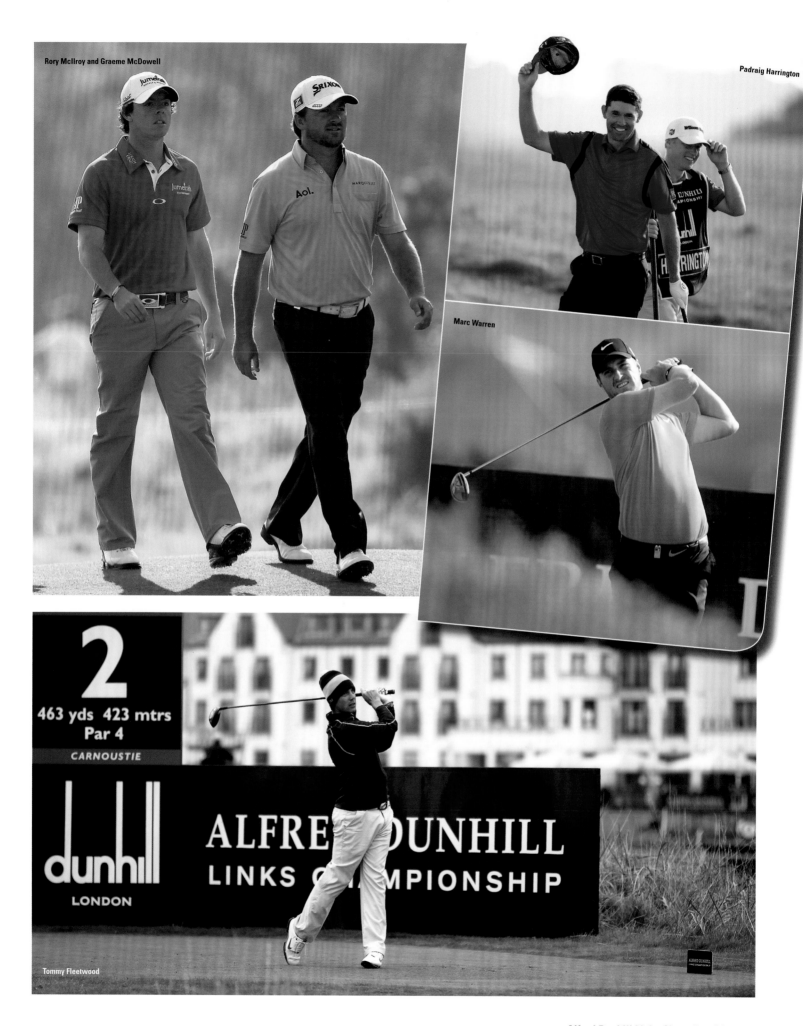

Rory McIlroy and Graeme McDowell

Padraig Harrington

Marc Warren

2
463 yds 423 mtrs
Par 4
CARNOUSTIE

dunhill
LONDON

ALFRED DUNHILL
LINKS CHAMPIONSHIP

Tommy Fleetwood

ALFRED DUNHILL
LINKS CHAMPIONSHIP

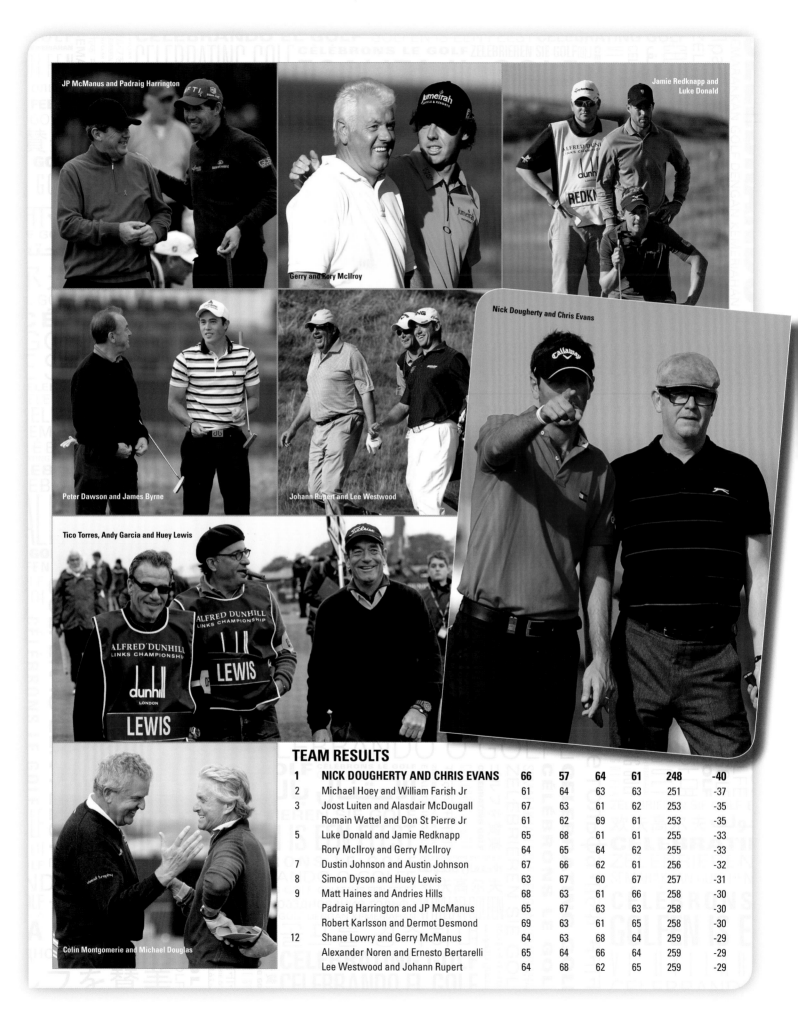

JP McManus and Padraig Harrington

Gerry and Rory McIlroy

Jamie Redknapp and Luke Donald

Nick Dougherty and Chris Evans

Peter Dawson and James Byrne

Johann Rupert and Lee Westwood

Tico Torres, Andy Garcia and Huey Lewis

Colin Montgomerie and Michael Douglas

TEAM RESULTS

1	**NICK DOUGHERTY AND CHRIS EVANS**	**66**	**57**	**64**	**61**	**248**	**-40**
2	Michael Hoey and William Farish Jr	61	64	63	63	251	-37
3	Joost Luiten and Alasdair McDougall	67	63	61	62	253	-35
	Romain Wattel and Don St Pierre Jr	61	62	69	61	253	-35
5	Luke Donald and Jamie Redknapp	65	68	61	61	255	-33
	Rory McIlroy and Gerry McIlroy	64	65	64	62	255	-33
7	Dustin Johnson and Austin Johnson	67	66	62	61	256	-32
8	Simon Dyson and Huey Lewis	63	67	60	67	257	-31
9	Matt Haines and Andries Hills	68	63	61	66	258	-30
	Padraig Harrington and JP McManus	65	67	63	63	258	-30
	Robert Karlsson and Dermot Desmond	69	63	61	65	258	-30
12	Shane Lowry and Gerry McManus	64	63	68	64	259	-29
	Alexander Noren and Ernesto Bertarelli	65	64	66	64	259	-29
	Lee Westwood and Johann Rupert	64	68	62	65	259	-29

George Murray

Style and Panache

Michael Hoey wrote another glorious chapter in the remarkable recent history of Northern Irish golf when he held off the challenge of compatriots Rory McIlroy and Graeme McDowell to win the Alfred Dunhill Links Championship.

The 32 year old, who began the week in 271st place in the Official World Golf Ranking but who ended it in 98th spot, carded a final round of 68 on the Old Course at St Andrews for a 22 under par total of 266 to claim his second European Tour title of the season.

The first place cheque - €588,149 – was some €471,483 more than the bounty he received for his first win of the season in the Madeira Islands Open in May and helped him move from 83rd to 15th in The Race to Dubai. It also allowed him to look forward to a place in the season-ending Dubai World Championship.

McIlroy finished two shots behind in second after a closing 65 with the man he succeeded as US Open champion, McDowell, sharing third alongside Scotland's George Murray, who did enough with his closing 67 to guarantee his card for next season.

Hoey began the final round five shots clear of McIlroy but a brilliant front nine of 30 followed by another birdie at the 11th, saw the 22 year old gain the initiative. However, McIlroy could not find another birdie in the closing seven holes, giving Hoey a chance he grasped with both hands; finishing birdie, birdie, par, birdie to win with considerable style and panache.

Louis Oosthuizen

BANKIA MADRID MASTERS
El Encín Golf Hotel
Alcalá de Henares, Spain
October 6–9, 2011

1	**LEE SLATTERY**		67	66	69	71	273	**-15**
2	Lorenzo Gagli		65	70	69	70	274	-14
3	Eduardo de la Riva		67	67	72	70	276	-12
	Cesar Monasterio		68	70	67	71	276	-12
5	Thomas Aiken		71	69	67	71	278	-10
6	Gonzalo Fernandez-Castaño		65	75	68	71	279	-9
	Oscar Floren		69	69	67	74	279	-9
	Peter Hanson		67	72	72	68	279	-9
	Benjamin Hebert		69	72	67	71	279	-9
	Francesco Molinari		67	67	71	74	279	-9

L-R: Percival Manglano, Consejero de Economía de la Comunidad de Madrid, Lee Slattery and Pilar Trucios, Directora General Adjunta de Comunicación y Marca de Bankia

Total Prize Fund €1,000,000   **First Prize** €166,660

"My mum and dad have done everything to help me and I got emotional coming down the last as I knew what a win would mean for them. I've never shaken so much as I did over the final putt – it was great to see it drop"

Lee Slattery

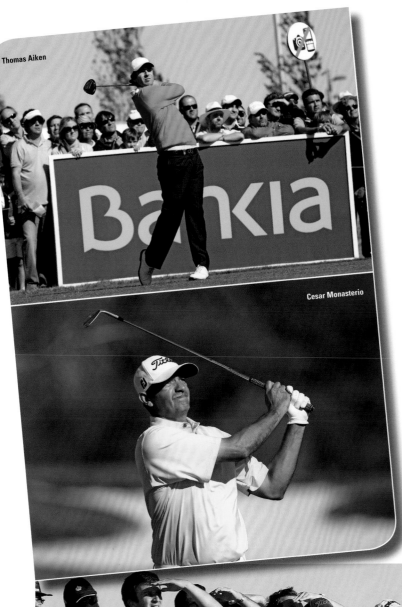

Thomas Aiken

Cesar Monasterio

Shaken not stirred

If anyone knows about the vagaries of professional golf it is Lee Slattery, which is perhaps why the Englishman's victory in the Bankia Madrid Masters was so well received across the game.

The affable 33 year old is one of the most popular figures on the circuit and everyone felt for him when he lost his playing privileges at the end of the 2007 season by a mere €77 and again by only 16 places at the culmination of 2009.

To his credit, however, he bounced back on both occasions, coming through the Qualifying School Final Stage in 2007 and the Challenge Tour Rankings last season before finally getting his European Tour reward at the end of a dramatic afternoon at El Encín Golf Hotel.

Having assumed the lead at the halfway stage, Slattery took a two shot advantage into the final round but an uncertain start allowed Argentina's Cesar Monasterio and Lorenzo Gagli of Italy to seize the initiative. The Englishman regained control with four birdies in five holes from the 11th and at three shots clear with three holes to play looked home and dry. However, the drama was not over.

On the par five 18th, Slattery's second shot drifted into sand from where his escape attempt flew into the water to the right of the putting surface. A penalty shot later, his chip found the green from where he two putted from ten feet for a double bogey seven, good enough to give him a one shot winning aggregate over Gagli.

Eduardo de la Riva

Lorenzo Gagli

PORTUGAL MASTERS
Oceânico Victoria Golf Course
Vilamoura, Portugal
October 13–16, 2011

1	TOM LEWIS		70	64	68	65	267	-21
2	Rafael Cabrera-Bello		69	65	64	71	269	-19
3	Felipe Aguilar		66	66	67	71	270	-18
	George Coetzee		70	69	66	65	270	-18
	Grégory Havret		66	69	71	64	270	-18
	David Lynn		70	68	68	64	270	-18
	Christian Nilsson		69	64	66	71	270	-18
8	Thomas Björn		65	69	66	71	271	-17
	Jamie Donaldson		69	68	67	67	271	-17
	Martin Kaymer		67	68	70	66	271	-17

L-R: Dr Cecilia Meireles, Secretaria de Estado do Turismo, Tom Lewis and George O'Grady, Chief Executive of The European Tour

Total Prize Fund €2,511,241   **First Prize** €416,660

"When George O'Grady came over at the end, shook my hand and said; 'Welcome to The European Tour', I was just thrilled. There were so many good players here, so to come out on top is just unbelievable"

Tom Lewis

David Lynn

Grégory Havret

Rafael Cabrera-Bello

10
406 Yds 371 Mtrs
PAR 4

TURISMO DE
PORTUGAL

PORTUGAL
MASTERS

oceânico   TURISMO DE PORTUGAL   TIVOLI

Breathtaking Landscapes

PORTUGAL

The beauty of simplicity

visitportugal.com

Portugal
Europe's West Coast™

TURISMO DE
PORTUGAL

Christian Nilsson

George Coetzee

Felipe Aguilar

A Star is Born

European Tour Chief Executive George O'Grady said it at the prize giving ceremony and those who witnessed Tom Lewis' stunning maiden European Tour triumph in the Portugal Masters agreed that, indeed, a star had been born at the Oceânico Victoria Golf Course.

The 20 year old Englishman was no stranger to the limelight before he arrived on the Algarve, having carded the lowest round by an amateur in Open Championship history at Royal St George's in July before helping Great Britain and Ireland defeat the United States to win the Walker Cup at Royal Aberdeen in September.

But, having turned professional, question marks were raised over whether or not he could cut it with the big boys in the paid ranks: it is fair to say he answered that question pretty emphatically.

Four shots off the pace at the start of the final round, Lewis' superb closing 65 saw him cut through the field to win by two shots from Spain's Rafael Cabrera-Bello, but it was his spectacular finish which drew most of the plaudits; birdies at the 12th, 14th, 15th, 16th and 17th holes blowing his nearest challengers away.

Tiger Woods needed five tournaments to land his first professional title, Matteo Mannasero needed ten, while Rory McIlroy did not taste success until his 38th outing. It was no surprise that Lewis' name was mentioned in such exalted company afterwards and, whatever happens in the future, he can always hold sway in this particular category; his triumph having come in his third professional tournament.

"I want to thank everyone – family, friends and sponsors – for supporting me through the last couple of years. They believed in me and I'm delighted to repay that faith with this win"

Sergio Garcia

CASTELLÓ MASTERS
Club de Campo del Mediterráneo
Castellón, Valencia, Spain
October 20–23, 2011

1	SERGIO GARCIA		67	63	64	63	257	-27
2	Gonzalo Fernandez-Castaño		69	66	69	64	268	-16
3	Alexander Noren		69	63	73	64	269	-15
	Richie Ramsay		72	64	68	65	269	-15
5	Thomas Aiken		68	69	70	63	270	-14
6	George Coetzee		67	70	69	66	272	-12
7	Marcel Siem		68	68	70	67	273	-11
8	Marcus Fraser		70	64	71	69	274	-10
	Ross McGowan		64	70	69	71	274	-10
	Romain Wattel		70	69	66	69	274	-10

Alberto Fabra, Presidente de La Generalitat Valenciana and Sergio Garcia

Total Prize Fund €2,000,000   **First Prize** €333,330

Swashbuckling Señor

If there were ever any doubts that Sergio Garcia was back to his swashbuckling best, they were dispelled with an astonishing triumph in the Castelló Masters.

The memory of almost three lean years were swept aside at his home Club de Campo del Mediterráneo course, where he first won the club championship as a 12 year old, as he turned an eight shot third round lead – thanks to rounds of 67-63-64 – into an 11 shot victory following another masterful closing round of 63.

Placing on the fairways denied Garcia's 27 under par 257 the opportunity to feature in The European Tour record books for all time, but it should nevertheless be noted that only one player in history – Ernie Els in the 2003 Johnnie Walker Classic at Lake

Karrinyup Country Club in Australia – had posted a lower winning tournament score, the South African being 29 under par that year at the Perth venue.

It was Garcia's ninth European Tour success and his first since winning the HSBC Champions tournament in China in November 2008. It not only lifted him back to just outside the top 30 on the Official World Golf Ranking but also into the top 15 of The Race to Dubai.

On a final day of exceptionally low scoring, second placed Gonzalo Fernandez-Castaño carded a 64 for a 16 under par total of 268 while Alex Noren (64) and Richie Ramsay (65) finished one shot further back. But they were merely supporting features to the main act.

Richie Ramsay

Thomas Aiken

Alex Noren

Gonzalo Fernandez-Castaño

"I don't really have words for this, it's been a very special two weeks. I have so much history here at Valderrama and to be the first Spaniard to win on the course is amazing"

Sergio Garcia

ANDALUCÍA MASTERS
Club de Golf Valderrama
Sotogrande, Spain
October 27–30, 2011

1	**SERGIO GARCIA**		**70**	**70**	**67**	**71**	**278**	**-6**
2	Miguel Angel Jiménez		71	70	68	70	279	-5
3	Richie Ramsay		65	72	73	70	280	-4
4	Shane Lowry		72	71	71	67	281	-3
5	Steve Webster		75	72	66	69	282	-2
6	Grégory Havret		68	71	76	68	283	-1
7	Alejandro Cañizares		71	72	71	70	284	0
	Christian Nilsson		73	71	65	75	284	0
9	Stephen Dodd		71	73	74	67	285	1
10	Peter Hanson		72	71	73	70	286	2
	Francesco Molinari		71	73	71	71	286	2

Sergio Garcia and Luciano Alonso, Consejero de Turismo, Comercio y Deporte de la Junta de Andalucía

Total Prize Fund €3,000,000   First Prize €500,000

Steve Webster

Shane Lowry

Richie Ramsay

Miguel Angel Jiménez

Battling triumph

Sergio Garcia's amazing resurgence continued when, only a week after claiming the Castelló Masters at his home course, he became the first Spanish golfer to win a stroke play tournament at the famed Club de Golf Valderrama with a battling triumph in the Andalucia Masters.

The 31 year old had endured the agony of being runner-up at the Sotogrande venue in 2004, 2005 and 2006 when the course played host to The European Tour season-ending Volvo Masters, but this time he put matters right with a closing level par 71 for a six under par total of 278 and a one shot winning margin over his fellow countryman Miguel Angel Jiménez.

Seven days previously, Garcia had coasted to an 11 shot win in Castellón, but this was always going to be closer.

Into the final round, birdies at the 11th and 14th, allied to Jiménez's bogeys at the 13th and 15th put Garcia three shots clear but Jiménez showed his battling qualities with birdies at the 16th and 17th to close the gap to one.

Another birdie at the 18th looked on the cards for the 47 year old when he found the fairway and green but he left his 15 foot putt agonisingly short. Garcia, in the final match behind, found the greenside fringe with his approach but bravely got up and down to triumph.

The win also saw Garcia become the first player since José María Olazábal in the 1992 Tenerife Open and the Open Mediterrania to win back-to-back events on Spanish soil.

"I played well today and it was great to see it all come together. With my Major win last year and now this, it is very satisfying to see my name on golf's biggest trophies"

Martin Kaymer

WGC - HSBC CHAMPIONS
Sheshan International Golf Club
Shanghai, China
November 3–6, 2011

1	**MARTIN KAYMER**		69	68	68	63	268	-20
2	Fredrik Jacobson		67	66	67	71	271	-17
3	Graeme McDowell		69	69	67	67	272	-16
4	Paul Casey		70	66	70	67	273	-15
	Rory McIlroy		70	69	65	69	273	-15
	Charl Schwartzel		70	69	69	65	273	-15
7	Hunter Mahan		71	67	69	67	274	-14
	Louis Oosthuizen		71	63	68	72	274	-14
	Justin Rose		68	70	70	66	274	-14
10	Jhonattan Vegas		69	73	65	68	275	-13

Peter Wong, Chief Executive HSBC, Asia Pacific and Martin Kaymer

Total Prize Fund €4,912,936   **First Prize €842,218**

Paul Casey

Rory McIlroy and Graeme McDowell

Charl Schwartzel

Fredrik Jacobson

Fireworks display

There were many impressive last round performances to win tournaments on The 2011 European Tour International Schedule but it could be argued that the best of the lot was provided by Martin Kaymer on an extraordinary afternoon in Shanghai which saw him claim the World Golf Championships – HSBC Champions title.

Having started the final day five shots adrift of leader Fredrik Jacobson and having begun with six straight par figures, there was little in the 26 year old German's play that gave any hint of the fireworks that were about to appear. But once he holed from a bunker at the seventh for a birdie three, the blue touchpaper was well and truly ignited.

From there to the finish Kaymer was immaculate; another birdie four following at the eighth before he launched a blistering assault on the Sheshan International Golf Club's back nine, birdieing seven of them to be home in 29 for a 63, a 20 under par total of 268 and a three shot winning margin over Jacobson who did nothing wrong in his closing 71, but who simply could not live with the scoring of the eventual champion.

At the end of a week when European Tour Members again occupied the top four slots in the Official World Golf Ranking, it was a similarly impressive showing in China as Tour Members Kaymer, Jacobson, Graeme McDowell, Paul Casey, Charl Schwartzel, Rory McIlroy, Justin Rose and Louis Oosthuizen filled eight of the top nine places.

"This is a great relief after all I've been through. Three years without a win is hard but I could see I was improving. To come out on top means so much to myself and my family"

Gonzalo Fernandez-Castaño

BARCLAYS SINGAPORE OPEN
Sentosa Golf Club (Tanjong and Serapong Courses)
Singapore
November 10–13, 2011

1	**GONZALO FERNANDEZ-CASTAÑO**		66	61	72	199	-14
2	Juvic Pagunsan		66	66	67	199	-14
3	Anthony Kim		70	66	64	200	-13
	Louis Oosthuizen		72	63	65	200	-13
5	Danny Lee		68	65	68	201	-12
	Joost Luiten		69	65	67	201	-12
	Edoardo Molinari		62	68	71	201	-12
8	James Morrison		62	68	72	202	-11
9	Justin Rose		69	65	69	203	-10
	Tjaart Van Der Walt		71	65	67	203	-10

Robert Morrice, Chairman and Chief Executive Asia Pacific, Barclays PLC and Gonzalo Fernandez-Castaño

Total Prize Fund €4,390,005   **First Prize** €720,877

Anthony Kim

Juvic Pagunsan

Joost Luiten

Back on Top

There have been several lengthy play-offs in the history of The European Tour but none which have taken 16 hours to complete. Yet that was exactly the situation which unfolded before Gonzalo Fernandez-Castaño finally laid claim to the Barclays Singapore Open.

In a tournament plagued by thunder and lightning interruptions, which eventually forced officials to cut it to 54 holes, the Spaniard and Filipino Juvic Pagunsan faced extra holes after both men finished on 14 under par 199. The play-off began at 4pm on Sunday afternoon, but more storms meant it did not finish until 8am on Monday morning following Fernandez-Castaño's ten-foot birdie putt on the second extra hole.

The Spaniard's delight was understandable because, six months ago, there were serious doubts as to whether he would play golf again beset, as he was, by back problems which led to a lengthy spell on the sidelines.

In addition to that, some serious woes with his putter blighted his return to the game although a recent conversion to the claw grip seemed to be paying dividends; illustrated by sixth, second and 12th place finishes in the three European Tour events in Spain in October.

His progress and renewed confidence in that department was highlighted, not only by his winning birdie putt, but also by the 20 foot curler he holed on the final green in regulation to force the play-off itself. There was disappointment for Pagunsan but some consolation in the fact that his runners-up cheque helped him move top of the Asian Tour Order of Merit.

Edoardo Molinari

Louis Oosthuizen

"I've been close a few times this year and so it was understandable I was a little nervous coming down the stretch. But now, to have finally won on The European Tour, is unbelievable"

Joost Luiten

ISKANDAR JOHOR OPEN
Horizon Hills Golf & Country Club
Johor, Malaysia
November 17–20, 2011

1	**JOOST LUITEN**		**63**	**70**	**65**	**198**	**-15**
2	Daniel Chopra		64	65	70	199	-14
3	Rhys Davies		70	65	65	200	-13
	Padraig Harrington		64	67	69	200	-13
	James Morrison		66	65	69	200	-13
6	Grégory Bourdy		64	67	70	201	-12
7	Søren Kjeldsen		71	64	67	202	-11
8	Fredrik Andersson Hed		68	67	68	203	-10
	Darren Beck		70	65	68	203	-10
	Marcus Fraser		64	70	69	203	-10
	José Manuel Lara		67	67	69	203	-10
	Louis Oosthuizen		69	67	67	203	-10

HE Dato' Abdul Ghani bin Othman, Chief Minister of Johor, Co-Chairman of Iskandar Regional Development Authority and Chairman of the IJO Organising Committee, Joost Luiten and HRH Tunku Ismail Idris ibni Sultan Ibrahim Ismail, Crown Prince of Johor

Total Prize Fund €1,459,861   **First Prize** €242,581

Daniel Chopra

Rhys Davies

James Morrison

Joost the ticket

Sometimes, if you knock on the door long enough it will open and so it was for Dutchman Joost Luiten who finally made his long-awaited European Tour breakthrough with victory in the Iskandar Johor Open.

It is arguable that there has been no more consistent player over the past five months with the 25 year old from Bleiswijk having finished in the top 15 on no less than eight of his previous 14 tournament outings. Despite that, the closest he had come to success was with his third place finishes in the Austrian GolfOpen and the BMW International Open in Germany, but he put all that behind him in Malaysia in a tournament cut to 54 holes due to numerous thunderstorm interruptions.

An opening 63 had seen Luiten lead but a second round 70 – salvaged by three closing birdies – dropped him back to such an extent that he began the third and final round four shots adrift of Sweden's Daniel Chopra who had begun with consistent rounds of 64-65.

The Dutchman knew he needed a fast start and got it with five birdies in a flawless outward half of 30 which saw him assume the lead as Chopra turned in 36.

Another bogey from the Swede at the tenth left Luiten firmly in control and an error free inward half saw him win by a shot, Chopra's birdie at the 18th helping lift him from the company of Rhys Davies, Padraig Harrington and James Morrison into second place on his own.

Padraig Harrington

"It was a battle but I just tried to play smart golf and I'm delighted to have come through. This win opens up a lot of opportunities for me and I'm looking forward to trying to take them"

Garth Mulroy

ALFRED DUNHILL CHAMPIONSHIP

ALFRED DUNHILL CHAMPIONSHIP
Leopard Creek Country Club
Malelane, South Africa
November 17-20, 2011

1	**GARTH MULROY**		**69**	**68**	**64**	**68**	**269**	**-19**
2	George Murray		66	69	69	67	271	-17
3	Felipe Aguilar		71	64	68	72	275	-13
	George Coetzee		66	71	69	69	275	-13
	Jaco Van Zyl		68	68	72	67	275	-13
	Peter Whiteford		73	67	64	71	275	-13
7	Hennie Otto		69	68	67	72	276	-12
	Andrea Pavan		68	70	68	70	276	-12
9	James Kamte		72	70	69	66	277	-11
	Jbe Kruger		64	67	73	73	277	-11
	Steven Tiley		70	69	70	68	277	-11

Garth Mulroy and Gaynor Rupert, wife of Johann Rupert, Executive Chairman and CEO Richemont

Total Prize Fund €1,000,000   **First Prize** €158,500

Felipe Aguilar

George Coetzee

Jaco Van Zyl

Peter Whiteford

100 not out

South Africa is unquestionably a proud cricketing nation in addition to its love of golf so it was appropriate that, using a favourite cricketing parlance, a century of winners for the country on The European Tour was brought up on home soil in the Alfred Dunhill Championship.

The man who notched the notable milestone was Garth Mulroy but the 33 year old had to battle hard throughout an enthralling final round at Leopard Creek Country Club before he finally got his hands on the silverware.

Two clear of the field going into Sunday's action, Mulroy was favourite to land his maiden European Tour title but he was caught in the early stages by fellow countryman Jbe Kruger before the latter's challenge faltered when he found the water en route to a double bogey six at the ninth.

Four birdies for Mulroy between the sixth and the 13th looked to have sealed the deal but when he bogeyed the 14th at the same time as, up ahead, George Murray notched an eagle three at the 15th, the three shot swing brought the Scotsman back level and firmly into the frame.

However, to his credit, Mulroy regained his composure and further birdies at the 15th and the 16th saw him move ahead once again and his closing 68 for a 19 under par total of 269 was good enough to win by two shots from Murray, the Scotsman's consolation being his best finish on The European Tour.

George Murray

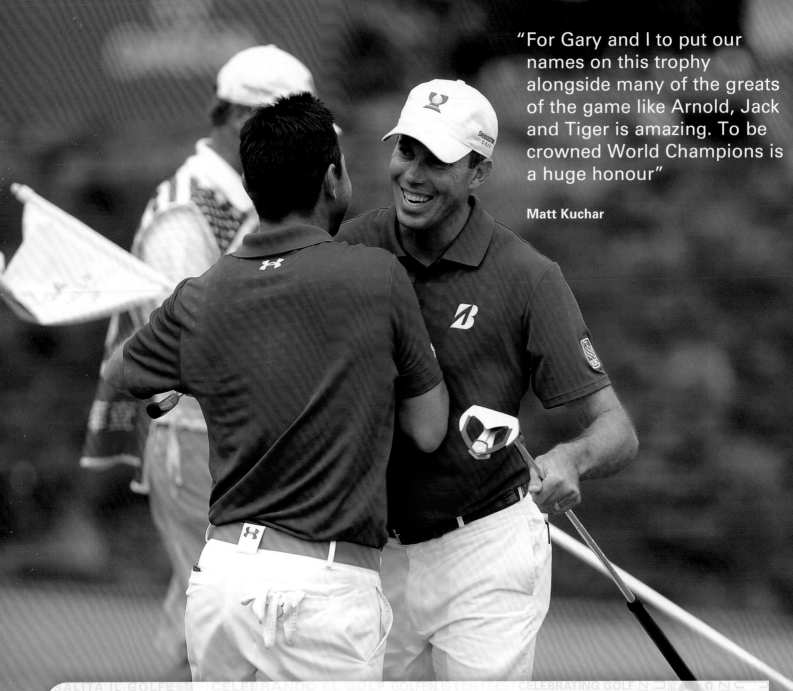

"For Gary and I to put our names on this trophy alongside many of the greats of the game like Arnold, Jack and Tiger is amazing. To be crowned World Champions is a huge honour"

Matt Kuchar

OMEGA MISSION HILLS WORLD CUP
Mission Hills Resort (Blackstone Course)
Hainan Island,China
November 24–27, 2011

1	**MATT KUCHAR / GARY WOODLAND**		64	70	63	67	264	-24
2	Alex Cejka / Martin Kaymer		65	71	61	69	266	-22
	Ian Poulter / Justin Rose		66	69	68	63	266	-22
4	Richard Green / Brendan Jones		61	70	67	69	267	-21
	Graeme McDowell / Rory McIlroy		63	68	64	72	267	-21
	Stephen Gallacher / Martin Laird		63	69	69	66	267	-21
	Robert-Jan Derksen / Joost Luiten		64	71	64	68	267	-21
8	Rhys Davies / Jamie Donaldson		67	69	65	67	268	-20
9	Miguel Angel Jiménez / Alvaro Quiros		65	69	68	67	269	-19
	Hyung-sung Kim / Sung Joon Park		66	71	64	68	269	-19

L-R: Stephen Urquhart, President of Omega, Gary Woodland, Matt Kuchar and Dr. Ken Chu, Chairman and CEO of Mission Hills Group

Total Prize Fund €5,588,132 **First Prize** €1,788,202 (Team)

Ireland: Rory McIlroy and Graeme McDowell

England: Ian Poulter and Justin Rose

Scotland: Martin Laird and Stephen Gallacher

Ω OMEGA
MISSION HILLS
WORLD CUP
欧米茄观澜湖高尔夫世界杯

Germany: Alex Cejka and Martin Kaymer

Netherlands: Robert-Jan Derksen and Joost Luiten

Mission Accomplished

The United States ended an 11 year wait for a 24th overall victory when Matt Kuchar and Gary Woodland won the Omega Mission Hills World Cup at the new Mission Hills Resort on Hainan Island.

The most successful nation in the history of the competition won their first World Cup since David Duval and Tiger Woods triumphed at the Buenos Aires Golf Club in 2000, as the two tournament debutants combined for a fine closing day 67 in the more demanding foursomes format on the spectacular Blackstone Course.

It gave the United States a 24 under par winning total of 264, two shots clear of the German duo of Alex Cejka and Martin Kaymer and the English pairing of Ian Poulter and Justin Rose who mounted

a stirring final day challenge with a remarkable 63, the best foursomes score of the week by some three shots.

After Saturday's fourball round, the Americans, the Germans and the South African duo of Louis Oosthuizen and Charl Schwartzel found themselves two shots adrift of the Irish pairing of Graeme McDowell and Rory McIlroy, many people's favourites to lift the title for the Emerald Isle for the first time since Padraig Harrington and Paul McGinley won at Kiawah Island in 1997.

But a three putt bogey at the first set the tone of their day and they could only finish tied fourth in the end alongside first round leaders Australia, the Netherlands and Scotland.

"There are such high standards in golf nowadays that to win is really something. But this victory is special as this is our national Open. You dream of winning this one so when it comes your way, you must relish it"

Hennie Otto

SA OPEN CHAMPIONSHIP
Serengeti Golf and Wildlife Estate
Ekurhuleni, South Africa
November 24-27, 2011

1	**HENNIE OTTO**		70	67	65	72	274	**-14**
2	Bernd Wiesberger		69	68	70	68	275	-13
3	Thomas Aiken		68	69	68	72	277	-11
	Richard McEvoy		70	70	69	68	277	-11
	Ockie Strydom		69	72	67	69	277	-11
6	Magnus A Carlsson		73	66	66	73	278	-10
	Trevor Fisher Jnr		68	72	70	68	278	-10
	Retief Goosen		66	68	71	73	278	-10
9	Jaco Ahlers		74	67	65	73	279	-9
	Branden Grace		69	68	74	68	279	-9
	Garth Mulroy		67	68	70	74	279	-9
	Lloyd Saltman		69	68	72	70	279	-9

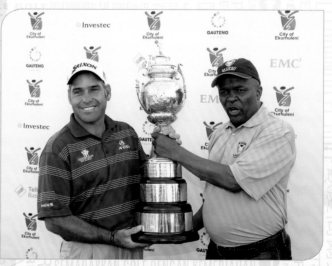

Hennie Otto and Mondli Gungubele, Mayor of Ekurhuleni

Total Prize Fund €1,000,200   **First Prize** €158,500

Retief Goosen

SA OPEN
CHAMPIONSHIP

10
417 yds 381 mtrs
Par 4

ROLEX

City of
Ekurhuleni

EKURHULENI
AEROTROPOLIS

Bernd Wiesberger

Sweet Sixteen

Hennie Otto overcame a nervous Sunday back nine to win his national title, the SA Open Championship, at the 16th time of asking. It was the 35 year old's second European Tour triumph, following his win in the 2008 Italian Open, and one which moved him into the top 60 in The Race to Dubai and in with a good chance of making his debut in the season-ending Dubai World Championship presented by DP World.

Three strokes clear of his nearest challenger going into the final round, his advantage remained intact with a mere six holes to play before he gave the challenging pack – led by Austrian Bernd Wiesberger – hope with bogeys at the 13th, 15th and 16th.

However, Otto steeled himself admirably and used his prodigious length from the tee to good effect at the 365 yard 17th, driving through the green before chipping and putting for a crucial birdie three.

There was still the water on the final hole to negotiate but from a perfect drive he found the green safely and two putted for par and the title by a shot from Wiesberger, who notched his second runners-up finish of the year having lost out to Thomas Björn in the play-off for the Johnnie Walker Championship at Gleneagles in August.

Joint third were South Africans Thomas Aiken and Ockie Strydom alongside Englishman Richard McEvoy who moved from 121st to 107th in The Race to Dubai, thus ensuring his playing privileges for the 2012 season.

Thomas Aiken

"I've wanted to win here so badly since I lost a play-off in 2008, because I just love Hong Kong. I knew I had to do it to keep alive my hopes of The Race to Dubai and you saw at the end how much it meant that I'd achieved it"

Rory McIlroy

UBS HONG KONG OPEN
Hong Kong Golf Club (New and Eden Courses)
Fanling, Hong Kong
December 1–4, 2011

1	**RORY MCILROY**		**64**	**69**	**70**	**65**	**268**	**-12**
2	Grégory Havret		70	69	66	65	270	-10
3	Peter Hanson		68	68	65	70	271	-9
4	Pariya Junhasavasdikul		70	65	67	70	272	-8
	Ian Poulter		71	68	67	66	272	-8
	Richie Ramsay		68	66	72	66	272	-8
7	Kiradech Aphibarnrat		68	69	70	66	273	-7
	Alvaro Quiros		64	69	67	73	273	-7
	Y E Yang		68	69	65	71	273	-7
10	Juvic Pagunsan		68	70	68	68	274	-6

Kathryn Shih, Chief Executive Officer, UBS, Asia Pacific and Rory McIlroy

Total Prize Fund €2,029,801   **First Prize** €341,724

Stunning Triumph

It is one thing winning on The European Tour International Schedule, it is quite another thing winning when you have to, which is why Rory McIlroy's stunning victory in the UBS Hong Kong Open was all the more impressive.

Knowing he had to succeed to keep alive his hopes of pipping Luke Donald to The Race to Dubai title, at five shots adrift midway through a misfiring third round, it looked like matters were going awry but McIlroy gritted his teeth and two late birdies brought him back in touch.

As leader Alvaro Quiros faltered in the final round, McIlroy saw his chance and powered forward, his main challengers into the home straight being playing partner Grégory Havret and Peter Hanson, two matches behind.

While Havret was steady, he could not get close enough, while Hanson's first bogey of the week on the back nine at the 14th stalled his progress, leaving the Northern Irishman one clear coming down the last.

McIlroy is already heralded as the most exciting talent the game has known in years and showed precisely why, holing from the bunker in front of the 18th green for a truly audacious birdie three. Now all eyes turn to Dubai and what will be a thrilling tussle down to the wire with Donald.

Further down the Hong Kong field, there was joy for another Ulsterman, Gareth Maybin, whose share of 39th place helped him move from 120th in The Race to Dubai to 117, thus keeping his playing privileges for next year – the unfortunate man to miss out and face a return to the Qualifying School being Chile's Mark Tullo, who dropped to 119th.

Brian Stevenson (centre), Chairman of the Hong Kong Jockey Club, was joined by Justin Rose, Ryder Cup captain José María Olazábal and Padraig Harrington at the Happy Valley Racecourse for the running of the inaugural European Tour Golf Cup

Ian Poulter

Richie Ramsay

Peter Hanson

Grégory Havret

Bravo Alvaro!

"This is unbelievable. To win such a big tournament will open many doors but for now I am just trying to stay in the moment. It's fair to say though, right now, I feel pretty good"

Alvaro Quiros

DUBAI WORLD CHAMPIONSHIP presented by DP World
Jumeirah Golf Estates (Earth Course)
Dubai, UAE
December 8-11, 2011

1	**ALVARO QUIROS**		**68**	**64**	**70**	**67**	**269**	**-19**
2	Paul Lawrie		65	73	66	67	271	-17
3	Luke Donald		72	68	66	66	272	-16
4	Peter Hanson		64	72	71	67	274	-14
5	Charl Schwartzel		69	71	68	67	275	-13
6	Francesco Molinari		71	68	68	69	276	-12
	Louis Oosthuizen		72	67	66	71	276	-12
8	Shane Lowry		69	70	68	70	277	-11
	Robert Rock		68	69	71	69	277	-11
10	Pablo Larrazábal		71	68	70	69	278	-10

L-R: George O'Grady, Chief Executive of The European Tour, Mohammed Sharaf, CEO of DP World and Alvaro Quiros

Total Prize Fund €5,487,710   **First Prize** €922,645

In a year when golf lost the most flamboyant and charismatic character the game has ever known, it was somehow fitting that The European Tour's glittering end of season tournament was won by a man cut from precisely the same cloth as Seve Ballesteros.

Alvaro Quiros not only shares the same handsome swarthy features and dazzling smile that, like Seve, lights up every room he enters, the 28 year old from Guadiaro also plays the game in precisely the same swashbuckling way his illustrious compatriot made famous worldwide.

Fairways and greens are anathema to a player whose triumph in the Dubai World Championship presented by DP World gave him his sixth European Tour title in total and his second in the Emirate this year following his win in the Omega Dubai Desert Classic in February.

Just like Ballesteros, wherever Quiros' ball might go from the tee or beyond, it invariably finds its way, somehow, to the bottom of the cup. Nowhere was that better illustrated than in the first three

holes of the final round on the Earth Course where trees, a greenside swale and a bunker were located in quick succession but which, nevertheless, did not stop birdie figures being recorded at each hole.

However such extravagance can, on occasion, lead to mistakes and having begun with a two shot lead, a front nine which featured only one par figure saw Quiros enter the final nine holes one behind a resurgent Paul Lawrie. The Scot had stepped into the winners' circle for the first time in almost nine years in Malaga in March and the confidence garnered from that victory was clearly flooding through the 42 year old whose focused and disciplined golf was a joy to watch.

Rory McIlroy

Peter Hanson

Paul Lawrie

The 1999 Open Champion battled gamely over the back nine but a bogey at the 12th, allied to Quiros' birdie at the 14th, saw the lead change hands once again and gave the Spaniard an advantage he managed to maintain until the pair stood on the last tee.

After a pushed drive Lawrie did admirably well to make birdie four, holing from 12 feet for a 67 to ensure second place on his own on 17 under par 271, a score which helped him rise to 18th place in The Race to Dubai, his best finish since the 2002 season. However, as he had been for most of the day, he was overshadowed by the finish of his playing partner.

A week ago Quiros took a lead into the final round of the UBS Hong Kong Open only to let it slip but ensured there would be no repeat this time round with a stunning eagle three to close, finding the right edge of the putting surface with a three wood before rattling the ball into the hole from fully 50 feet for his own

67 and a winning total of 19 under par 269. How Seve would have loved it; the majesty and the theatre of it all.

At the start of the week the majority of the attention, understandably, had focused on Luke Donald and Rory McIlroy and their tussle for The Race to Dubai, a battle intensified thanks to the Northern Irishman's thrilling victory in Hong Kong.

Donald had already won the Money List on the US PGA Tour and was looking to become the first player to top the pile on both sides of the Atlantic in the same season. To do so, the arithmetic was simple; finish in the top nine so that not even a McIlroy victory could deny him his place in history.

The 34 year old Englishman admitted feeling the pressure and that showed in a hesitant opening 72 which was pushed even further into the shade by McIlroy's excellent 66. However, there is simply no better player in golf in compiling a 72 hole

score than Donald and steadily, as the week progressed, the undisputed World Number One began to turn things around.

With a fatigued McIlroy visibly wilting, despite the on-course support of girlfriend Caroline Wozniacki, the World Number One tennis player, Donald took advantage. Rounds of 68-66 saw him breeze past the Northern Irishman and indeed gave him hope of even lifting the tournament title itself when he began the final round in fourth place only four shots adrift of Quiros.

Yet despite another flawless 66 – meaning he had played the final 47 holes of the tournament bogey-free – he came up just short, finishing on 16 under par 272, two ahead of fourth placed Peter Hanson but one behind Lawrie and three adrift of Quiros.

Aside from making golfing history, Donald also had the knowledge he had set a new season's earnings record by a

DUBAI
WORLD CHAMPIONSHIP
JUMEIRAH GOLF ESTATES

PRESENTED BY

DP WORLD

EADER BOARD

		1	2	3	4	5	6	7	8	9	10	11	12	13	14	15	16	17	18
PAR		4	5	4	3	4	3	5	4	4	4	4	4	3	5	4	4	3	5
ORS	-8	3	5	3	3	3	3	5	4	4	3	4	4	3	5	4	4	4	4
	-8	4	4	3	3	4	2	4	5	3	4	2	6	3	5	3	5
RSSON HED	-6	4	5	4	3	5	3	4	3	4	4	3	4	4	3	2	5
GAERTS	-6	4	5	3	3	3	3	4	5	3	5	3	4	3	5
EN	-6	3	5	3	3	4	3	5	4	3	3	5
ZEE	-5	4	5	3	2	4	2	5	2	5	4	4	3	5
	-5	5	4	4	3	4	3	4	3	5	4	4	2	5
LTER	-5	4	5	4	3	4	3	5	3	5	4	4	4

	AFTER	DONALD			
	AFTER	LAWRIE PA			-17

Luke Donald

Francesco Molinari

Charl Schwartzel

Louis Oosthuizen

Member on The European Tour, his final haul of €5,323,400 comfortably passing the previous best of €4,461,011 set by Germany's Martin Kaymer last year.

Befitting the stature of the tournament, the week of the Dubai World Championship presented by DP World featured almost as much excitement off the course as inside the ropes and while the Tuesday night beach party at the Atlantis Palm and the Thursday night horse racing at Meydan were relished, it was an announcement on Sunday afternoon which resonated the most.

With Dubai emerging from an uncertain global financial climate, European Tour Chief Executive George O'Grady was delighted to announce a significant three-year agreement to extend The Race to Dubai through to the end of the 2014 season with a new name and title sponsor for the season-ending finale, which will be known, from 2012, as the DP World Tour Championship, Dubai.

The next three editions of the DP World Tour Championship, Dubai, will return to Jumeirah Golf Estates with the prize fund increasing by US$500,000 to a total of $8 million, and the winner's cheque rising from $1.25 million to $1.33 million.

"In DP World and Nakheel we have two incredibly strong partners who are fully dedicated to the future success of The Race to Dubai and the DP World Tour Championship, Dubai," said O'Grady. "We thank them for their continued backing of our season's finale at Jumeirah Golf Estates and we look forward to further strengthening our association with them when our leading world-ranked players return to compete in Dubai over the next three years."

If those tournaments are anything like the most recent four days on the Earth Course, everyone is already counting down the days.

Scott Crockett

L-R: Mohammed Sharaf, CEO of DP World, George O'Grady, Chief Executive of The European Tour, Sanjay Manchanda, Interim CEO of Nakheel, Saeed Harib, Managing Director of Nakheel Marine and Leisure and Keith Waters, Chief Operating Officer of The European Tour at the announcement of a further three years of sponsorship. From 2012 the tournament will be known as the DP World Tour Championship, Dubai

THE RACE TO DUBAI ON THE 2011 EUROPEAN TOUR INTERNATIONAL SCHEDULE

Pos	Name	Country	Played	€	Pos	Name	Country	Played	€	Pos	Name	Country	Played	€
1	Luke DONALD	(ENG)	(13)	5,323,400.36	51	Ernie ELS	(RSA)	(16)	591,507.72	101	Graeme STORM	(ENG)	(31)	311,307.67
2	Rory MCILROY	(NIR)	(19)	4,002,168.00	52	Ross FISHER	(ENG)	(25)	583,568.56	102	Colin MONTGOMERIE	(SCO)	(23)	300,287.17
3	Martin KAYMER	(GER)	(22)	3,489,033.01	53	Hennie OTTO	(RSA)	(27)	583,295.93	103	David HOWELL	(ENG)	(31)	294,081.01
4	Charl SCHWARTZEL	(RSA)	(18)	2,929,829.25	54	Felipe AGUILAR	(CHI)	(29)	573,085.80	104	David DRYSDALE	(SCO)	(35)	292,749.62
5	Lee WESTWOOD	(ENG)	(19)	2,439,601.15	55	Justin ROSE	(ENG)	(13)	571,283.12	105	Michael JONZON	(SWE)	(32)	285,713.76
6	Alvaro QUIROS	(ESP)	(23)	2,259,242.40	56	Rhys DAVIES	(WAL)	(31)	571,088.45	106	Victor DUBUISSON	(FRA)	(21)	285,400.66
7	Anders HANSEN	(DEN)	(22)	2,074,366.12	57	James MORRISON	(ENG)	(32)	556,549.30	107	Joel SJÖHOLM	(SWE)	(30)	280,311.31
8	Sergio GARCIA	(ESP)	(13)	1,962,723.19	58	Peter LAWRIE	(IRL)	(26)	546,660.15	108	Richard MCEVOY	(ENG)	(35)	277,098.21
9	Thomas BJÖRN	(DEN)	(23)	1,814,115.07	59	Scott JAMIESON	(SCO)	(31)	523,754.28	109	Søren HANSEN	(DEN)	(33)	272,637.00
10	Simon DYSON	(ENG)	(29)	1,694,779.16	60	Christian NILSSON	(SWE)	(29)	521,586.71	110	Brett RUMFORD	(AUS)	(29)	271,782.22
11	Darren CLARKE	(NIR)	(22)	1,590,414.68	61	Stephen GALLACHER	(SCO)	(28)	499,387.10	111	Oscar FLOREN	(SWE)	(27)	264,782.66
12	Miguel Angel JIMÉNEZ	(ESP)	(29)	1,570,454.38	62	Steve WEBSTER	(ENG)	(31)	480,689.18	112	Carlos DEL MORAL	(ESP)	(29)	262,964.84
13	Peter HANSON	(SWE)	(24)	1,500,590.48	63	Peter WHITEFORD	(SCO)	(31)	478,674.41	113	Keith HORNE	(RSA)	(35)	261,804.31
14	Alexander NOREN	(SWE)	(28)	1,427,643.05	64	Bernd WIESBERGER	(AUT)	(33)	469,498.68	114	Marc WARREN	(SCO)	(23)	258,971.20
15	Louis OOSTHUIZEN	(RSA)	(22)	1,409,126.35	65	Richard GREEN	(AUS)	(19)	461,579.65	115	Damien MCGRANE	(IRL)	(33)	258,938.67
16	Graeme MCDOWELL	(NIR)	(18)	1,230,461.34	66	Tom LEWIS	(ENG)	(8)	459,265.92	116	Markus BRIER	(AUT)	(25)	258,513.20
17	Pablo LARRAZÁBAL	(ESP)	(33)	1,183,039.55	67	Padraig HARRINGTON	(IRL)	(18)	457,389.34	117	Gareth MAYBIN	(NIR)	(28)	254,807.28
18	Paul LAWRIE	(SCO)	(24)	1,142,012.74	68	Marcus FRASER	(AUS)	(21)	457,248.35	118	Phillip PRICE	(WAL)	(31)	252,083.35
19	Gonzalo FDEZ-CASTAÑO	(ESP)	(14)	1,114,060.09	69	Søren KJELDSEN	(DEN)	(30)	452,146.94	119	Mark TULLO	(CHI)	(28)	250,806.50
20	Nicolas COLSAERTS	(BEL)	(23)	1,091,504.16	70	Anthony WALL	(ENG)	(30)	449,266.24	120	Simon KHAN	(ENG)	(25)	250,131.87
21	Francesco MOLINARI	(ITA)	(22)	1,087,852.04	71	Robert COLES	(ENG)	(29)	437,585.79	121	Shiv KAPUR	(IND)	(31)	236,970.14
22	Thomas AIKEN	(RSA)	(29)	1,055,893.71	72	Pablo MARTIN	(ESP)	(29)	437,131.62	122	Simon WAKEFIELD	(ENG)	(25)	226,794.64
23	Ian POULTER	(ENG)	(16)	1,015,670.94	73	Ryan MOORE	(USA)	(8)	432,999.52	123	Stephen DODD	(WAL)	(32)	225,206.58
24	Joost LUITEN	(NED)	(27)	976,539.68	74	Richard FINCH	(ENG)	(28)	425,528.70	124	Matthew ZIONS	(AUS)	(33)	218,452.12
25	Michael HOEY	(NIR)	(30)	967,667.78	75	James KINGSTON	(RSA)	(28)	405,962.16	125	Scott STRANGE	(AUS)	(25)	215,548.63
26	George COETZEE	(RSA)	(29)	913,127.93	76	Kenneth FERRIE	(ENG)	(30)	405,148.89	126	John PARRY	(ENG)	(35)	209,111.77
27	Grégory HAVRET	(FRA)	(29)	906,859.38	77	José Manuel LARA	(ESP)	(30)	403,370.29	127	Alvaro VELASCO	(ESP)	(30)	206,169.94
28	Richie RAMSAY	(SCO)	(32)	904,001.85	78	Gary BOYD	(ENG)	(28)	395,923.79	128	Jamie ELSON	(ENG)	(20)	204,145.05
29	Paul CASEY	(ENG)	(15)	879,088.23	79	Robert-Jan DERKSEN	(NED)	(27)	395,503.67	129	Robert ALLENBY	(AUS)	(7)	199,637.13
30	Rafael CABRERA-BELLO	(ESP)	(33)	862,684.57	80	S S P CHOWRASIA	(IND)	(22)	392,701.69	130	Oliver WILSON	(ENG)	(31)	199,003.54
31	Matteo MANASSERO	(ITA)	(22)	859,461.43	81	George MURRAY	(SCO)	(28)	386,710.03	131	Steven O'HARA	(SCO)	(34)	198,148.08
32	Mark FOSTER	(ENG)	(27)	853,840.26	82	Lee SLATTERY	(ENG)	(31)	380,086.90	132	Niclas FASTH	(SWE)	(30)	196,937.77
33	Y E YANG	(KOR)	(14)	846,230.00	83	Martin WIEGELE	(AUT)	(33)	372,252.82	133	Lloyd SALTMAN	(SCO)	(26)	195,965.29
34	Robert ROCK	(ENG)	(32)	818,013.96	84	Danny LEE	(NZL)	(15)	358,477.47	134	Magnus A CARLSSON	(SWE)	(23)	193,636.14
35	David LYNN	(ENG)	(24)	788,412.55	85	Thongchai JAIDEE	(THA)	(27)	357,602.23	135	Mikael LUNDBERG	(SWE)	(8)	189,840.00
36	Raphaël JACQUELIN	(FRA)	(28)	783,817.24	86	Seung-yul NOH	(KOR)	(19)	348,140.04	136	Henrik STENSON	(SWE)	(14)	189,831.47
37	Robert KARLSSON	(SWE)	(14)	773,347.00	87	Marcel SIEM	(GER)	(29)	343,653.77	137	Gary ORR	(SCO)	(22)	187,908.86
38	Jamie DONALDSON	(WAL)	(26)	771,563.22	88	Alejandro CAÑIZARES	(ESP)	(33)	342,928.03	138	Rafa ECHENIQUE	(ARG)	(33)	175,242.12
39	Fredrik ANDERSSON HED	(SWE)	(28)	769,849.17	89	Chris WOOD	(ENG)	(23)	339,533.94	139	David DIXON	(ENG)	(31)	175,108.03
40	Johan EDFORS	(SWE)	(27)	764,807.20	90	Romain WATTEL	(FRA)	(29)	337,475.78	140	Alastair FORSYTH	(SCO)	(20)	174,783.34
41	Shane LOWRY	(IRL)	(25)	764,777.78	91	Danny WILLETT	(ENG)	(30)	333,727.13	141	Robert DINWIDDIE	(ENG)	(30)	170,706.63
42	Retief GOOSEN	(RSA)	(19)	752,572.84	92	Jbe KRUGER	(RSA)	(20)	332,289.12	142	Daniel GAUNT	(AUS)	(33)	167,053.08
43	David HORSEY	(ENG)	(28)	718,444.17	93	Jean-Baptiste GONNET	(FRA)	(27)	330,408.18	143	Tjaart VAN DER WALT	(RSA)	(7)	160,060.84
44	Fredrik JACOBSON	(SWE)	(5)	709,444.59	94	Jeev Milkha SINGH	(IND)	(30)	329,261.72	144	Tetsuji HIRATSUKA	(JPN)	(12)	156,797.12
45	Thomas LEVET	(FRA)	(23)	695,396.59	95	Oliver FISHER	(ENG)	(33)	328,221.73	145	Christian CÉVAËR	(FRA)	(30)	155,602.90
46	Edoardo MOLINARI	(ITA)	(21)	686,390.93	96	Bradley DREDGE	(WAL)	(30)	324,853.48	146	Kiradech APHIBARNRAT	(THA)	(8)	154,895.03
47	Grégory BOURDY	(FRA)	(30)	650,863.47	97	Ignacio GARRIDO	(ESP)	(31)	323,794.88	147	Jason KNUTZON	(USA)	(21)	152,930.92
48	Thorbjørn OLESEN	(DEN)	(30)	637,703.21	98	Tano GOYA	(ARG)	(31)	315,164.67	148	Tommy FLEETWOOD	(ENG)	(8)	151,969.40
49	Lorenzo GAGLI	(ITA)	(25)	622,845.74	99	Ricardo GONZALEZ	(ARG)	(18)	314,713.40	149	Maarten LAFEBER	(NED)	(31)	144,897.58
50	Jaco VAN ZYL	(RSA)	(23)	611,280.16	100	Fabrizio ZANOTTI	(PAR)	(29)	314,124.21	150	Scott HEND	(AUS)	(18)	144,119.32

Pos	Name	Country	Played	€
151	Ross McGOWAN	(ENG)	(30)	143,390.87
152	Paul MCGINLEY	(IRL)	(24)	141,384.34
153	Barry LANE	(ENG)	(13)	141,035.16
154	Rikard KARLBERG	(SWE)	(18)	139,282.55
155	Thomas NØRRET	(DEN)	(23)	138,438.36
156	Florian FRITSCH	(GER)	(19)	138,423.99
157	Anthony KANG	(USA)	(36)	131,914.93
158	Jeppe HULDAHL	(DEN)	(37)	131,370.24
159	Alexandre KALEKA	(FRA)	(27)	128,734.67
160	Andrew DODT	(AUS)	(26)	124,089.41
161	Mark BROWN	(NZL)	(34)	121,005.22
162	Richard BLAND	(ENG)	(35)	117,725.65
163	Seve BENSON	(ENG)	(29)	116,923.51
164	Manuel QUIROS	(ESP)	(22)	116,176.67
165	Thaworn WIRATCHANT	(THA)	(8)	114,499.75
166	Mikko KORHONEN	(FIN)	(22)	113,821.11
167	Cesar MONASTERIO	(ARG)	(9)	113,657.50
168	Chinnarat PHADUNGSIL	(THA)	(9)	108,587.56
169	José María OLAZÁBAL	(ESP)	(18)	103,843.79
170	Niklas LEMKE	(SWE)	(8)	103,750.00
171	Floris DE VRIES	(NED)	(23)	99,107.62
172	Pariya JUNHASAVASDIKUL	(THA)	(7)	98,751.20
173	Prayad MARKSAENG	(THA)	(6)	97,285.81
174	Chapchai NIRAT	(THA)	(7)	93,152.94
175	Matt HAINES	(ENG)	(35)	88,800.42
176	Tim SLUITER	(NED)	(22)	88,689.11
177	Oskar HENNINGSSON	(SWE)	(30)	86,504.33
178	Paul BROADHURST	(ENG)	(19)	84,703.85
179	Branden GRACE	(RSA)	(8)	80,005.00
180	Darren BECK	(AUS)	(6)	79,583.91
181	Michael CAMPBELL	(NZL)	(23)	77,803.58
182	Wade ORMSBY	(AUS)	(24)	77,020.20
183	Matthew NIXON	(ENG)	(24)	75,314.29
184	Alfredo GARCIA-HEREDIA	(ESP)	(17)	70,280.00
185	Stuart MANLEY	(WAL)	(23)	68,638.77
186	Rick KULACZ	(AUS)	(17)	64,716.12
187	Marco RUIZ	(PAR)	(12)	62,770.66
188	Himmat Singh RAI	(IND)	(4)	62,427.91
189	Peter KARMIS	(RSA)	(11)	61,965.26
190	Chris GANE	(ENG)	(4)	61,693.50
191	Liam BOND	(WAL)	(23)	60,671.25
192	Todd HAMILTON	(USA)	(13)	59,992.64
193	Mark F HAASTRUP	(DEN)	(17)	57,941.30
194	Andreas HARTØ	(DEN)	(21)	57,333.63
195	Benjamin HEBERT	(FRA)	(11)	57,228.50
196	Tom WATSON	(USA)	(2)	56,632.43
197	Simon THORNTON	(IRL)	(7)	55,963.64
198	Elliot SALTMAN	(SCO)	(18)	55,775.77
199	John DALY	(USA)	(11)	52,455.53
200	Andrew MARSHALL	(ENG)	(11)	51,318.33

FLAGS OF THE WORLD

	Abu Dhabi		Kazakhstan
	Argentina		Kenya
	Australia		Malaysia
	Austria		Mauritius
	Bahrain		Morocco
	Barbados		Netherlands
	Belgium		New Zealand
	Brunei		Northern Ireland
	Chile		Norway
	China		Paraguay
	Chinese Taipei		Phillipines
	Colombia		Poland
	Czech Republic		Portugal
	Denmark		Qatar
	Dubai		Russia
	England		Scotland
	Estonia		Singapore
	Fiji		South Africa
	Finland		South Korea
	France		Spain
	Germany		Sweden
	Hong Kong		Switzerland
	Iceland		Taiwan
	India		Thailand
	Indonesia		Trinidad & Tobago
	Ireland		USA
	Italy		Venezuela
	Jamaica		Wales
	Japan		Zimbabwe

Stroke Average

Pos	Name	Stroke Average	Total Strokes	Total Rounds	Pos	Name	Stroke Average	Total Strokes	Total Rounds	Pos	Name	Stroke Average	Total Strokes	Total Rounds
1	Luke DONALD	69.12	2834	41	51	Marcus FRASER	70.94	4682	66	76	Robert COLES	71.22	6267	88
2	Rory MCILROY	69.16	4703	68	52	Raphaël JACQUELIN	70.96	6528	92	77	Colin MONTGOMERIE	71.25	4774	67
3	Charl SCHWARTZEL	69.44	4305	62	53	Johan EDFORS	70.98	6175	87	78	Edoardo MOLINARI	71.26	4846	68
4	Sergio GARCIA	69.56	3617	52	54	Grégory HAVRET	70.99	6460	91	79	Bradley DREDGE	71.27	6414	90
5	Lee WESTWOOD	69.79	4397	63	55	Ross FISHER	70.99	5253	74	80	Søren KJELDSEN	71.27	6486	91
6	Fredrik JACOBSON	69.94	1259	18	56	Chapchai NIRAT	71.00	1420	20	81	Tetsuji HIRATSUKA	71.28	2851	40
7	Martin KAYMER	70.11	5188	74	57	Graeme MCDOWELL	71.00	3834	54	82	Graeme STORM	71.29	6915	97
8	Joost LUITEN	70.15	6454	92	58	Justin ROSE	71.00	2698	38	83	Shane LOWRY	71.29	5133	72
9	Branden GRACE	70.17	1684	24	59	Alvaro QUIROS	71.01	5255	74	84	Darren FICHARDT	71.32	1569	22
10	Peter HANSON	70.24	5549	79	60	Robert-Jan DERKSEN	71.01	6178	87	85	Tommy FLEETWOOD	71.32	1355	19
11	Retief GOOSEN	70.31	3867	55	61	Richard GREEN	71.02	4190	59	86	Jyoti RANDHAWA	71.33	1284	18
12	Louis OOSTHUIZEN	70.33	4642	66	62	Steve WEBSTER	71.02	6818	96	87	Barry LANE	71.35	3282	46
13	Francesco MOLINARI	70.35	4995	71	63	Grégory BOURDY	71.03	6322	89	88	Søren HANSEN	71.36	6351	89
14	Jamie DONALDSON	70.41	6337	90	64	Robert ROCK	71.03	8097	114	89	Alejandro CAÑIZARES	71.37	7422	104
15	Tjaart VAN DER WALT	70.42	1831	26	65	Y. E. YANG	71.03	2770	39	90	Peter WHITEFORD	71.37	6780	95
16	Jbe KRUGER	70.44	4790	68	66	José Manuel LARA	71.07	6467	91	91	Rikard KARLBERG	71.37	3069	43
17	Anders HANSEN	70.47	5074	72	67	Paul CASEY	71.07	3269	46	92	Oscar FLOREN	71.38	5282	74
18	Alexander NOREN	70.52	6770	96	68	Jean-Baptiste GONNET	71.10	5688	80	93	Tano GOYA	71.38	6781	95
19	Thomas AIKEN	70.52	6699	95	69	Jeev Milkha SINGH	71.10	6328	89	94	Miguel Angel JIMÉNEZ	71.39	6568	92
20	Lorenzo GAGLI	70.54	6419	91	70	James KINGSTON	71.11	6044	85	95	Ian POULTER	71.40	3427	48
21	Simon DYSON	70.54	7054	100	71	Brett RUMFORD	71.12	5832	82	96	Gary ORR	71.42	4428	62
22	Richie RAMSAY	70.60	7413	105	72	Chris WOOD	71.14	4980	70	97	Ignacio GARRIDO	71.44	6358	89
23	George COETZEE	70.61	6637	94	73	Danny WILLETT	71.16	6262	88	98	James MORRISON	71.46	6646	93
24	Mark FOSTER	70.64	6499	92	74	Felipe AGUILAR	71.20	6408	90	99	Jason KNUTZON	71.46	4359	61
25	Robert KARLSSON	70.65	3391	48	75	Thongchai JAIDEE	71.20	6266	88	100	Simon THORNTON	71.46	1858	26
26	Richard FINCH	70.66	6077	86										
27	Thaworn WIRATCHANT	70.68	1555	22										
28	Nicolas COLSAERTS	70.69	5443	77										
29	David LYNN	70.71	5445	77										
30	Jaco VAN ZYL	70.71	5515	78										
31	Padraig HARRINGTON	70.71	3677	52										
32	Pablo LARRAZÁBAL	70.76	7571	107										
33	Peter LAWRIE	70.77	6582	93										
34	Darren BECK	70.79	1345	19										
35	Kiradech APHIBARNRAT	70.81	1487	21										
36	Ernie ELS	70.82	3541	50										
37	Ricardo GONZALEZ	70.83	3754	53										
38	Paul LAWRIE	70.85	5739	81										
39	Stephen GALLACHER	70.85	6235	88										
40	Anthony WALL	70.88	6875	97										
41	Christian NILSSON	70.88	6237	88										
42	Prayad MARKSAENG	70.88	1205	17										
43	Thomas BJÖRN	70.88	5174	73										
44	Rafael CABRERA-BELLO	70.89	7514	106										
45	Matteo MANASSERO	70.90	5530	78										
46	David HORSEY	70.91	6524	92										
47	Gonzalo FDEZ-CASTAÑO	70.91	3049	43										
48	Victor DUBUISSON	70.91	4822	68										
49	Hennie OTTO	70.92	6454	91										
50	Danny LEE	70.93	2908	41										

Alvaro Quiros of Spain received his Driving Distance Category Award from Peter Barrett, Managing Director of Genworth Financial at the Genworth Statistics Awards annual dinner held during the Dubai World Championship presented by DP World.

Driving Distance (yds)

Pos	Name	Average Yards	Stats Rounds
1	Alvaro QUIROS	312.7	54
2	Pelle EDBERG	308.6	20
3	Daniel VANCSIK	308.5	22
4	Lloyd SALTMAN	306.9	73
5	Seung-yul NOH	304.8	34
6	Elliot SALTMAN	304.7	36
7	Nicolas COLSAERTS	303.8	73
8	Sebi GARCIA	302.9	33
9	Scott HEND	302.3	45
10	Stephen GALLACHER	302.1	80
11	Victor DUBUISSON	301.8	60
12	Clodomiro CARRANZA	301.6	33
13	Pedro ORIOL	300.9	38
14	Rory MCILROY	300.9	44
15	Shaun NORRIS	300.8	38
16	George COETZEE	300.7	79
17	Padraig HARRINGTON	300.7	32
18	Romain WATTEL	299.0	80
19	Tim SLUITER	298.5	57
20	Bernd WIESBERGER	298.4	94
21	Gaganjeet BHULLAR	298.4	18
22	Danny WILLETT	298.1	78
23	Julien GUERRIER	297.8	20
24	Steve WEBSTER	297.8	91
25	Charl SCHWARTZEL	297.3	34

Driving Accuracy (%)

Pos	Name	%	Stats Rounds
1	Luke DONALD	75.6	19
2	Richie RAMSAY	75.1	100
3	Peter LAWRIE	74.4	89
4	Francesco MOLINARI	72.8	53
5	Michael CAMPBELL	72.0	52
6	Anders HANSEN	71.7	54
7	Matteo MANASSERO	70.6	64
8	Lorenzo GAGLI	70.3	88
9	Phillip PRICE	70.0	87
10	Martin WIEGELE	69.7	98
11	Stephen DODD	69.7	85
12	Simon WAKEFIELD	69.5	65
13	Anthony WALL	69.4	95
14	Jaco VAN ZYL	69.2	73
15	Felipe AGUILAR	69.0	86
16	Joost LUITEN	68.9	84
17	Colin MONTGOMERIE	68.7	67
18	Marcus FRASER	68.6	62
19	Liam BOND	68.5	50
20	Matthew NIXON	68.5	52
21	Søren KJELDSEN	68.4	86
22	Borja ETCHART	68.2	23
23	David DRYSDALE	68.1	105
24	Jason KNUTZON	67.9	55
25	Justin ROSE	67.9	18

Average Putts Per Round

Pos	Name	Putts per Round	Stats Rounds
1	Retief GOOSEN	28.3	38
2	Tetsuji HIRATSUKA	28.4	29
3	Brett RUMFORD	28.5	81
4	Thaworn WIRATCHANT	28.6	22
5	David HOWELL	28.7	81
6	Marcus FRASER	28.7	62
7	George COETZEE	28.8	79
8	Mark F HAASTRUP	28.8	35
9	Carlos DEL MORAL	28.9	83
10	David HORSEY	28.9	84
11	Luke DONALD	28.9	19
12	Jarmo SANDELIN	29.0	33
13	Miguel Angel JIMÉNEZ	29.0	70
14	Robert KARLSSON	29.0	26
15	S.S.P CHOWRASIA	29.0	44
16	Sam HUTSBY	29.0	19
17	Daniel VANCSIK	29.1	22
18	Francesco MOLINARI	29.1	53
19	Graeme MCDOWELL	29.1	36
20	Grégory BOURDY	29.1	79
21	Jamie ELSON	29.1	52
22	Jeev Milkha SINGH	29.1	84
23	Markus BRIER	29.1	60
24	Romain WATTEL	29.1	80
25	Charl SCHWARTZEL	29.2	34

Greens In Regulation (%)

Pos	Name	%	Stats Rounds
1	Luke DONALD	77.5	19
2	Justin ROSE	77.2	18
3	Lorenzo GAGLI	77.1	88
4	Rory MCILROY	76.4	44
5	Chapchai NIRAT	76.4	20
6	Louis OOSTHUIZEN	76.3	45
7	Richie RAMSAY	75.9	100
8	Ernie ELS	75.6	31
9	Nicolas COLSAERTS	75.4	73
10	Sergio GARCIA	75.3	31
11	Ian POULTER	75.2	28
12	Jbe KRUGER	75.1	41
13	Peter HANSON	74.5	59
14	Joost LUITEN	74.1	84
15	Richard FINCH	73.9	74
16	Charl SCHWARTZEL	73.7	34
17	Steven O'HARA	73.6	84
18	Stephen GALLACHER	73.5	80
19	Mardan MAMAT	73.1	19
20	Ross FISHER	73.1	60
21	Pablo LARRAZÁBAL	73.0	91
22	Martin KAYMER	72.9	54
23	Steve WEBSTER	72.8	91
24	Johan EDFORS	72.4	79
25	Lee WESTWOOD	72.4	41

Sand Saves (%)

Pos	Name	%	Stats Rounds
1	Luke DONALD	78.6	19
2	Ian POULTER	69.4	28
3	Tetsuji HIRATSUKA	68.4	29
4	Miguel Angel JIMÉNEZ	68.1	70
5	Marcus FRASER	67.6	62
6	Oliver WILSON	66.2	84
7	George COETZEE	65.9	79
8	David HORSEY	65.7	84
9	Gonzalo FDEZ-CASTAÑO	65.6	43
10	Jeev Milkha SINGH	65.5	84
11	Pablo LARRAZÁBAL	65.5	91
12	Peter HANSON	64.1	59
13	Thomas AIKEN	64.0	81
14	Chinnarat PHADUNGSIL	63.6	25
15	Oliver FISHER	63.6	75
16	Thomas BJÖRN	63.5	55
17	Robert COLES	63.4	81
18	Robert KARLSSON	63.2	26
19	Padraig HARRINGTON	62.5	32
20	Wade ORMSBY	62.5	55
21	Stephen GALLACHER	62.2	80
22	Charl SCHWARTZEL	61.7	34
23	Jamie DONALDSON	61.5	84
24	Gary ORR	61.4	60
25	Fredrik ANDERSSON HED	60.7	73

Putts Per Green In Regulation

Pos	Name	Putts per GIR	Stats Rounds
1	Luke DONALD	1.694	19
2	Thaworn WIRATCHANT	1.696	22
3	Retief GOOSEN	1.719	38
4	Charl SCHWARTZEL	1.727	34
5	Brett RUMFORD	1.736	81
6	Graeme MCDOWELL	1.739	36
7	Martin KAYMER	1.742	54
8	Tetsuji HIRATSUKA	1.742	29
9	Robert KARLSSON	1.743	26
10	Rory MCILROY	1.744	44
11	Fredrik ANDERSSON HED	1.749	73
12	David HOWELL	1.750	81
13	Sergio GARCIA	1.750	31
14	Alexander NOREN	1.753	78
15	George COETZEE	1.753	79
16	David HORSEY	1.754	84
17	Alvaro QUIROS	1.755	54
18	Paul CASEY	1.755	24
19	Robert COLES	1.755	81
20	Danny LEE	1.756	41
21	Francesco MOLINARI	1.756	53
22	Kiradech APHIBARNRAT	1.756	20
23	Lloyd SALTMAN	1.756	73
24	Pablo MARTIN	1.757	64
25	Peter HANSON	1.757	59

Scrambles

Pos	Name	%	AVE SPR	AVE Missed GPR	Total Missed GIR	Total Scrambles	Stats Rounds
1	Sergio GARCIA	65.2	2.9	4	138	90	31
2	Marcus FRASER	64.1	3.9	6	376	241	62
3	Retief GOOSEN	63.1	3.6	6	214	135	38
4	Francesco MOLINARI	62.8	3.2	5	269	169	53
5	Rory MCILROY	62.0	2.6	4	187	116	44
6	Miguel Angel JIMÉNEZ	61.9	3.7	6	420	260	70
7	Wade ORMSBY	61.3	4.1	7	367	225	55
8	Martin KAYMER	61.2	3.0	5	263	161	54
9	Padraig HARRINGTON	61.1	3.1	5	162	99	32
10	Simon DYSON	61.1	3.2	5	435	266	82
11	Jaco VAN ZYL	60.9	3.5	6	414	252	73
12	Paul CASEY	60.7	3.1	5	122	74	24
13	David LYNN	60.6	3.5	6	424	257	73
14	Robert KARLSSON	60.6	3.2	5	137	83	26
15	Tetsuji HIRATSUKA	60.2	4.1	7	196	118	29
16	Grégory HAVRET	59.7	3.4	6	461	275	81
17	Jeev Milkha SINGH	59.7	3.8	6	531	317	84
18	Raphaël JACQUELIN	59.7	3.2	5	432	258	81
19	Robert-Jan DERKSEN	59.5	3.4	6	479	285	83
20	Simon THORNTON	59.5	3.7	6	163	97	26
21	Anders HANSEN	59.4	3.1	5	278	165	54
22	Jean-Baptiste GONNET	59.4	3.4	6	409	243	71
23	Christian NILSSON	59.2	3.3	6	463	274	84
24	Jyoti RANDHAWA	59.2	3.2	5	98	58	18
25	Rikard KARLBERG	59.2	3.2	5	147	87	27

Average One Putts Per Round

Pos	Name	One Putts Average	Stats Rounds
1	Thaworn WIRATCHANT	6.86	22
2	Luke DONALD	6.84	19
3	Kiradech APHIBARNRAT	6.75	20
4	Darren BECK	6.58	19
5	Tetsuji HIRATSUKA	6.55	29
6	Grégory BOURDY	6.54	79
7	Alexander NOREN	6.53	78
8	S.S.P CHOWRASIA	6.39	44
9	Jamie DONALDSON	6.29	84
10	Seung-yul NOH	6.29	34
11	Wade ORMSBY	6.25	55
12	Oliver WILSON	6.24	84
13	Graeme MCDOWELL	6.22	36
14	Lee WESTWOOD	6.22	41
15	Rory MCILROY	6.20	44
16	Thomas BJÖRN	6.16	55
17	Jyoti RANDHAWA	6.11	18
18	Marco RUIZ	6.10	29
19	Jamie ELSON	6.08	52
20	Christian NILSSON	6.04	84
21	Robert COLES	6.04	81
22	Miguel Angel JIMÉNEZ	5.97	70
23	David DRYSDALE	5.89	105
24	Lee SLATTERY	5.89	83
25	Carlos DEL MORAL	5.88	83

THE 2011 EUROPEAN TOUR INTERNATIONAL SCHEDULE

Date		Event	Venue
Dec '10	9-12	**Alfred Dunhill Championship**	Leopard Creek CC, Malelane, South Africa
	16 - 19	**South African Open Championship**	Durban CC, Durban, South Africa
Jan '11	6 - 9	**Africa Open**	East London GC, East London, Eastern Cape, South Africa
	13 - 16	**Joburg Open**	Royal Johannesburg & Kensington GC, Johannesburg, South Africa
	20 - 23	**Abu Dhabi HSBC Golf Championship**	Abu Dhabi GC, Abu Dhabi, UAE
	27 - 30	**Volvo Golf Champions**	The Royal GC, Kingdom of Bahrain, Bahrain
Feb	3-6	**Commercialbank Qatar Masters presented by Dolphin Energy**	Doha GC, Doha, Qatar
	10-13	**Omega Dubai Desert Classic**	Emirates GC, Dubai, UAE
	17 - 20	**Avantha Masters**	DLF G&CC, New Delhi, India
	23 - 27	**WGC - Accenture Match Play Championship**	Ritz-Carlton GC, Dove Mountain, Marana, Arizona, USA
Mar	10-13	**WGC - Cadillac Championship**	Doral Golf Resort & Spa, Doral, Florida, USA
	17 - 20	**Sicilian Open**	Donnafugata Golf Resort & Spa, Sicily, Italy
	24 - 27	**Open de Andalucía de Golf by Turkish Airlines**	Parador de Málaga Golf, Málaga, Spain
	31 - 3 Apr	**Trophée Hassan II**	Golf du Palais Royal & Golf de L'Ocean, Agadir, Morocco
Apr	7-10	MASTERS TOURNAMENT	Augusta National GC, Georgia, USA
	14 - 17	**Maybank Malaysian Open**	Kuala Lumpur G&CC, Kuala Lumpur, Malaysia
	21 - 24	**Volvo China Open**	Luxehills International CC, Chengdu, China
	28 -1 May	**Ballantine's Championship**	Blackstone GC, Icheon, Seoul, South Korea
May	5 - 8	**Open de España**	Real Club de Golf El Prat, Terrassa, Barcelona, Spain
	12-15	**Iberdrola Open**	Pula GC, Son Servera, Mallorca, Spain
	19 - 22	**Madeira Islands Open**	Porto Santo Golfe, Madeira, Portugal
	19 - 22	**Volvo World Match Play Championship**	Finca Cortesin, Casares, Andalucía, Spain
	26 - 29	BMW PGA CHAMPIONSHIP	Wentworth Club, Surrey, England
June	2 - 5	**Saab Wales Open**	The Celtic Manor Resort, City of Newport, Wales
	9-12	**BMW Italian Open presented by CartaSi**	Royal Park I Roveri, Turin, Italy
	16 - 19	**SAINT-OMER OPEN presented by Neuflize OBC**	Aa Saint Omer GC, Lumbres, France
	16 - 19	U.S. OPEN CHAMPIONSHIP	Congressional CC, Bethesda, Maryland, USA
	23 - 26	**BMW International Open**	Golfclub München Eichenried, Munich, Germany
	30 - 3 Jul	**Alstom Open de France**	Le Golf National, Paris, France
July	7 - 10	**Barclays Scottish Open**	Castle Stuart Golf Links, Inverness, Scotland
	14 - 17	THE 140th OPEN CHAMPIONSHIP	Royal St George's GC, Sandwich, Kent, England
	21 - 24	**Nordea Masters**	Bro Hof Slott GC, Stockholm, Sweden
	28 - 31	**Irish Open presented by Discover Ireland**	Killarney Golf & Fishing Club, Killarney, Co. Kerry, Ireland
Aug	4 - 7	**WGC - Bridgestone Invitational**	Firestone CC, Akron, Ohio, USA
	11-14	US PGA CHAMPIONSHIP	Atlanta Athletic Club, Johns Creek, Georgia, USA
	18 - 21	**Czech Open**	Prosper Golf Resort, Čeladná, Czech Republic
	25 - 28	**Johnnie Walker Championship at Gleneagles**	The Gleneagles Hotel, Perthshire, Scotland
Sept	1 - 4	**Omega European Masters**	Crans-sur-Sierre, Crans Montana, Switzerland
	8 - 11	**KLM Open**	Hilversumsche GC, Hilversum, The Netherlands
	15 - 18	**Vivendi Seve Trophy***	Saint-Nom-la-Bretèche, Paris, France
	22 - 25	**Austrian GolfOpen presented by Lyoness**	Diamond CC, Atzenbrugg, Austria
	29 - 2 Oct	**Alfred Dunhill Links Championship**	Old Course, St Andrews, Carnoustie & Kingsbarns, Scotland
Oct	6 - 9	**Bankia Madrid Masters**	El Encín Golf Hotel, Alcalá de Henares, Spain
	13 - 16	**Portugal Masters**	Oceânico Victoria Golf Course, Vilamoura, Portugal
	20 - 23	**Castelló Masters**	Club de Campo del Mediterráneo, Castellón, Valencia, Spain
	27 - 30	**Andalucía Masters**	Club de Golf Valderrama, Sotogrande, Spain
Nov	3 - 6	**WGC - HSBC Champions**	Sheshan International GC, Shanghai, China
	10-13	**Barclays Singapore Open**	Tanjong & Serapong, Sentosa GC, Singapore
	17 - 20	**Iskandar Johor Open**	Horizon Hills G&CC, Johor, Malaysia
	17 - 20	**Alfred Dunhill Championship**	Leopard Creek CC, Malelane, South Africa
	24 - 27	**Omega Mission Hills World Cup***	Mission Hills Resort, Hainan Island, China
	24 - 27	**SA Open Championship**	Serengeti Golf & Wildlife Estate, Ekurhuleni, South Africa
Dec	1 - 4	**UBS Hong Kong Open**	Hong Kong GC, Fanling, Hong Kong
	8 - 11	DUBAI WORLD CHAMPIONSHIP presented by DP World	Jumeirah Golf Estates, Dubai, UAE

* Denotes Approved Special Event   ** Denotes Play-off

^^ Reduced to 54 holes because of inclement weather

+ Capped for The Race to Dubai €566,660 / €2,571,390

• Each member of the winning team received €65,000. Each member of the losing team received €50,000

Winner	Score	First prize / Prize Fund
Pablo Martin, ESP	69-70-68-70=277 (-11)	€158,500 / €1,000,000
Ernie Els, RSA	65-65-64-63=257 (-25)	€158,500 / €1,006,182
Louis Oosthuizen**, RSA	70-67-69-70=276 (-16)	€158,000 / €1,001,700
Charl Schwartzel, RSA	68-61-69-67=265 (-19)	€206,050 / €1,302,210
Martin Kaymer, GER	67-65-66-66=264 (-24)	€334,398 / €2,006,391
Paul Casey, ENG	67-67-66-68=268 (-20)	€283,330 / €1,705,097
Thomas Björn, DEN	74-65-66-69=274 (-14)	€303,113 / €1,835,034
Alvaro Quiros, ESP	73-68-68-68=277 (-11)	€301,353 / €1,808,148
S S P Chowrasia, IND	70-69-67-67= 273 (-15)	€300,000 / €1,829,535
Luke Donald, ENG bt Martin Kaymer, GER	3 and 2	€1,027,923 / €6,240,960
Nick Watney, USA	67-70-68-67=272 (-16)	€999,572 / €5,984,757
Raphaël Jacquelin, FRA	66-69-69-68=272 (-12)	€166,660 / €1,005,982
Paul Lawrie, SCO	66-67-65-70=268 (-12)	€166,660 / €1,001,500
David Horsey**, ENG	67-71-67-69=274 (-13)	€250,000 / €1,517,916
Charl Schwartzel, RSA	69-71-68-66=274 (-14)	€1,011,691 / €5,660,915
Matteo Manassero, ITA	66-71-67-68=272 (-16)	€288,466 / €1,741,188
Nicolas Colsaerts, BEL	65-67-66-66=264 (-24)	€350,946 / €2,118,298
Lee Westwood, ENG	72-68-69-67=276 (-12)	€367,500 / €2,211,611
Thomas Aiken, RSA	68-68-72-70=278 (-10)	€333,330 / €2,000,000
Darren Clarke, NIR	65-70-70-69=274 (-6)	€166,660 / €1,000,000
Michael Hoey, NIR	72-68-67-71=278 (-10)	€116,660 / €702,097
Ian Poulter, ENG bt Luke Donald, ENG	2 and 1	€800,000 / €3,400,000+
Luke Donald**, ENG	64-72-72-70=278 (-6)	€750,000 / €4,500,000
Alexander Noren, SWE	67-67-71-70=275 (-9)	€344,358 / €2,040,689
Robert Rock, ENG	64-68-68-67= 267 (-21)	€250,000 / €1,504,497
Matthew Zions, AUS	68-72-67-69=276 (-8)	€100,000 / €606,237
Rory McIlroy, NIR	65-66-68-69=268 (-16)	€1,003,414 / €5,574,524
Pablo Larrazábal**, ESP	68-67-69-68=272 (-16)	€333,330 / €1,992,550
Thomas Levet, FRA	70-70-67-70=277 (-7)	€500,000 / €3,000,000
Luke Donald^^, ENG	67-67-63=197 (-19)	€550,250 / €3,331,167
Darren Clarke, NIR	68-68-69-70=275 (-5)	€999,540 / €5,435,665
Alexander Noren, SWE	67-66-63-77=273 (-15)	€250,000 / €1,500,000
Simon Dyson, ENG	70-65-67-67=269 (-15)	€250,000 / €1,500,000
Adam Scott, AUS	62-70-66-65=263 (-17)	€972,148 / €5,804,071
Keegan Bradley**, USA	71-64-69-68 272= (-8)	€1,028,126 / €5,645,086
Oliver Fisher, ENG	71-67-68-69=275 (-13)	€250,000 / €1,500,000
Thomas Björn**, DEN	68-69-71-69=277 (-11)	€266,629 / €1,587,270
Thomas Björn, DEN	68-68-66-62=264 (-20)	€333,330 / €2,000,000
Simon Dyson, ENG	65-66-71-66=268 (-12)	€300,000 / €1,805,397
Great Britain & Ireland def Continental Europe	15½ - 12½	€65,000 / €1,150,000•
Kenneth Ferrie**, ENG	72-70-67-67=276 (-12)	€166,660 / €1,007,470
Michael Hoey, NIR	66-66-66-68=266 (-22)	€588,149 / €3,528,893
Lee Slattery, ENG	67-66-69-71=273 (-15)	€166, 660 / €1,000,000
Tom Lewis, ENG	70-64-68-65=267 (-21)	€416,000 / €2,511,241
Sergio Garcia, ESP	67-63-64-63=257 (-27)	€333,330 / €2,000,000
Sergio Garcia, ESP	70-70-67-71=278 (-6)	€500,000 / €3,000,000
Martin Kaymer, GER	69-68-68-63=268 (-20)	€842,218 / €4,912,936
Gonzalo Fernandez-Castaño**^^, ESP	66-61-72=199 (-14)	€720,878 / €4,390,005
Joost Luiten^^, NED	63-70-65=198 (-15)	€242,581 / €1,459,861
Garth Mulroy, RSA	69-68-64-68=269 (-19)	€158,500 / €1,000,000
Matt Kuchar & Gary Woodland, USA	64-70-63-67=264 (-24)	€1,788,202 / €5,588,132
Hennie Otto, RSA	70-67-65-72=274 (-14)	€158,500 / €1,000,200
Rory McIlroy, NIR	64-69-70-65=268 (-12)	€341,724 / €2,029,801
Alvaro Quiros, ESP	68-64-70-67=269 (-19)	€922,645 / €5,487,710

Proving Ground

Oli Fisher

THE EUROPEAN TOUR QUALIFYING SCHOOL
PGA Catalunya Resort, Girona, Spain

L-R: Mike Stewart, Qualifying School Director, Simon Wakefield and Angel Gallardo, Vice-Chairman of The PGA European Tour Board of Directors

Oli Fisher is recognised for becoming in 2006 the youngest British player to win Membership of The European Tour at the Qualifying School where he played as an amateur, claimed the fifth available card and promptly turned professional.

Fisher's impact was immediate as he climbed from 109th in 2007 to 51st the following year in The Race to Dubai, but he was compelled to go through the stomach-churning heartache of losing his card before achieving his maiden victory.

This was made all the more frustrating for Fisher as he had arrived on the scene with amateur credentials comparable to Rory McIlroy and Matteo Manassero. His career had stalled but all that was transformed in one glorious week in 2011 at the Prosper Golf Resort where he won the Czech Open.

"I was nervous," he confessed. "I didn't know how I'd handle the chance of winning but as it turned out I loved it. Absolutely loved it."

The importance of The European Tour Qualifying School Finals as a proving ground for champions of the future is recognised by all involved in the game.

Victories by Louis Oosthuizen, Charl Schwartzel, Alvaro Quiros, Raphaël Jacquelin, Paul Lawrie. Nicolas Colsaerts, Lee Westwood, Thomas Aiken, Michael Hoey, Ian Poulter, Robert Rock, Matthew Zions, Pablo Larrazábal, Thomas Levet, Darren Clarke, Simon Dyson, Kenneth Ferrie, Lee Slattery, Gonzalo Fernandez-Castaño, Hennie Otto and Fisher took to 549 by

153 different players the number of triumphs by Qualifying School graduates on The European Tour International Schedule.

Hoey's success in the Madeira Islands Open, followed by a landmark win in the Alfred Dunhill Links Championship, is a case in point of how The European Tour Qualifying School can resurrect a career. His arrival as a professional in 2002 followed a stellar amateur career.

He had underlined his huge promise by winning the Amateur Championship in 2001 and then helping Great Britain and Ireland overcome the United States in the Walker Cup. Furthermore he gave a clear indication of his huge potential by finishing 11th as an amateur in the Scottish Open at Loch Lomond that same year after a closing 64.

Yet despite winning three times on the European Challenge Tour, Hoey was compelled to return to the Qualifying School in 2008. He graduated and, with his confidence renewed, he achieved the breakthrough he deserved by holding off the challenge of Gonzalo Fernandez-Castaño in a play-off to win the 2009 Estoril Open de Portugal. His second win on The European Tour International Schedule in the 2011 Madeira Islands Open demonstrated again Hoey's huge potential which he underlined in style

PGA Catalunya Resort

with his victory at St Andrews ahead of Rory McIlroy in second with Graeme McDowell tied third, so continuing another famous year for players from Northern Ireland.

Hoey said: "It's taken a long time but in a weird way you enjoy it more because of the struggling. Six years at the Qualifying School is not nice though it opens the door to winning Tour titles and it's just amazing what that can do for you. I've watched all the great events over the years on TV; now I'm finally playing in them. Getting into the Dubai World Championship was one of my goals and I made it by moving from 83rd to 15th in The Race to Dubai with the win in the Alfred Dunhill Links Championship."

In 2010, England's Simon Wakefield triumphed with a 21 under par total of 407, finishing ahead of Spain's Carlos del Moral, Finland's Mikko Korhonen, England's Adam Gee and Jaco Van Zyl of South Africa. Wakefield became the second consecutive Englishman called Simon to win the Qualifying School – Simon Khan had triumphed in 2009 and followed that by winning the 2010 BMW PGA Championship, The European Tour's flagship event.

The opportunity for players to live their dream emerged once again when the 36th European Tour Qualifying School was staged in December, 2011, for a fourth successive year at the PGA Catalunya Resort near Girona, northern Spain, with two world-class courses, the Tour and the Stadium, hosting the six-round event from which the leading 30 players and ties earned their playing privileges for The 2012 European Tour International Schedule.

Michael Hoey

The 2012 Ryder Cup

Medinah Country Club, Medinah, Illinois: September 28-30

Aerial image of the Clubhouse in the 1960's

Medinah Country Club - The Next Chapter

William S Barbee has no chance of being held in the same high esteem as Bobby Jones but, similar to Jones discovering Fruitland Nurseries on which Augusta National was born, when Barbee's car stalled on a blustery May day in 1923, he happened upon a tract of land where the world's greatest golfers would one day come to exhibit their prodigious skills.

Medinah Country Club might not be home to the Masters Tournament, but as host to three US Opens and two US PGA Championships, it has thoroughly earned its place in golfing history. Moreover, another illustrious chapter is on the cusp of being written with the playing of The 2012 Ryder Cup on the famed No. 3 course at the venue 35 minutes from downtown Chicago.

With his car stuck in the mud, Barbee had set off in search of help but his attention swiftly turned to the picturesque countryside. He instantly recognised exactly the kind of land that he and his colleagues were seeking to create a new golfing complex. Together with Charles H Canode, owner of a printing company, Theodore R Heman, a real estate entrepreneur, and banker Frederick N Peck, Barbee, a real estate man with a previous affiliation to the theatre, acquired an option on that land so that by March 1, 1924, they began offering memberships, initially exclusively, to a group of Chicago Shriners.

The Shriners – members of the Ancient Arabic Order of Nobles of the Mystic

Shrine of North America – are an offspring of Europe's freemasons who trace their lineage back to the construction of Solomon's Temple. Not a religious sect – the heart of their activities is philanthropy – their charitable arm is The Shriners Hospitals for Children, and the Justin Timberlake Shriners Hospital for Children Open is played annually on the US PGA Tour.

With the promise of a self-sufficient country retreat for themselves and their families, including a 45-hole golf complex as its cornerstone, it was not difficult to see why the Chicago Shriners were swift to invest US $1,000 each to be a member at such a grand country club. It was the start of Medinah Country Club, but all

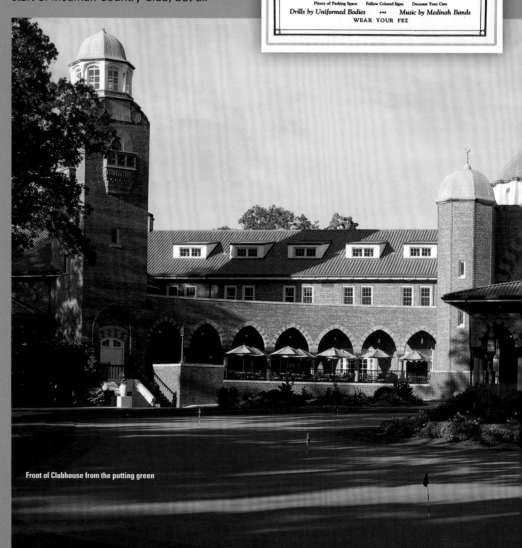

Front of Clubhouse from the putting green

The ballroom, elegantly appointed from floor to painted ceiling, was done in a Louis XIV style

was not as it seemed. It was with money brought in from the membership fees received that Barbee, Canode, Heman and Peck used to buy the land.

According to 'The Spirit of Medinah', a brilliantly researched book, in which author Tim Cronin chronicles the history and the development of the club, the four not only diverted US $419,340 of the US $1,928,000 fees received by January 18, 1927, their own way but also collected another US $142,560 by charging commission and administrative fees.

What is more, while the clubhouse – formally opened on September 25, 1926 – was built, and two 18 hole courses laid out, The Irving Lake Land Association, the company formed by the four founders, had secretly kept titles to 77 acres of land adjacent to the property as a potential housing community.

All was eventually uncovered by a Committee of Twelve, who interviewed the four founders, looked over the books,

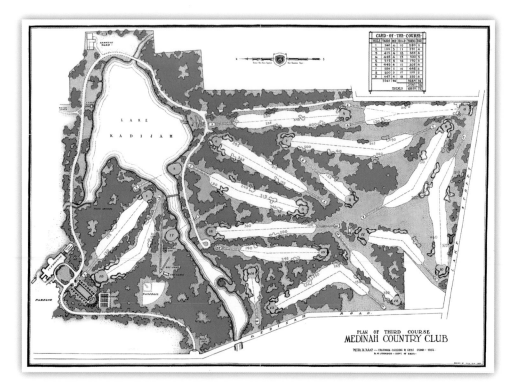

PLAN OF THIRD COURSE
MEDINAH COUNTRY CLUB

examined the maps and the property transactions and came to the conclusion that the club had been fleeced. After protracted negotiations, including the filing of a law suit, an agreement was reached whereby the four would keep every dollar of the half million or so they had paid themselves but, among other things, they would turn over clear title to the remaining 77 acres.

This land proved essential to Medinah's future, for it was where the famous No. 3 course would bloom and where Europe will seek to retain Sam Ryder's golden chalice against the United States from September 28-30, 2012.

Tom Bendelow, born in Aberdeen on September 2, 1868, and one of nine children of parents who owned a pie shop in the Scottish town, had been contracted to build two 18 hole courses and a nine hole ladies course. Bendelow, who became known as the Johnny Appleseed of American golf and who designed more than 600 courses, had indicated from the start that, in his opinion, a third 18 hole course was required if Medinah was to achieve its full potential as a country club.

How Bendelow came to be in Chicago is an interesting tale in itself. He had taken up the game with his father at Royal

Aberdeen but, in 1892, moved to New York for work and joined the New York Herald as a linotype operator. There he intercepted an advert to teach a Long Island family how to play golf. They asked him to layout six holes on their estate, which became the Nassau Country Club. Then, in 1894, they introduced him to A G Spalding and he joined the Spalding Sporting Goods Company, moving with them to Chicago in 1901.

Bendelow served as Editor of Spalding's Official Golf Guide from 1907 to 1917 and he also sold golf balls and clubs, offered

lessons, organised events, and designed courses. Bendelow even caddied for Harry Vardon, also a Spalding man, when he beat J H Taylor at Chicago Golf Club to win the 1900 US Open.

At Medinah, construction on No. 1 began on June 26, 1924, and the course was opened on September 5, 1925, with some 2,500 people on hand. The No. 2 course was completed in 1926. Meanwhile, construction on No. 3 stalled, which was hardly a revelation with financial turmoil building across the United States. Barbee announced on January 19, 1927, "We will have to go to the bank in the morning and borrow some money; there is nothing in the kitty."

Work on No. 3 did not resume until September 1927, and it fully opened on September 23, 1928. Bendelow, however, was not a happy man. He was, by now, recognised as one of the most renowned architects of his time, and quality and perfection were key words in his vocabulary. He never drank alcohol, but he was a workaholic. He did not design or play golf on Sundays, he never uttered swear words or told crude stories and his only vice was a penchant for smoking huge cigars.

Bendelow, however, was not convinced by No. 3. Even though the original concept was for this to be a

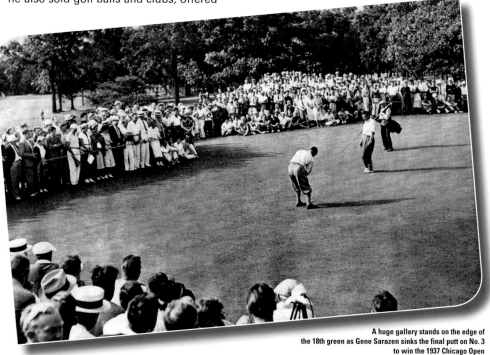

A huge gallery stands on the edge of the 18th green as Gene Sarazen sinks the final putt on No. 3 to win the 1937 Chicago Open

course for women – "a sporty little course that will become famous the country over" – Bendelow would present a new design, a makeover described as being as brilliant as it was extensive. In fact, he had completed his redesign even before Gene Sarazen headed a star-studded field of 62 professionals and five amateurs in the 36 hole Medinah Open with a prize fund of US $3,000 on September 22, 1930. At the culmination of the tournament, the members were equally convinced that No. 3 required extensive strengthening after Harry Cooper, the club professional at nearby Glen Oak, shot a second round 63 to win.

The renovation only became possible with the financial settlements that gave the club the use of the additional land. So, where Bendelow had jammed his original design into an area too compact for a course of real quality, he was now able to go to town with the design he had on the backburner. The remodeled No. 3, with eight new holes and two others upgraded, was opened on June 19, 1932. The original course had measured 6,215 yards; the new one stretched 6,768 yards with a par of 71 for the Championships and 72 for the members. Medinah now had its 'monster' – four of the par fours measuring more than 440 yards, the par fives 500, 515 and 580 yards and in total off the very back tees the course could play to more than 7,000 yards. Cooper won the Medinah Open again in 1935 – but with a five over par score of 289. Mission accomplished.

What was initially the third ranked course at Medinah Country Club was now the best. In fact, No. 3 was now rated a rival to No. 4 at the nearby Olympia Fields Club, which had hosted the US Open and the US PGA Championship. Bendelow had been paid US $1,000 for the redesign. There is a school of thought that it is the best US $1,000 any club ever paid an architect.

So Medinah had started life in the Roaring Twenties, survived the Great Depression of the early 1930s, and, although still strapped for cash, had become a country club of which its members could truly feel proud.

Tommy Armour, seen here with his brother Sandy watching, was a man for all climates. As the palm trees in the background indicate, Armour wintered in Florida although in the 1930s he became the public face of Medinah CC

In fairness to the four founders, the concept had been grand from the start. They billed the club as 'By Shriners for Shriners' and they did not do things by half – more than 15,000 turned up when the cornerstone was laid in 1924 and a 60 foot long pit was used to roast whole steers, hogs and lambs so that no-one went home hungry.

The plans, too, were grand. They had diligently researched Europe and the Middle East so that the proposed brick clubhouse – Moorish and Italianate, with a touch of Byzantine, and a ballroom to make Louis XIV proud – would fit the visionary design of Richard Gustav Schmid.

They did their work well, testimony to that being the fact that the original main electrical panel did not require enlarging until 1977. They used a Turkish mosque as a template; the building had crowned archways, a pair of deliberately mismatched towers, an elegant ballroom, a chimney originally disguised as a minaret, a big front porch, four floors and a dome reaching 60 feet towards the heavens.

There was also a health club, a locker room to accommodate 1,500 members with their families and guests, a bowling alley, an outdoor dance pavilion with room for 1,000 couples that would double as a roller skating facility, gun and equestrian clubs, an outdoor swimming pool, facilities for boating on Lake Kadijah, a 56 acre artificial lake named after the wife of the prophet Mohammed, ice skating, cross country skiing, ski jumping and tobogganing. The clubhouse alone, measuring 112,000 square feet, cost US $822,975 to build. Today, it would cost more than US $30 million to replace.

Those early days, even when the club discovered it was in debt, were fun-filled. Medinah was the home of dancing girls, slot machines, a bear cub and even a camel.

It would appear that on 'Camel Trail Day', otherwise known as 'Men's Party Day', the golf was enlivened by a 'shapely adorable' wearing little more than a bath towel – sometimes less – who would jump out and surprise the golfers just as they were about to tee off. The beer flowed from 6:30am and the girls made return performances in the evening by kicking their heels high on stage at the stag dinner. The 'Dawn to Dawn Party' in 1933 was billed as "combining the attractions of a major professional golf tournament with a night of whoopee that will rival the streets of Paris." The day was reserved entirely for men – no female members were admitted into the grounds until much later.

Those early days of razzamatazz helped to fund the club's income, as did the slot machines – to be found in the hallway of the locker room level. The live bear cub was embraced until deemed too dangerous when a little girl was mauled and a camel called Miss Medinah took its place. The camel, too, eventually left for nearby Lincoln Park Zoo.

Even so, Medinah Country Club was struggling through the Depression to keep members, and to keep functioning. It succeeded at long odds because of the tenaciousness of its members and also, in the opinion of many, because of the arrival in the spring of 1933 of a man born in Edinburgh and described as a champion golfer, an innovative teacher, a more than occasional drinker and someone who dressed the part, silk handkerchief and all.

Chicago Mayor Anton Cermak (left), a Medinah member, poses with Miss Medinah - the camel - and James Triner in the early 1930s

Tommy Armour, wounded in World War I when he lost the sight in one eye, found himself in the right city, at the right time, and at the right club. Medinah and Armour was a marriage made in Chicago. The Silver Scot, as he was known, had won the US Open in 1927, the US PGA Championship in 1930, beating Gene Sarazen by one hole in the 36-hole final, and The Open Championship at Carnoustie in 1931. This was the era of the champion club professional, but Armour was much, much more than that, with a playing record known around the world, and as the fifth Head Professional at Medinah, he was the one who became its public face and made the club known for golf.

Medinah No. 3 was on the way to earning a reputation. In 1937, the club hosted the Chicago Open with a prize fund of US $10,000. This time Sarazen won, and then in 1939 Byron Nelson claimed the Western Open. Nelson returned after the Second World War in 1946 to notch another important triumph – capturing the Chicago Victory Open with a five under par 279 against a field that included Ben Hogan.

The year of 1949 marked Medinah's silver anniversary and there was good reason to celebrate with the US Open being played there for the first time. The winner was Cary Middlecoff. He earned US $2,000 and 30,000 spectators attended who, between them, consumed 100,000 bottled beverages and 26,000 sandwiches. The US Open would next return in 1975 – the Western Open had been played in 1962 and again in 1966 when Billy Casper won – and Lou Graham beat John Mahaffey in a play-off. The course now measured 7,032 yards, following renovations by George Fazio, the winning score was a three over par 287 and Graham won the play-off with a score of 71 to Mahaffey's 73.

Even so, that US Open uncovered a problem. The 18th hole had room to seat only 700 spectators and the United States Golf Association, who also considered the

In 1937 a $10,000 prize fund was worth shouting about!

finish to be less than challenging, rejected Medinah's offer to host the US Open again in 1980.

P J Boatwright Jr., then the USGA's Executive Director, Rules and Competitions, said: "We told Medinah we felt the 18th was a very weak hole. And we told them we didn't want to go back until something was done to alleviate the problem. They decided on their own to do much more."

Eventually, following much discussion and some resistance from the membership, another remodeling of the No. 3 course was approved. The remodeling of the back nine, essential to ensure a new 18th, would cost the membership US $1.2 million. Chicago architect, Roger Packard, did not touch the course's most famous hole – the par three 17th over Lake Kadijah – but it became instead the 'signature' 13th. He did not touch the old 13th – a 452-yard par four, and regarded as one of the toughest holes in America – but it became the 16th. The first 11 holes remained in sequence. The old 16th became the 12th, the old 15th was lengthened from a 326 yards par four to a 583 yards par five and became the 14th, and the old 12th became the 15th.

18th hole

Aberdeen-born Tom Bendelow designed No. 3 and became recognised as one of the most renowned architects of his time

Cary Middlecoff, winner of the United States Open at Medinah in 1949, collected the trophy – and a kiss from his wife, Edith

of Lake Kadijah. It had been deemed a dull hole in 1999, when the green had been moved to a hillside, thus taking the water out of play. Now, the water was very much back in play and a new tee on top of the hill made for an imposing shot.

The one hole Jones did not touch was the 12th, which many regard as setting the most difficult approach shot on the course. The second and the 13th – like the 17th – are both played over water, and the 17th is bookended by the dogleg 16th, requiring a risk and reward drive and an approach to an elevated green, and the 18th, with a Jones-themed elevated green, in a challenging finish.

Jones put the devil into the second hole – flattening the green slightly and pushing it to the left to bring the water into play with a new bunker behind the putting surface – and he reshaped the bunkers at the sixth to cause more trouble at a

Packard designed two new holes – the 17th a par three of 165 yards over Lake Kadijah and the 18th, a brash 440 yards par four that could accommodate a gallery of several thousand. Two of the weakest holes had been removed, replaced by two very strong holes. The revamped course measured 7,667 yards from the back tees, compared to, 7056 yards – although for the 1990 US Open it would measure 7,185 yards - and No. 3 moved that year from 26th to 12th in the biennial rankings of America's best courses in one magazine. Packard had supervised the renovation; executing the job with the reverence of a preservationist.

The changes caught the attention of the USGA, and the US Open returned in 1990 when Hale Irwin won, and Medinah's reputation was further enhanced when Tiger Woods edged Sergio Garcia in the 1999 US PGA Championship. Woods won that title again on the No. 3 course in 2006. In 2006, however, the golfers faced a different course than 1999 as the fabled architect Rees Jones had renovated 17 of the 18 holes, including laying out seven new greens. The Championship course now measured 7,561 yards – the longest ever for a Major Championship.

A key change was the return of the 17th green to the spot just in front of the shore

This pewter case was Tom Bendelow's reward for caddieing for winner Harry Vardon in the 1900 United States Open at Chicago G.C. in Wheaton

hole where, with out of bounds to the left and trees along the right, it is easy to understand why some refer to No. 3 as a torture chamber.

A new Championship tee added 25 yards to the 11th which doglegs to the left with a fairway bunker restricting bailouts and the bunkers moved closer to the green, while the 13th received a new tee and a new, flatter green that demanded a longer shot made tougher by three guarding bunkers.

History, however, dictates that a club such as Medinah, the Chicago area's best known and most frequent major championship venue, does not rest on its laurels. On June 13, 2009, Medinah's membership voted by a margin of four to one to spend upwards of US $1.1 million on a new greens project, and shortly afterwards approved a US $380,000 plan to dramatically improve the 15th hole. Rees Jones, who has overseen all architectural design aspects of Medinah's three courses since 2000, had long envisioned the major change for the 15th – transforming it into a drivable par four by reducing the length by 100 yards and adding a new two acre lake that borders dangerously on the right side of the fairway and green.

For The 2012 Ryder Cup, it is poised to come at that time in a round when the match play strategy demands that such risk-reward options will place a premium

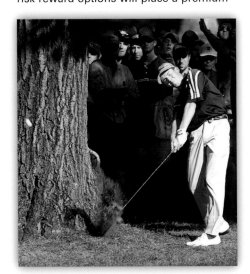

Sergio Garcia produced one of the most audacious shots in golfing history – closing his eyes, slicing a six iron to the green 189 yards away at the 16th at Medinah where he finished runner-up to Tiger Woods. The tree lived a full life – around 400 years – but it was recently taken down as disease had made it a safety hazard.

on the boldness as the players enter that formidable home stretch. A new forward tee will allow for the hole to be set up as short as 308 yards and by moving the green to the left, Jones also made way for the creation of a new back tee for the tree-lined 16th which will bring the dogleg very much back into play from the new championship tee at 482 yards.

Jones said: "I felt that the 15th was a hole where the risk-reward challenge could be strengthened. I felt a water hazard adjacent to the green would increase that risk-reward element in a fashion similar to the 12th. It is now an important part of the round and extends one of the great finishing tests in golf."

The redesign of the 15th took place concurrently with a major greens project – the course was closed for almost a year – in which 11 of No. 3's original 18 greens and the main putting green were rebuilt to USGA specifications. Jones redesigned the contours of all 11 newly built greens, with the exception of the fifth. The other seven greens, which had been rebuilt to USGA standards in 2002, also were re-grassed, and the 15th green was rebuilt.

Joe Ebner, the Medinah Country Club President, said: "We are thrilled with the changes to the 15th and with the completion of the greens renovation. The membership embraced and supported these course improvements in order to keep Medinah among the world's elite championship golf courses."

Medinah now features 4,200 trees – more than 200 a hole – comprising mostly of Red, White and Bur Oak. There are 60 bunkers in strategic positions and the greens average 5,450 square feet.

In 1984 Bill Willy set to music the lyrics of the aptly-named Melody Weber for the song "Medinah"

The largest putting surface is the 12th at 6,400 square feet, and the smallest, the 11th, which covers 4,000.

Chicago might be famous as one of the world's top ten global financial centres, but as a powerhouse to sports the town takes some beating. If you are a baseball fan, then the choice is simple – head to Wrigley Field to see the Cubs or to US Cellular Field for the Chicago White Sox. At Soldier Field, you can see the Bears in the NFL, or if basketball is your game, then it's the Chicago Bulls. Finally, in hockey, it's the Chicago Blackhawks.

Even so, Chicago is steeped in golfing history – the Chicago Golf Club in Wheaton was, in 1895, the first 18-hole course built in the United States – and Chicagoans love their golf. They will tell you that they have an unbeatable collection of public courses, and remind you that the Western Open is second only to the US Open as the oldest tournament in the country.

What no Chicagoan has witnessed, however, is The Ryder Cup in their own backyard. Now, as hosts, Medinah Country Club will provide that opportunity.

Mitchell Platts

Carries golfers, bags **and your operation to a new level.**

CAN A GOLF CAR REALLY DO THAT?

Increase revenues, reduce expenses, manage your key assets and deliver a superior customer experience. Only a Club Car fleet can deliver all of these. Sound too good to be true? Contact your Club Car representative today.

YES, IF IT'S A

Card of the No. 3 Course

Hole	Yards	Metres	Par
1	443	405	4
2	192	176	3
3	412	377	4
4	463	423	4
5	536	490	5
6	509	465	4
7	617	564	5
8	201	184	3
9	432	395	4
Out:	3,805	3,479	36
10	578	529	5
11	440	402	4
12	476	435	4
13	245	224	3
14	609	557	5
15	391	358	4
16	482	441	4
17	193	176	3
18	449	411	4
In:	3,863	3,533	36
Total:	7,668	7,012	72

Ryder Cup Results: 1979-2010

1979 The Greenbrier, White Sulphur Springs, West Virginia, USA
Europe: 11 –USA 17

1981 Walton Heath, Surrey, England
Europe 9½ - USA 18½

1983 PGA National Golf Club, Palm Beach Gardens, Florida, USA
Europe 13½ - USA 14½

1985 The Belfry, Sutton Coldfield, West Midlands, England
Europe 16½ - USA 11½

1987 Muirfield Village, Columbus, Ohio, USA
Europe 15 - USA 13

1989 The Belfry, Sutton Coldfield, West Midlands, England
Europe 14 - USA 14 (Europe retained Cup)

1991 Ocean Course, Kiawah Island, South Carolina, USA
Europe 13½ - USA 14½

1993 The Belfry, Sutton Coldfield, West Midlands, England
Europe 13 - USA 15

1995 Oak Hill Country Club, Rochester, New York, USA
Europe 14½ - USA 13½

1997 Club de Golf Valderrama, Sotogrande, Spain
Europe 14½ - USA 13½

1999 The Country Club, Brookline, Massachusetts, USA
Europe 13½ - USA 14½

2002 The Belfry, Sutton Coldfield, West Midlands, England
Europe 15½ - USA 12½

2004 Oakland Hills Country Club, Bloomfield Township, Michigan, USA
Europe 18½ - USA 9½

2006 The K Club, Straffan, Co. Kildare, Ireland
Europe 18½ - USA 9½

2008 Valhalla Golf Club, Louisville, Kentucky, USA
Europe 11½ - USA 16½

2010 The Celtic Manor Resort, City of Newport, Wales
Europe 14½ - USA 13½

The Ryder Cup - Future Venues

2014	The Gleneagles Hotel, Perthshire, Scotland
2016	Hazeltine National Golf Club, Chaska, Minnesota, USA
2018	Le Golf National, Paris, France
2020	Whistling Straits, Kohler, Wisconsin, USA

L-R: George O'Grady, Chief Executive of The European Tour, Pascal Grizot, Chairman of the French Ryder Cup Bid, Chantal Jouanno the French Minister for Sport and Richard Hills Ryder Cup Director, Europe

France will host The Ryder Cup for the first time in 2018. The historic announcement, which will see golf's greatest team event return to the Continent of Europe for the first time in 21 years, was made by Ryder Cup Europe on May 17, 2011, at Wentworth Club, Surrey, England.

Le Golf National on the outskirts of Versailles near Paris, the well-established home of the Alstom Open de France, will become only the second Continental venue – following Club de Golf Valderrama, in Spain in 1997 - when the 42nd edition of The Ryder Cup between Europe and the United States is contested in the autumn of 2018.

Five nations – France, Germany, Holland, Portugal and Spain – had participated in an exhaustive and comprehensive Bid Process – the first conducted by Ryder Cup Europe - to identify the country best qualified to follow Medinah Country Club; Gleneagles in 2014 and Hazeltine in 2016 as host of the biennial contest.

Hole by Hole guide by Mike Scully,
Director of Golf, Medinah Country Club

Hole 12

Hole 1 – Par 4 – 443 Yards: 405 Metres

This opening hole requires an accurate tee shot with either a driver or fairway wood which must avoid the bunker on the left and trees on the right side in order to leave a short iron approach to a left to right angled green. Any ball long and left will go into the grass swale and leave a challenging recovery. Bunkers on both the front left and right call for an accurate approach.

Hole 2 – Par 3 – 192 Yards: 176 Metres

The first of four very challenging par threes. This is the first real view and challenge of Lake Kadijah that sits menacingly between the tee and green and wraps all down the left edge of the green. A deep bunker awaits any shot that goes beyond the green. This picturesque hole calls for an accurate mid-iron shot struck to the centre of the green from where birdies are possible.

Hole 3 – Par 4 – 412 Yards: 377 Metres

A short dog-leg to the left that requires a fairway wood from the tee to a narrow landing area protected on the right by three bunkers and on the left by numerous overhanging trees. This newly contoured green now demands a precise short iron approach shot that must stay below the hole for a good opportunity for a birdie.

Hole 4 – Par 4 – 463 Yards: 423 Metres

This hole calls for a driver to be hit so that players can get as close to the elevated green as possible. The second shot requires a pin point distance control iron shot in order to have a realistic birdie opportunity. The most difficult hole locations are on the front half of the green as there is a severe false front which causes any ball that is short to roll off the green back down the steep fairway slope.

Hole 5 – Par 5 – 536 Yards: 490 Metres

This reachable par five provides an exciting opportunity for a birdie but also can create a lot of risk. The fairway landing area is heavily bunkered on the right side and is heavily tree lined on the left so hitting the fairway is a pre-requisite. From there, it requires an accurate uphill second shot to a heavily bunkered and very challenging putting surface. This will be a very interesting hole to watch and see how the players from each team choose to play it.

Hole 6 – Par 4 – 509 Yards: 465 Metres

The addition of a new teeing ground back and to the right of the former tee now makes this dog-leg right long par four play even more difficult. In addition, the green has been re-contoured to provide plenty of challenges to the player once they make it there. The opening into the green is fairly wide and does allow for a ball to run up if a player finds the rough from the tee. A truly challenging hole.

Hole 13

Hole 7 – Par 5 – 617 Yards: 564 Metres

This long and demanding par five that bends from left to right will provide plenty of challenges. It requires a long and fading tee shot, an accurate second shot followed by a precise approach to a wonderful green complex. Throughout the entire length of the hole there are bunkers, trees and dog-legs so players must be alert. If the tees are moved forward, it may be possible to reach the green in two shots but again, there are lots of risks involved in doing so.

Hole 8 – Par 3 – 201 Yards: 184 Metres

The only par three on No. 3 that does not have any water in play. Nevertheless, the elevated teeing ground provides a nice view to this downhill hole that will require a mid-iron to a well bunkered green. Like all the par threes at Medinah, the middle of the green is a good place to aim although this being match play the pin will no doubt be attacked.

Hole 9 – Par 4 – 432 Yards: 395 Metres

This slightly uphill sharp dog-leg to the left does not require a driver from the tee but players must hit the fairway that is heavily lined by trees on either side. The short second shot requires an accurate approach to a back to front and right to left sloping green. This is a good birdie opportunity.

Hole 10 – Par 5 – 578 Yards: 529 Metres

The tenth hole is the furthest point from the clubhouse and has the club boundary fence running down the entire left side of the hole. It is a reachable par five in favourable weather conditions but often the prudent play is to lay up and hit a short approach to one of the most severe greens on the course.

Witnessing History. Priceless.®

There are some things money can't buy.
For golf fans everywhere, there's MasterCard.®

Hole 15

Hole 11 – Par 4 - 440 Yards: 402 Metres

Another dog-leg to the left which requires an accurate tee shot that must hit the fairway. There are a number of large trees that eat into and overhang the left side of the fairway that can force players to be blocked out when hitting to the green. The green itself is the smallest on the course and new contours on it have created some very interesting challenges.

Hole 12 – Par 4 – 476 Yards: 435 Metres

The only hole on the course that does not have any bunkers. Despite that, it still is a wonderful golf hole. A severely left to right sloping fairway means the majority of tee shots finish on the right side. The mid iron approach shot is also a challenge as anything that misses the green to the right will roll almost 40 yards down the steep slope to the edge of the lake. On the green, there are a lot of subtle and challenging slopes that will test even the best of putters.

Hole 13 – Par 3 – 245 Yards: 224 Metres

This truly dramatic and picturesque par three crosses Lake Kadijah and provides a stern test. It requires a long iron or hybrid to reach this well bunkered green complex. Any shot that comes up short could well go into the Lake while deep bunkers surrounding the green offer a difficult recovery to get the ball up and down to save par.

Hole 14 – Par 5 – 609 Yards: 557 Metres

Another long and difficult par five that requires a straight tee shot again crossing Lake Kadijah. The second shot is usually a layup into a narrow, tree lined and sloping landing area. This sets up a short approach to a challenging green complex that is heavily bunkered at the front and has some deceptive and deceiving slopes. This will be another interesting hole to monitor how each player unravels the challenge.

Hole 15 – Par 4 – 391 Yards: 358 Metres

This hole has been totally rebuilt since the US PGA Championship was played in 2006. A large pond has been added on the right side of the fairway and runs all the way up to the green, which itself has one deep bunker at the rear left side as well as a deep grass chipping swale at the right rear. If the rear tee is used, then players will lay up to their favorite distance leaving a short iron approach to the challenging green complex. If the tee is moved forward, then the players will be faced with the ultimate risk/reward decision as to whether or not to try to drive the green.

Hole 16 – Par 4 – 482 Yards: 441 Metres

A new tee has extended this very challenging hole by over 20 yards and demands an accurate right to left shaped tee shot that must avoid overhanging trees on both the left and right sides of the fairway. It is on the right side of this fairway that Sergio Garcia hit his famous "closed eyes" shot from behind a tree in the 1999 PGA Championship. The second shot to an elevated green requires accuracy and precision.

Hole 17 – Par 3 – 193 Yards: 176 Metres

The final par three once again crosses over Lake Kadijah but this time the water is right up to the front and right edge of the putting green which means the tee shot cannot be short. The elevated tee makes the shot play shorter than the actual yardage but swirling winds can make judging the distance very difficult indeed. A great spectator viewing hole where a number of matches may conclude during The Ryder Cup.

Hole 17

Hole 18 – Par 4 – 449 Yards: 411 Metres

The closing hole requires an accurate tee shot to a narrow landing area that must avoid the three fairway bunkers. Once in position, a medium or short iron approach to an elevated green will provide a lot of excitement in any tension filled match that comes down to this final hole.

FONDÉ EN 1743

MOËT & CHANDON
CHAMPAGNE

TRIANON, MAISON MOËT & CHANDON, ÉPERNAY FRANCE

José María Olazábal –
The 2012 European Ryder Cup Captain

A quarter of a century on from the flamenco dance that heralded history, José María Olazábal is seeking to choreograph another chapter of Ryder Cup glory.

The Spaniard's hip-wiggling performance alongside his celebrating team-mates remains the iconic memory of Europe's first victory on American soil. "Whenever I see the video I cannot believe it is me, but that tells you everything about The Ryder Cup," he said. "When you win, the joy is beyond imagination. You are with 11 other players plus their wives and girlfriends and all the backroom staff and there is nothing to compare. You feel for each other. The Ryder Cup has been special to me; to my life. It is welded to my heart."

Historians of the game will, of course, always point to the 1987 match at Muirfield Village in Ohio as being the birth of the game's most charismatic and successful partnership.

Seve Ballesteros and Olazábal bonded their individuality in such a zealous manner that they galvanised their colleagues into sharing their belief that, displaying such unashamed care and emotion, significantly increased the impetus generated by their special precocious talents.

No player was closer to Ballesteros than Olazábal and no player instilled into Olazábal the importance of The Ryder Cup more than Ballesteros.

"I didn't know what The Ryder Cup was in 1987, but then I played with Seve," he said. "I saw the way he played, what it meant to him. He passed that attitude onto me. And he passed it on to others. I know just how much impact Seve had with the phone call he made to our team during the match at Celtic Manor in 2010 – he reached out to the players; it was very emotional."

Sadly, as we know, Seve will not be at Medinah. He lost his fight with cancer on May 7, 2011 and Olazábal said: "The best tribute we can pay to Seve is to go on playing for him, although no tribute will ever do justice to everything he did for golf and to everything he gave us."

Even so, Olazábal owes his allegiance to the game to his upbringing, not to Ballesteros. He was born to play golf – arriving in this world on February 5, 1966, in a 250-year-old traditional, picturesque Basque farmhouse 100 yards from the clubhouse at the Réal Golf Club de San Sebastian where his father, Gaspar, and mother, Julia, both worked. There, in the beautiful countryside in the hamlet of Hondarribia at the foot of the Jaizkibel mountains, Olazábal, aged two, hit his first shots on the rich pasture lands on which golfers now fight to master the game where once livestock roamed.

Olazábal, of course, achieved that better than any of the other members. Yet one of those members was to play a vital role as the young señor matured. Sergio Gomez, former medical student, rugby forward, salesman, lover of classical music and 13 handicap golfer, would become Olazábal's chaperon, caddie, chauffeur, companion and confidant. Gomez likened it to being a minister without portfolio. The timing was perfect.

Progressing through the Spanish age group system, Olazábal won the Under 9s National Infantile Championship aged seven before graduating in style to make his first international appearance aged 15 in the Spanish Under-18 team. At 16 he journeyed with his best friend Ignacio 'Nacho' Gervas to the Junior World Cup at the Atlanta Athletic Club where he hit a three wood of such beauty out of the rough at that last hole that Spain won the title. Byron Nelson, the winner of five Major Championships and the 1965 winning United States Ryder Cup captain, called it "one of the greatest shots I've ever seen."

Gomez offered to help with his entry letters to big competitions as Olazábal embarked on creating history by becoming the first golfer to complete the 'Triple Crown' of the British Boys' Championship, the British Youths' Championship and The Amateur Championship.

The career of a professional was looming and Olazábal's family life – he grew up with his mother, father, grandmother Sabina, grandfather José Maria and sister Sabina in the harbour fronted village where they lived – would need to be exchanged for a gypsy-like existence once he won the European Tour Qualifying School at La Manga in 1985, only weeks after losing a play-off to Ballesteros in the Spanish PGA Championship.

Olazábal could not have chosen a finer place to win his first tournament and look into the future than halfway up the Swiss Alps – his 1986 victory at the European Masters on the Crans-sur-Sierre course in Switzerland, being the first of 23 European Tour wins and 30 in all worldwide. His Masters Tournament success in 1994 secured global acclaim and his second in 1999 was emotionally received after his well-documented recovery from rheumatoid polyarthritis.

Even so, The Ryder Cup, with seven appearances, a record 11 wins and two halves from 15 matches in partnership with Ballesteros, followed by roles as vice-captain in 2008 and 2010, has been a major part of his life. Now, the next chapter waits to unfold at Medinah Country Club.

Mitchell Platts

We're on course to finish a great front nine.

What great club selection.

Ryder Cup Travel Services have been the Official Travel Services Operator for the Ryder Cup since 1997. Over the years we have ensured over 50,000 people have been in the thick of the action as the drama and spectacle of this, unique of all, golf events unfolds.

We have a great travel programme in place for the next US Matches at Medinah Country Club, Chicago, Illinois, for 2012 and our plans for 2014 and the European Match at Gleneagles, Scotland, are also being formulated.

All details of these value travel opportunities can be found on our website. Why not book yourself a greenside seat to cheer on the very best golfers in the world battle head to head for that precious Team victory.

www.rcts.co.uk

Davis Love III –
The 2012 United States Ryder Cup Captain

Destiny decreed that Davis Love III would one day be Captain America. He learned to crawl in a house crammed with golf instruction books and clubs of all shapes and sizes. He struck his first shots at the ripe old age of 18 months and by the age of five he was honing the swing which, in pre-technology days, would make him the longest hitter in world golf with drives booming more than 300 yards.

His father – Davis Love Jnr – quit the US PGA Tour and became a master teacher or, as many of the observers of the game at that time agreed, one of the great technicians. He gave his son – his number one pupil and his life's work – all the attention he could. And more. Rarely in the Royal and Ancient game has there been such a bonding and mutual respect between father and son. Then, one night in 1988, a single engine plane went down in a fog bank at Jacksonville Airport, Florida, killing all four occupants. Davis Love Jnr was one of them.

"When I decided to play the game seriously, Dad told me that if I was going to do it, then I should do it right," said Love. "He told me that, otherwise, I should just play for fun. He didn't want me to be anywhere in-between. He was terrific, my Dad – my teacher, my coach, my father."

There had been no prouder man on planet earth on April 19, 1987, than Davis Love Jnr when his son captured the MCI Heritage Classic on the Harbour Town Golf Links not far from the family home. Nearly a quarter of a century later, Davis Love Jnr would have been even prouder to hear Allen Wronowski, the 37th President of the PGA of America, introduce Davis Love III as the Captain of the United States team for The 2012 Ryder Cup.

Wronowski said: "The Ryder Cup is an event that demands both an experienced and strong leader and we have found that individual. He is the son of one of the most renowned PGA teaching professionals of our generation. He has exemplified enthusiasm for this job by competing on six Ryder Cup teams. He has been one of the most focused American competitors in memory at The Ryder Cup and his competitiveness and passion for the game, particularly The Ryder Cup, makes him the consummate captain to guide our next American team."

Love responded: "Winning the 1997 US PGA Championship was a thrill, especially being the son of a PGA member. To be named Ryder Cup captain is a thrill I never thought I would have. I would love to share that with my father and I know that somehow I am. I'm thrilled to represent the PGA of America and thrilled to represent all of the men and women PGA professionals. As we have said a lot of times, there's not a Tour player out there that plays one Tour event or plays six Ryder Cups that doesn't have a PGA professional that led them to that position. So I thank all the PGA professionals, including my Dad."

Davis Milton Love III was born in Charlotte, North Carolina, on April 13, 1964 – the day after Arnold Palmer became the first four time winner of the Masters Tournament. His father shared the first round lead that year with Palmer but, understandably nervous about his wife, Penta, giving birth, tumbled out of contention. "By the age of nine there was no doubt I wanted to follow Dad and become a pro," he said. "I didn't have a lot of success in junior golf but when I went to the University of North Carolina, I was ready. With Dad I had built a swing that would last."

Love turned professional in 1985 with great credentials including, that year, being a member of the United States Walker Cup team. The rest as they say is history. Love has won 20 US PGA Tour titles; 31 titles in all worldwide. His latest success in the Children's Miracle Network Classic in 2008 arrived shortly after he received the Payne Stewart Award presented annually to a player sharing Stewart's respect for the traditions of the game, his commitment to uphold the game's heritage of charitable support and the professional and meticulous presentation of himself and the sport through his dress and conduct.

Much respected in the golf community, and rightly so, Love made his 90th appearance in a Major Championship when he teed-up in the 2011

Open Championship at Royal St George's and soon followed that with his 91st in the US PGA Championship at Atlanta Athletic Club. His respect and love for the game of golf has no boundaries along with his appreciation of The Ryder Cup and Medinah.

"It's the biggest sporting event in the world," he said. "Medinah is iconic to Major Championship golf. My wife, Robin, said if the PGA of America offered me The Ryder Cup in Chicago then I was to take it! There is so much history and tradition associated with the competition and the venue. It's special. It'll be a tough competition. But José María and I go way back. He has been a good friend; he's always been respectful and supportive of my career. I look forward to competing against him; to us leading our teams together.

"I know Thursday at the Opening Ceremony we'll be friends and on Sunday night when we get done we'll still be friends. It's going to be a lot of fun."

Mitchell Platts

Wins Around the World

European Tour Members have always prided themselves in the global contribution they make to the game of golf and never has this fact been more conclusively proven than during the 2011 season when Members garnered trophies across all five continents. From February to December silverware was hoisted high, with once again the United States, Asia and Africa proving fertile hunting grounds.

In the United States, pride of place went to Luke Donald whose stunning victory in the Children's Miracle Network Hospitals Classic helped him top the US PGA Tour Money List, while Justin Rose showed he was back in form with victory in the BMW Championship during the FedEx Cup Series

In South Africa, Hennie Otto won twice – in the Dimension Data Pro-Am and the Platinum Classic – while George Coetzee also had double reason to celebrate, on his own in the Telkom PGA Championship and together with Mark James in the Gary Player Invitational presented by Coca-Cola.

In Asia, the success was widespread with Paul Casey winning in Korea, Rory McIlroy triumphing in China, David J Russell winning in Japan and Lee Westwood topping the pile in Indonesia, a victory which helped him return to World Number One.

With victories for Englishman Gary Wolstenholme down under in the ISPS Handa Australian Senior Open allied to triumphs in their own national PGA Championships for Welshman Stephen Dodd and Irishman Simon Thornton, it truly was a year to remember.

Luke Donald - Children's Miracle Network Hospitals Classic

Thaworn Wiratchant - Indonesia Open presented by Enjoy Jakarta

Darren Fichardt - Vodacom Origins of Golf Wild Coast and Suncoast Classic

James Kamte - BMG Classic

Rory McIlroy - Lake Malaren Shanghai Masters

Paul Casey - The 27th Shinhan Donghae Open

Stephen Dodd - Welsh National PGA Championship

Tetsuji Hiratsuka - Asia-Pacific Panasonic Open

Mark McNulty and David Eger - Liberty Mutual Legends of Golf

Bernhard Langer - ACE Group Classic

Kiradech Aphibarnrat - SAIL Open

Hennie Otto - Dimension Data Pro-Am and Platinum Classic presented by UD Trucks (below)

Julian Etulain - TLA Televisa Players Championship

Fredrik Jacobson - Travelers Championship

David J Russell - Fuji Film Senior Championship

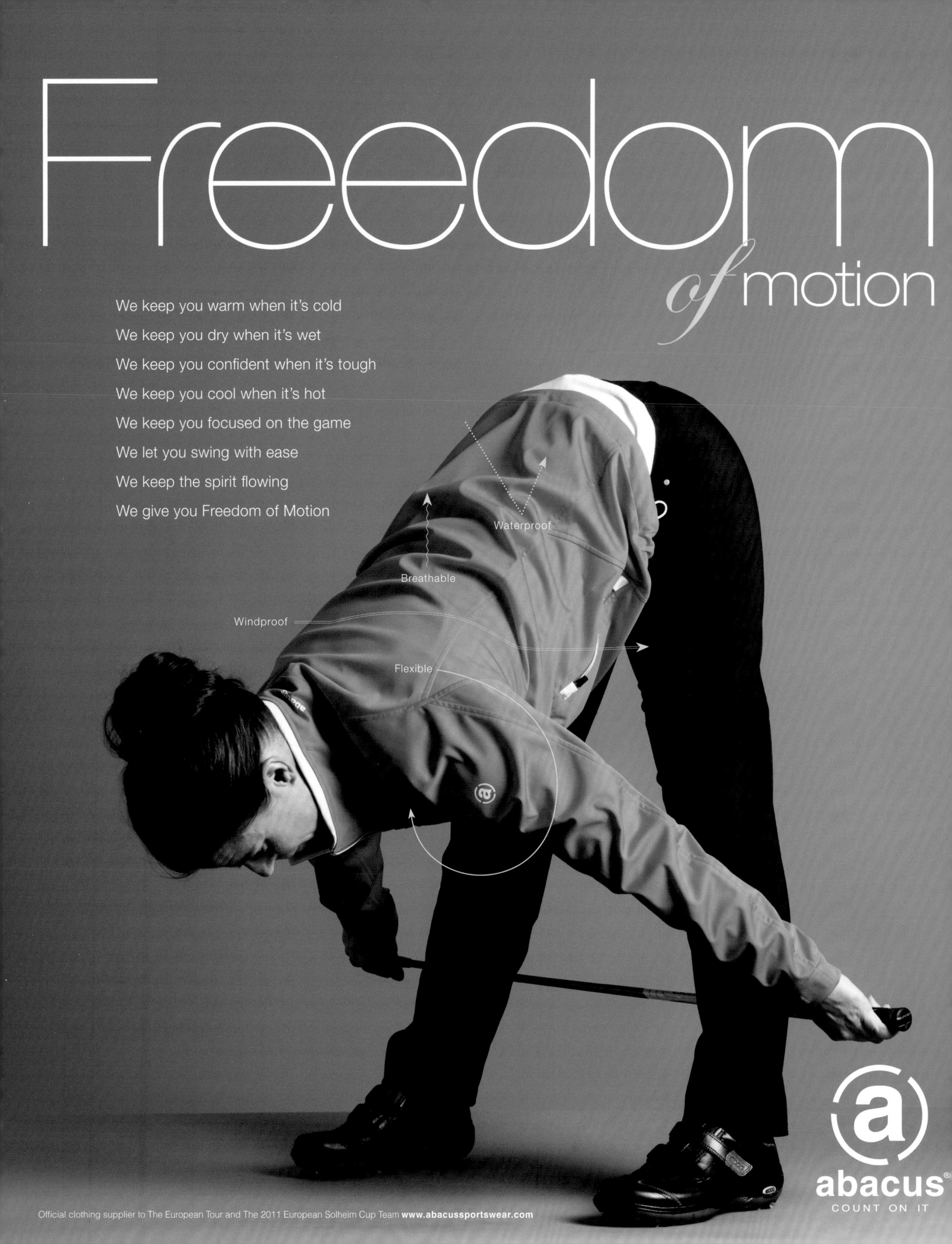
Freedom
of motion
We keep you warm when it's cold
We keep you dry when it's wet
We keep you confident when it's tough
We keep you cool when it's hot
We keep you focused on the game
We let you swing with ease
We keep the spirit flowing
We give you Freedom of Motion
Waterproof
Breathable
Windproof
Flexible
abacus®
COUNT ON IT
Official clothing supplier to The European Tour and The 2011 European Solheim Cup Team www.abacussportswear.com

Fabrizio Zanotti - Stella Artois: Tigo Carlos Franco Invitational

George Coetzee (right) with Mark James – Gary Player Invitational presented by Coca-Cola. Coetzee also won the Telkom PGA Championship

Simon Thornton - 101st Irish PGA Championship

Lee Westwood - Indonesian Masters and Nedbank Challenge (below)

Shaun Norris - Nashua Masters

Justin Rose - BMW Championship

Gary Wolstenholme - ISPS Handa Australian Senior Open

Jaco Van Zyl - Telkom PGA Pro-Am

Danny Lee - WNB Golf Classic

Rollercoaster Ride

Peter Fowler

Barry Lane

There is an old adage that applies to both golf and general life that 'hard work pays off' and for self-proclaimed workaholic Peter Fowler, the 2011 European Senior Tour campaign was the season when his tireless dedication to the game was finally rewarded.

Two victories, 13 top ten finishes in 18 appearances and, most significantly of all, the John Jacobs Trophy now resting on his mantelpiece underlined a year defined by the consistency the Australian has always strived for, but feared he might never achieve.

Seventeen years had passed between Fowler's zenith on The European Tour in 1993 – when he held off Major Champions Bernhard Langer and Ian Woosnam to win the BMW International Open in Munich – and his dominance of the Senior Tour's 20th anniversary season.

During that time Fowler rode the rollercoaster of golfing emotions, from the wilderness of seven seasons in a row outside the top 100 on The European Tour in the years immediately following his sole victory, to a renaissance at the start of the new century.

Even at his lowest ebb, which included a three year return to teaching from 1996 to 1998, Fowler's devotion to the game never diminished and neither did his determination to succeed – characteristics of a man who has overcome his fair share of adversity, including a career-threatening back injury that struck just days before his Senior Tour debut in 2009.

Andy Stubbs, Managing Director of the European Senior Tour, presents the 2011 John Jacobs Trophy to Peter Fowler

"The struggles that I've had over the years makes this all the sweeter," said the 52 year old. "The guys who win work hard and I have had a long struggle, so it does feel very special to win the John Jacobs Trophy and join all the great names on there."

Fowler's victory in the ISPS Handa Senior Masters presented by The Stapleford Forum in June was his first in 18 years and he claimed a second the following month when he overhauled a seven shot deficit in the final round of Bad Ragaz PGA Seniors Open.

Having seized control of the Order of Merit, he never relinquished it and despite the formidable challenge of former Ryder Cup player Barry Lane who along with Carl Mason was the only other two-time winner in 2011, Fowler was anointed the new Senior Tour Number One at the culmination of the MCB Tour Championship in Mauritius.

"It was a great tussle with Barry but fortunately when he had his two wins I finished second and third so I managed to stay close enough," he said. "The more the year went on, the more exhausted I was. Then I suffered some back problems again in Portugal in October so it was good to see the job through."

Battling is certainly an adjective that could be used to describe the remarkable turnaround in Fowler's fortunes. Gary Player once said: "You have to work hard to become a natural golfer," and Fowler has been a fully subscribed pupil to that particular school of golfing thought throughout a career that has endured highs and lows in equal measure.

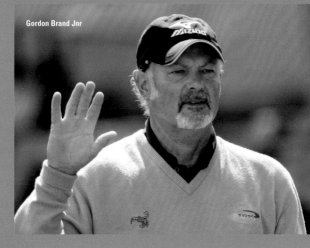

Gordon Brand Jnr

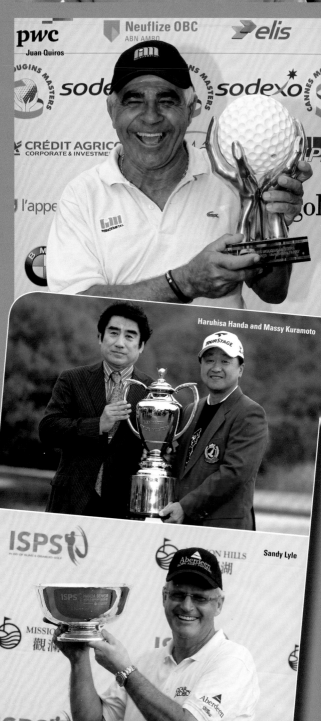

Juan Quiros

Haruhisa Handa and Massy Kuramoto

Sandy Lyle

Peter Senior

Chris Williams

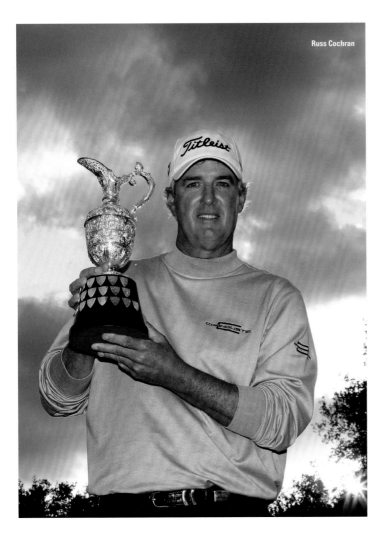
Russ Cochran

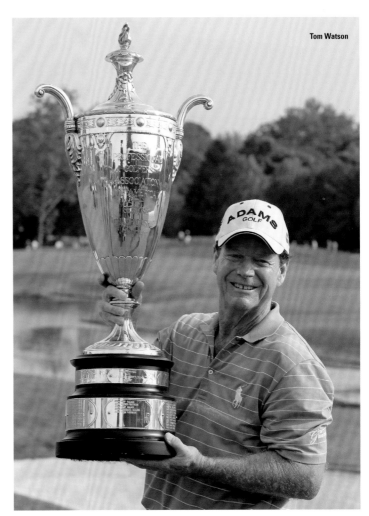
Tom Watson

Born Peter Randall Fowler on September 9, 1959, in Sydney, the man nicknamed 'Chook' turned professional in 1977 and won his maiden professional title in the 1983 Australian Open before partnering Wayne Grady to World Cup glory at Las Brisas in 1989, when he also took the individual award.

He ended the 1989 season in a career high 22nd on The European Tour Order of Merit before, having finished runner-up six times on The European Tour between 1984 and 1992, he finally made his breakthrough on that memorable afternoon in Germany.

It proved to be his only European Tour victory and after subsequent spells on the European Challenge Tour and numerous trips to the Qualifying School, he found his game returning. However, just as he was preparing for the dawn of a new career on the Senior Tour in 2009, disaster struck.

Ironically, Fowler was at La Moye Golf Club in Jersey for his Senior Tour debut – the same venue he had made his first European Tour appearance 23 years earlier – when he suffered a debilitating disc problem in his back that threatened to end his career for good.

"My back and hips had been stiff for years but my back went in practice before my debut in Jersey," he said. "I didn't know how bad it was at the time and I played four events that season but I was hopeless. I had a nerve problem and I had to have surgery sooner rather than later.

"At that stage I didn't know if I was going to play again. I worked hard after that and was out for 12 months. I came back for the 2010 US Senior PGA Championship and I was going to see how it went but I managed to play through until the end of the season and finished 29th. I battled and got through but it wasn't until November that year

Tom Lehman

Gary Wolstenholme

that I felt strong. I did a lot of hard work before the 2011 season and it has really paid off."

After starting the 2011 season with a share of sixth place in the ISPS Handa Senior Australian Open, Fowler went on to finish inside the top ten in all but five of his 18 appearances in 2011. Even when Lane won twice in three events, successfully defending his Cleveland Golf/Srixon Scottish Senior Open title and winning the Casa Serena Open to pile on the pressure, Fowler did not falter nor let injury woes deter him.

Heading into the MCB Tour Championship, the Australian had a €25,569 advantage and after opening with a 73, he ignored the lure of the Mauritius beach and headed straight to the practice ground for yet more "grinding" as he fondly calls it.

The result was a 13th top ten finish of the season as Lane's own challenge faded, with an emotional Fowler eventually taking his 2011 earnings to €302,327. He ended the campaign €31,154 clear of Lane to become only the third Australian to win the Senior Tour Order of Merit after Noel Ratcliffe in 2000 and Ian Stanley in 2001, and it was a personal triumph that Fowler himself admits was founded on his insatiable work ethic.

Aside from the tussle between Fowler and Lane, the landmark 2011 season will be remembered for the record breaking achievements of Mason, now the Senior Tour's most successful player.

Having equalled Tommy Horton's benchmark of 23 Senior Tour victories in 2010, the Englishman became the most prolific winner in Senior Tour history with a four stroke victory in the OKI Open de España Senior by Cleveland Golf/Srixon in May. The 58 year old then made it 25 titles in nine seasons when he returned to Spain in October to win the Benahavis Senior Masters.

It was also a notable year for former Open and Masters Champion Sandy Lyle, who claimed his first tournament title since 1992 when he won the ISPS Handa Senior World Championship presented by Mission Hills China.

Carl Mason

Ian Woosnam

Des Smyth

Andrew Oldcorn

Roger Chapman

David Frost

Mark Mouland

Lyle and Fowler were two of 11 first time winners in 2011, joining Peter Senior (Handa Australian Senior Open), Massy Kuramoto (Handa Cup Senior Masters), David Frost (Mauritius Commercial Bank Open) and Chris Williams (Aberdeen Brunei Senior Masters presented by The Stapleford Forum) in a run of five consecutive maiden champions at the start of the season.

Other first time winners were Andrew Oldcorn, who claimed a PGA double by adding the De Vere Club PGA Seniors Championship to the PGA Championship he won ten years previously at Wentworth Club, Mark Mouland (Belas Clube de Campo Senior Open de Portugal) and Chien Soon Lu (Fubon Senior Open), while Americans Russ Cochran and Olin Browne won The Senior Open Championship played at Walton Heath Golf Club in Surrey, England, and US Senior Open respectively in consecutive weeks in July.

The evergreen Tom Watson had earlier captured the season's first Major, winning the US Senior PGA Championship at the age of 61, while Des Smyth, at 58, also showed his longevity, winning the Van Lanschot Senior Open in the Netherlands in June.

Juan Quiros denied Smyth a second title, defeating the Irishman in a play-off to win the Cannes Mougins Masters, while two former winners of the John Jacobs Trophy, Ian Woosnam and Boonchu Ruangkit, also joined the 2011 champions roll call, claiming the Berenberg Bank Masters and the Travis Perkins plc Senior Masters respectively.

It then left former Open Champion Tom Lehman, winner of the US Champions Tour Money List in 2011, to bring the curtain down on the 2011 season by finishing one stroke clear of South African David Frost in the MCB Tour Championship in Mauritius in the final event of the campaign.

However, in the year the Senior Tour started its 20th anniversary season down under in Australia, it was entirely fitting that it was an Antipodean who eventually stood tallest at the end.

Steve Todd

Sam Torrance
Mark James
Mike Harwood

Chien Soon Lu

Olin Browne

Boonchu Ruangkit

	Date	Event	Venue	Winner	Score	First prize / Prize fund
Nov 10	19-21	Handa Australian Senior Open	Royal Perth GC, Perth, Australia	Peter Senior, AUS	65-70-72=207 (-9)	€54,498 / €248,567
	25-28	Handa Cup Senior Masters	Ohmurasaki GC, Saitama, Japan	Masahiro Kuramoto, JPN	69-71-66-65=271 (-17)	€188,960 / €1,031,510
Dec 10	10-12	Mauritius Commercial Bank Open	Constance Belle Mare Plage, Poste de Flacq, Mauritius	David Frost, RSA**	70-64-69=203 (-13)	€42,000 / €279,720
Mar 11	4-6	Aberdeen Brunei Senior Masters presented by The Stapleford Forum	The Empire Hotel & Country Club, Bandar Seri Begawan, Brunei Darussalam	Chris Williams, RSA	68-69-64=201 (-12)	€34,689 / €231,264
	11-13	ISPS Handa Senior World Championship presented by Mission Hills China	World Cup Course, Mission Hills, Shenzhen, China	Sandy Lyle, SCO	68-66-70=204 (-12)	€37,483 / €249,892
May	18-20	OKI Open de Espana Senior by Cleveland Golf/Srixon	El Valle Golf Resort, Murcia, Spain	Carl Mason, ENG	67-65-68=200 (-13)	€30,000 / €200,000
	26-29	US SENIOR PGA CHAMPIONSHIP	Valhalla GC, Louisville, Kentucky, USA	Tom Watson, USA**	70-70-68-70=278 (-10)	€254,650/ €1,466,132
Jun	3-5	ISPS Handa Senior Masters presented by The Stapleford Forum	Stapleford Park, Melton Mowbray, England	Peter Fowler, AUS	68-71-70=209 (-10)	€34,436 / €229,572
	9-12	De Vere Club PGA Seniors Championship	Hunting Course, De Vere Slaley Hall, Hexham, England	Andrew Oldcorn, SCO	73-66-68-70= 277 (-11)	€45,646 / €285,290
	17-19	Berenberg Bank Masters	Cologne Golf und Land Club, Cologne, Germany	Ian Woosnam, WAL	71-70-66=207 (-9)	€60,000 / €400,000
	24-26	Van Lanschot Senior Open	Royal Haagsche G&CC, The Hague, Netherlands	Des Smyth, IRL	71-74-65=210 (-6)	€37,500 / €249,750
Jul	1-3	Bad Ragaz PGA Seniors Open	Golf Club Bad Ragaz, Bad Ragaz, Switzerland	Peter Fowler, AUS	66-65-65=196 (-14)	€37,500 / €250,000
	21-24	THE SENIOR OPEN CHAMPIONSHIP	Walton Heath GC, Surrey, England	Russ Cochran, USA	72-70-67-67 =(-12)	€220,962 / €1,406,343
	28-31	US SENIOR OPEN*	Inverness Club, Toledo, Ohio, USA	Olin Browne, USA	64-65-69-71=269 (-15)	$2,600,000
Aug	19-21	Cleveland Golf/Srixon Scottish Senior Open	Fairmont St. Andrews, Fife, Scotland	Barry Lane, ENG	67-69-66=202 (-14)	€42,930 / €286,729
Sep	2-4	Travis Perkins plc Senior Masters	Duke's Course, Woburn GC, Woburn, England	Boonchu Ruangkit, THA	68-68-71=207 (-9)	€48,192 / €321,280
	16-18	Casa Serena Open	Casa Serena Golf, Kutna Hora, Czech Republic	Barry Lane, ENG	67-62-69=198 (-15)	€40,000 / €400,000
	22-24	Cannes Mougins Masters	Cannes Mougins, Cannes, France	Juan Quiros, ESP**	69-68-69=206 (-10)	€38,826 / €250,000
	29-1 Oct	Belas Clube de Campo Senior Open de Portugal	Belas Clube de Campo, Lisbon, Portugal	Mark Mouland, WAL	70-69-68=207 (-9)	€40,000 / €300,555
Oct	14-16	Benahavis Senior Masters	La Quinta G&CC, Benahavis, Spain	Carl Mason, ENG	70-65-69=204 (-9)	€27,000 / €180,171
Nov	18-20	Fubon Senior Open	Miramar G&CC, Taipei, Taiwan	Chien Soon lu, TPE	64-71-69=204 (-12)	€52,398 / €274,763
Dec	9-11	MCB Tour Championship	Constance Belle Mare Plage, Poste de Flacq, Mauritius	Tom Lehman, USA	65-68-71=204 (-12)	€61,722 / €400,000

** denotes play-off
* Money won does not count towards the 2011 European Senior Tour Order of Merit

THE 2011 EUROPEAN SENIOR TOUR ORDER OF MERIT

	Pos	Name	Country	Played	€		Pos	Name	Country	Played	€
	1	Peter FOWLER	(AUS)	(18)	302326.62		56	Steve VAN VUUREN	(RSA)	(15)	27813.37
	2	Barry LANE	(ENG)	(15)	271172.75		57	Massy KURAMOTO	(JPN)	(6)	27560.03
	3	Andrew OLDCORN	(SCO)	(17)	188980.98		58	Delroy CAMBRIDGE	(JAM)	(19)	25805.38
+	4	Gary WOLSTENHOLME	(ENG)	(21)	181636.68		59	Horacio CARBONETTI	(ARG)	(14)	24631.57
	5	Ian WOOSNAM	(WAL)	(14)	179160.08		60	Mike CLAYTON	(AUS)	(10)	23299.63
	6	Boonchu RUANGKIT	(THA)	(14)	148387.24		61	Jeb STUART	(USA)	(17)	23002.10
	7	David FROST	(RSA)	(6)	147986.03		62	Jean Pierre SALLAT	(FRA)	(9)	20741.37
	8	Mike HARWOOD	(AUS)	(16)	143789.40		63	Manuel MORENO	(ESP)	(16)	20700.96
	9	Juan QUIROS	(ESP)	(18)	140511.09		64	Wayne GRADY	(AUS)	(6)	19650.64
	10	Carl MASON	(ENG)	(15)	136161.71		65	Fraser MANN	(SCO)	(15)	19452.35
	11	Roger CHAPMAN	(ENG)	(11)	129816.10		66	Denis DURNIAN	(ENG)	(16)	19060.67
	12	Des SMYTH	(IRL)	(15)	122652.62		67	Peter DAHLBERG	(SWE)	(18)	19002.46
	13	Gordon BRAND JNR	(SCO)	(11)	121428.80		68	Andrew MURRAY	(ENG)	(5)	18494.81
+	14	Mark MOULAND	(WAL)	(13)	117767.85		69	Giuseppe CALI	(ITA)	(14)	18225.48
	15	Sandy LYLE	(SCO)	(10)	113203.48		70	John CHILLAS	(SCO)	(13)	17293.78
	16	Chris WILLIAMS	(RSA)	(22)	113174.93		71	Steve CIPA	(ENG)	(10)	15857.79
	17	Angel FRANCO	(PAR)	(18)	105375.23	+	72	Paul CURRY	(ENG)	(3)	15390.81
	18	Marc FARRY	(FRA)	(19)	103428.92	**	73	Claude GRENIER	(AUT)	(6)	14139.56
	19	Ross DRUMMOND	(SCO)	(16)	98771.05		74	Eamonn DARCY	(IRL)	(6)	13104.41
	20	Sam TORRANCE	(SCO)	(17)	95800.62		75	Jim RHODES	(ENG)	(11)	12019.16
	21	Mark JAMES	(ENG)	(11)	83485.03		76	Manuel PIÑERO	(ESP)	(12)	11384.03
	22	Bob CAMERON	(ENG)	(16)	82925.77	+	77	François ILLOUZ	(FRA)	(7)	11151.31
	23	Bill LONGMUIR	(SCO)	(20)	81911.28		78	Stephen BENNETT	(ENG)	(12)	9122.45
+	24	Tim THELEN	(USA)	(12)	80109.79		79	Jimmy HEGGARTY	(NIR)	(11)	8535.50
	25	David MERRIMAN	(AUS)	(18)	79021.48		80	Joe STANSBERRY	(USA)	(9)	8291.09
	26	Angel FERNANDEZ	(CHI)	(12)	75964.16	+	81	Hiroshi UEDA	(JPN)	(1)	7952.06
	27	Nick JOB	(ENG)	(20)	73077.07		82	Matt BRIGGS	(ENG)	(7)	7377.40
	28	Bobby LINCOLN	(RSA)	(19)	68409.59	**	83	Peter A SMITH	(SCO)	(4)	6729.32
	29	Mike CUNNING	(USA)	(16)	67283.43	**	84	Lyndsay STEPHEN	(AUS)	(6)	6521.24
	30	David J RUSSELL	(ENG)	(17)	64788.35		85	Tony CHARNLEY	(ENG)	(11)	6474.48
	31	George RYALL	(ENG)	(17)	63705.63		86	Antonio GARRIDO	(ESP)	(14)	5700.30
	32	John HARRISON	(ENG)	(19)	61693.65		87	Maurice BEMBRIDGE	(ENG)	(11)	5255.53
	33	Gordon J BRAND	(ENG)	(20)	60526.49	**	88	James MURPHY	(ENG)	(2)	4837.64
+	34	Gordon MANSON	(AUT)	(16)	60425.23		89	Jeff HALL	(ENG)	(5)	3498.63
	35	Graham BANISTER	(AUS)	(17)	58978.47		90	Emilio RODRIGUEZ	(ESP)	(6)	3254.10
	36	Kevin SPURGEON	(ENG)	(20)	56025.61		91	Mike MILLER	(SCO)	(8)	2881.57
	37	Katsuyoshi TOMORI	(JPN)	(12)	54550.12		92	Martin GRAY	(SCO)	(5)	2788.50
	38	Bertus SMIT	(RSA)	(17)	52718.12		93	Eddie POLLAND	(NIR)	(8)	2626.32
	39	Mark BELSHAM	(ENG)	(19)	52401.26		94	Glyn DAVIES	(WAL)	(5)	2546.84
	40	Adan SOWA	(ARG)	(16)	48795.70		95	Victor GARCIA	(ESP)	(8)	2481.07
	41	José RIVERO	(ESP)	(14)	48006.90		96	Mitch KIERSTENSON	(ENG)	(6)	2382.31
	42	Costantino ROCCA	(ITA)	(14)	47264.21		97	Bill HARDWICK	(CAN)	(8)	2369.04
+	43	Andrew SHERBORNE	(ENG)	(16)	47126.35		98	Mike WILLIAMS	(ZIM)	(3)	1847.12
	44	Tony JOHNSTONE	(ZIM)	(13)	45259.03		99	Terry BURGOYNE	(SCO)	(6)	1769.42
	45	Jerry BRUNER	(USA)	(20)	45233.82	**	100	Ken TARLING	(CAN)	(2)	1717.49
	46	Denis O'SULLIVAN	(IRL)	(18)	42098.76		101	Barrie STEVENS	(ENG)	(5)	1524.50
	47	Peter MITCHELL	(ENG)	(12)	41691.25	**	102	Ian ESPITALIER NOEL	(MUS)	(2)	1350.70
	48	Rodger DAVIS	(AUS)	(13)	40183.29		103	Doug YOUNG	(ENG)	(4)	939.20
	49	Luis CARBONETTI	(ARG)	(14)	38137.77		104	Ian MOSEY	(ENG)	(5)	647.06
	50	John GOULD	(ENG)	(18)	37311.14		105	Stephen SHIELDS	(ENG)	(3)	490.00
	51	Noel RATCLIFFE	(AUS)	(13)	35847.12			Neville CLARKE	(RSA)	(3)	490.00
	52	Domingo HOSPITAL	(ESP)	(11)	34820.02		107	TR JONES	(USA)	(5)	336.00
	53	Doug JOHNSON	(USA)	(12)	34812.19		108	Chris LINSTEAD	(ENG)	(4)	308.00
	54	Glenn RALPH	(ENG)	(19)	33089.03	**	109	Ian DOUGAN	(SCO)	(2)	294.00
+	55	Anders FORSBRAND	(SWE)	(11)	29269.79						

+ Denotes rookie
** Denotes affiliate member

Fearlessness and Flair

Tommy Fleetwood

A thrilling 2011 European Challenge Tour campaign reached a fitting climax on the final afternoon of the Apulia San Domenico Grand Final, when young guns Tommy Fleetwood and Andrea Pavan went head to head in a duel for the right to be crowned Number One.

With a combined age of just 42 and with the golfing world at their feet, the duo displayed all the elements we have come to associate with the Challenge Tour: fearlessness, flair and, above all, pure golfing talent.

Ultimately it was 20 year old Englishman Fleetwood who prevailed although Pavan, the 22 year old from Rome with the model looks and silky smooth swing, had the consolation of winning the tournament at San Domenico Golf, the course in southern Italy to which he is attached. Indeed it was Pavan's second victory of the season, following his debut win at the Norwegian Challenge in August.

Fleetwood might have lost that battle but he won the war, his second place finish in Italy good enough to see him end the season with €148,912 – some €15,860 ahead of Pavan – to become the youngest winner of the Challenge Tour Rankings in its 22 year history.

Having carried the prolific promise of a stellar amateur career into the professional arena, there is genuine excitement to what Fleetwood can now go on to achieve in a game which has been in his blood for as long as he can remember.

"My dad and brother were good players and I grew up in Southport, which is a great golfing area," he said. "So from a young age, it became pretty obvious where my future might lie. From about five, I played nine holes every Monday,

and two years later I entered my first national tournament."

The record books show he carded 130 but, despite being the youngest player there by some six years, he did not finish in last place. It would be the only time

Andrea Pavan

Sam Little

Danny Denison

Jamie Moul

Anthony Snobeck

he would come even remotely close to taking the wooden spoon.

Guided by his father Pete, a constant presence at his son's side during his formative years, Fleetwood soon started making waves in the amateur game. Aged 11 he joined Formby Hall Golf Club, spending countless hours on the course and practice range perfecting the technique which led to a call-up from the English Golf Union to play for his country.

Triumphant appearances for Great Britain and Ireland in the Jacques Léglise Trophy in 2007 and 2008 followed before, a year later, he tasted individual success in the Scottish Amateur Open Stroke Play Championship at Murcar, winning by a handsome eight stroke margin.

Having achieved his boyhood dream of competing in the Walker Cup in 2009, he rounded off his amateur career the

following year in some style by winning the English Amateur Championship at Little Aston – a performance which helped him depart at the top of the World Amateur Ranking.

The game is littered with tales of players who have struggled to convert amateur excellence to professional achievements, but there was no danger of Fleetwood adding to them – especially after proving he could cut it in the paid ranks in the 2010 English Challenge, where he narrowly missed out on becoming only the fourth amateur to win on the Challenge Tour.

Another runner-up finish – this time as a professional – soon followed at the M2M Russian Challenge Cup, a performance which effectively secured him a full category for the 2011 Challenge Tour season. Given such achievements, he understandably came into the campaign as one of the favourites.

His initial results were steady rather than spectacular, but that all changed in August. With his confidence buoyed by victory in a EuroPro Tour event at his home club, Fleetwood embarked on a run of form which would propel him to the very top.

Having narrowly missed out at the Rolex Trophy, he made amends at the most lucrative regular tournament on the Challenge Tour Schedule, the Kazakhstan Open. After taking charge of the €400,000 event with a sumptuous round of 66 on the third day, he managed to keep calm on a tense final day until reaching the 18th green, where he was left with two putts from 25 feet to take the title and, with it, the €64,000 winner's cheque.

As the enormity of the situation dawned on him, by his own admission Fleetwood felt the pressure. But he overcame it in emphatic fashion, finding the middle of the cup with a birdie putt which summed up the man himself: deadly.

No sooner had the champagne on his shirt dried out than he was plotting his next move: to gain some invaluable experience on The European Tour. If finishing tied tenth in the Austrian GolfOpen presented by Lyoness was one thing, finishing joint fifth – higher than a multitude of Major winners – in the Alfred Dunhill Links Championship the following week was quite another.

It took his season's earnings on both Tours through the €250,000 barrier and, perhaps more importantly, it proved to Fleetwood – and everyone else – that he belonged in such elevated company.

Ricardo Santos

Benjamin Hebert

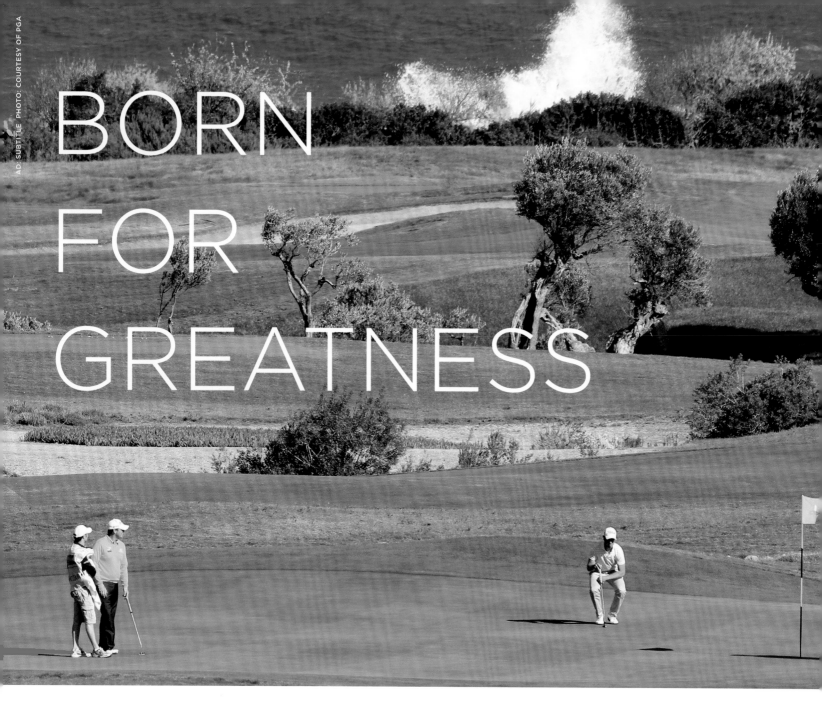

BORN
FOR
GREATNESS

A LAND THAT NURTURES ANCIENT HISTORY, A TIME HONOURED CUISINE, NATURE'S FINEST INGREDIENTS AND A SUN BLESSED CLIMATE IS NOW A DESTINATION FOR GREAT GOLF.

Sitting on the edge of the sea whilst it winds through a grove of timeless olive trees, San Domenico championship golf course (home to the European Challenge Tour Grand Final) together with its fine hotels Borgo Egnazia and Masseria Cimino offer a golfing experience to remember.

San Domenico Hotels
WWW.SANDOMENICOHOTELS.COM

San Domenico Golf
SAVELLETRI DI FASANO - PUGLIA

WWW.SANDOMENICOGOLF.COM

"Playing with Padraig Harrington in the last round on the Old Course was a great experience, and something I'll never forget," he said. "Some members from Formby Hall came along to watch so I treated them to dinner on Sunday night – nothing too fancy, mind!"

You see Fleetwood, as down to earth and grounded as they come, does not do fancy. Indeed, his reward for earning €126,334 at the Alfred Dunhill Links Championship was to splash out £200 on a computer games console. But if he leads a humble existence away from the course, anyone who has witnessed him wield a golf club will have come to expect extraordinary feats from the young man on it.

The second day of the Apulia San Domenico Grand Final is a case in point; where a stunning round of 61 proved the catalyst for glory. Now, however, the hard work really begins as he prepares for life week in, week out with the big boys of The European Tour.

As well as Pavan, whose stunning victory in Italy helped him finish second in the Rankings with €133,052,

Fleetwood will be joined on The 2012 European Tour International Schedule by 18 other worthy graduates including Benjamin Hebert and Sam Little who certainly know what winning is all about.

Between them, the Frenchman and the Englishman – who ended the season in fifth and third place respectively on the Rankings – won almost a quarter of the events on the 2011 Challenge Tour in two blistering spells of form. Hebert's zenith came in July and August when he won three tournaments out of five; the Credit Suisse Challenge, the English Challenge and the Rolex Trophy, where he pipped Fleetwood for the silverware.

Not to be outdone, Little then took up the baton in September and October and repeated the extraordinary feat of winning three times in five weeks; starting with back-to-back triumphs in the M2M Russian Challenge Cup and the ALLIANZ Golf Open Grand Toulouse before ending with victory in the Roma Golf Open.

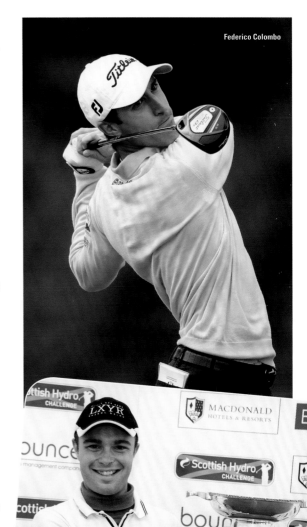

Federico Colombo

Edouard Dubois

Andrew Tampion

Julien Quesne

Chris Gane

Craig Lee

Michael Hoey

Pelle Edberg

Simon Thornton

The 2011 European Challenge Tour graduates.
L-R back:- Pelle Edberg, Craig Lee, Federico Colombo, Alessandro Tadini, Sam Walker, Julien Quesne, Chris Gane, Ricardo Santos, Jamie Moul, Matthew Baldwin, Daniel Denison, Benjamin Hebert, Sam Little, Simon Thornton.
L-R front:- Tommy Fleetwood, Jorge Campillo, Andrea Pavan, Edouard Dubois, Andrew Johnston, Charles-Edouard Russo.

Portugal's Ricardo Santos, who captured his debut title in The Princess by Schüco in June, was sandwiched between the three time winners in fourth place on the final Rankings, while England's Danny Denison finished sixth thanks chiefly to his victory in the ECCO Tour Championship hosted by Thomas Björn & Mercedes-Benz in July, a performance which proved, finally, the 26 year old had recovered from the nasty car accident which halted his career progress in the summer of 2007.

Denison's compatriots Jamie Moul (eighth in the Rankings) and Matthew Baldwin (tenth) secured their maiden professional titles at the Acaya Open in July and the

Fred Olsen Challenge de España in September respectively, whilst Italian Federico Colombo and Spaniard Jorge Campillo were rewarded for their consistent seasons, completing the top ten in seventh and ninth place.

Aside from Hebert, Little and Pavan, the only other multiple winner this year was Frenchman Edouard Dubois, who won the Kärnten Golf Open presented by Mazda at the start of June and followed that with success in the Scottish Hydro Challenge at the end of that month en route to finishing in 11th place in the Rankings.

Having finished 13th and 17th respectively, his fellow

Charles-Edouard Russo

Joaquin Estevez

Matthew Zions

Alessandro Tadini

Sam Walker

Gaganjeet Bhullar

Frenchmen Julien Quesne, winner of the ALLIANZ Golf Open de Lyon in October, and Charles-Edouard Russo will also be playing on European golf's top tier next term; as will Ireland's Simon Thornton (12th), Scotland's Craig Lee (14th), the English trio of Andrew Johnston (15th), Sam Walker (16th) and Chris Gane (19th), Sweden's Pelle Edberg (18th) and Italian Alessandro Tadini (20th).

Aside from the 23 regular tournaments on the 2011 European Challenge Tour, there were also two dual ranking events during the course of the season; with Northern Ireland's Michael Hoey and Australia's Matt Zions already plying their trade on The European Tour after winning the Madeira Islands Open in May and the SAINT-OMER OPEN presented by Neuflize OBC in June respectively.

But India's Gaganjeet Bhullar (winner of the season-opening Gujarat Kensville Challenge), Argentine Joaquin Estévez (Abierto International Copa Antioquia), South Africa's Michiel Bothma (Barclays Kenya Open), Germany's Nicolas Meitinger (ALLIANZ Challenge de France), Frenchman Anthony Snobeck (Mugello Tuscany Open), Australian Andrew Tampion (Telenet Trophy) and England's Phillip Archer (ALLIANZ Open Cotes d'Armor Bretagne) all missed out on promotion to the top tier despite their tournament triumphs, thus once again emphasising the strength in depth, and fiercely competitive nature, of the modern day European Challenge Tour.

Paul Symes

Michiel Bothma

Andrew Johnston

Phillip Archer

Nicolas Meitinger

Matthew Baldwin

Jorge Campillo

THE 2011 EUROPEAN CHALLENGE TOUR

	Date	Event	Venue	Winner	Score	First prize / Prize fund
Jan	13 - 16	Gujarat Kensville Challenge	Kensville GC, Ahmedabad, India	Gaganjeet Bhullar, IND	70-70-68-75=283 (-5)	€32,000 / €201,740
Mar	10-13	Abierto International Copa Antioquia	Club Campestre, La Macarena, Colombia	Joaquin Estévez**, ARG	68-69-70-67=274 (-10)	€26,274 / €165,184
	31-3 April	Barclays Kenya Open	Muthaiga GC, Nairobi, Kenya	Michiel Bothma, RSA	66-67-69-68=270 (-14)	€30,400 / €194,446
May	5-8	ALLIANZ Challenge de France	Golf Disneyland, Paris, France	Nicolas Meitinger,** GER	71-63-67-68=269 (-15)	€24,000 / €150,000
	12-15	Mugello Tuscany Open	Poggio dei Medici GC, Scarperia, Florence, Italy	Anthony Snobeck, FRA	71-69-65-67=272 (-12)	€24,000 / €151,305
	19 - 22	Madeira Islands Open*	Porto Santo Golfe, Madeira, Portugal	Michael Hoey, NIR	72-68-67-71=278 (-10)	€116,660 / €702,097
	26-29	Telenet Trophy	Royal Waterloo GC, La Marache Course, Lasne, Belgium	Andrew Tampion, AUS	70-72-72-66=280 (-8)	€25,600 / €161,824
Jun	2-5	Kärnten Golf Open presented by Mazda	GC Klagenfurt-Seltenheim, Klagenfurt, Austria	Edouard Dubois, FRA	70-67-65-63=265 (-23)	€25,600 / €163,392
	9-12	ALLIANZ Open Cotes d'Armor Bretagne	Golf Blue Green de Pléneuf Val André, Le Val André, France	Phillip Archer, ENG	69-67-61-76 = 273 (-7)	€24,000 / €152,475
	16-19	SAINT-OMER OPEN presented by Neuflize OBC *	Aa St Omer GC, Lumbres, France	Matthew Zions, AUS	68-72-67-69=276 (-8)	€100,000 / €606,237
	23-26	Scottish Hydro Challenge	Macdonald Spey Valley GC, Aviemore, Scotland	Edouard Dubois, FRA	67-69-66-69=271 (-13)	€35,200 / €220,660
	30-3 July	The Princess by Schüco	Lakes Course, PGA of Sweden National, Bara, Sweden	Ricardo Santos, POR	73-68-65-66=272 (-16)	€32,000 / €203,300
July	7-10	Acaya Open 2011	Acaya Golf Resort, Lecce, Puglia, Italy	Jamie Moul, ENG	65-71-71-65=272 (-8)	€25,600 / €162,240
	14-17	Credit Suisse Challenge	Golf Sempachersee, Hildisrieden, Switzerland	Benjamin Hebert, FRA	67-67-67-71=272 (-12)	€24,000 / €154,125
	21-24	English Challenge	Stoke by Nayland Hotel, Golf & Spa, Colchester, England	Benjamin Hebert, FRA	71-66-69-70=276 (-12)	€25,600 / €161,392
Aug	11-14	Norwegian Challenge	Hauger Golf Klubb, Slattum, Norway	Andrea Pavan**, ITA	70-71-68-70=279 (-9)	€28,000 / €179,462
	17-20	ECCO Tour Championship hosted by Thomas Björn & Mercedes-Benz	Lübker Golf Resort, Nimtofte, Denmark	Daniel Denison^^, ENG	73-66-69=208 (-8)	€25,600 / €162,640
	24-27	Rolex Trophy	Golf Club de Genève, Geneva, Switzerland	Benjamin Hebert, FRA	66-65-71-67=269 (-19)	€24,400 / €190,240
Sep	8-11	Kazakhstan Open	Nurtau GC, Almaty, Kazakhstan	Tommy Fleetwood, ENG	68-69-66-70=273 (-15)	€64,000 / €406,600
	15-18	M2M Russian Challenge Cup	Tseleevo Golf & Polo Club, Moscow, Russia	Sam Little, ENG	74-69-66=277 (-11)	€40,000 / €252,175
	22-25	ALLIANZ Golf Open Grand Toulouse	Golf de Toulouse-Seilh, Seilh, France	Sam Little, ENG	66-68-66-68=268 (-16)	€25,600 / €162,240
	29-2 Oct	Fred Olsen Challenge de España	Tecina Golf, La Gomera, Canary Islands, Spain	Matthew Baldwin**, ENG	63-67-65-68=263 (-21)	€24,000 / €152,475
Oct	6-9	ALLIANZ Golf Open de Lyon	Golf du Gouverneur, Monthieux, France	Julien Quesne, FRA	66-67-67-68=268 (-16)	€24,000 / €153,825
	13-16	Roma Golf Open	Olgiata GC, Rome, Italy	Sam Little**, ENG	66-68-71-68=273 (-11)	€25,600 / €162,640
Nov	2-5	Apulia San Domenico Grand Final	San Domenico Golf, Puglia, Italy	Andrea Pavan, ITA	66-65-65-71=267 (-17)	€56,650 / €330,000

* Dual ranking event, for Ranking purposes the prize fund will be capped at €500,000

** denotes play-off

^^ Reduced to 54 holes due to inclement weather

THE 2011 EUROPEAN CHALLENGE TOUR RANKINGS

Pos	Name	Country	Played	€	Pos	Name	Country	Played	€
1	Tommy FLEETWOOD	(ENG)	(19)	148912.71	51	Benn BARHAM	(ENG)	(19)	33034.39
2	Andrea PAVAN	(ITA)	(19)	133052.10	52	Joaquin ESTEVEZ	(ARG)	(21)	32911.45
3	Sam LITTLE	(ENG)	(18)	130797.58	53	Bjorn ÅKESSON	(SWE)	(20)	32623.06
4	Ricardo SANTOS	(POR)	(22)	97516.00	54	Christophe BRAZILLIER	(FRA)	(22)	32005.92
5	Benjamin HEBERT	(FRA)	(15)	91293.17	55	Colm MORIARTY	(IRL)	(15)	31139.52
6	Daniel DENISON	(ENG)	(21)	86897.60	56	Daniel VANCSIK	(ARG)	(18)	30687.70
7	Federico COLOMBO	(ITA)	(20)	81833.67	57	Maximilian KIEFFER	(GER)	(20)	29950.17
8	Jamie MOUL	(ENG)	(20)	80771.00	58	Pierre RELECOM	(BEL)	(16)	29604.50
9	Jorge CAMPILLO	(ESP)	(22)	80040.63	59	Adrien BERNADET	(FRA)	(23)	29544.56
10	Matthew BALDWIN	(ENG)	(23)	76971.75	60	Gary LOCKERBIE	(ENG)	(20)	29111.50
11	Edouard DUBOIS	(FRA)	(22)	75623.37	61	James HEATH	(ENG)	(20)	27818.17
12	Simon THORNTON	(IRL)	(12)	74711.71	62	Anders Schmidt HANSEN	(DEN)	(20)	26787.29
13	Julien QUESNE	(FRA)	(24)	74026.92	63	Roland STEINER	(AUT)	(13)	26457.00
14	Craig LEE	(SCO)	(24)	73792.46	64	Sion E BEBB	(WAL)	(18)	26079.64
15	Andrew JOHNSTON	(ENG)	(10)	70987.07	65	Alastair FORSYTH	(SCO)	(9)	25684.50
16	Sam WALKER	(ENG)	(14)	67584.00	66	Garry HOUSTON	(WAL)	(21)	25477.32
17	Charles-Edouard RUSSO	(FRA)	(22)	67191.69	67	Charlie FORD	(ENG)	(21)	25035.00
18	Pelle EDBERG	(SWE)	(14)	66282.21	68	Chris PAISLEY	(ENG)	(10)	24926.29
19	Chris GANE	(ENG)	(19)	64487.67	69	Olly WHITELEY	(ENG)	(9)	24646.00
20	Alessandro TADINI	(ITA)	(22)	62629.99	70	Andreas HARTØ	(DEN)	(7)	24076.00
21	Anthony SNOBECK	(FRA)	(25)	61828.52	71	Jordi GARCIA	(ESP)	(17)	23768.18
22	Florian PRAEGANT	(AUT)	(19)	61725.17	72	Andrea PERRINO	(ITA)	(20)	22724.04
23	José-Filipe LIMA	(POR)	(17)	61291.56	73	Mikael LUNDBERG	(SWE)	(15)	22310.46
24	Branden GRACE	(RSA)	(21)	60241.83	74	Andrew MCARTHUR	(SCO)	(13)	21871.71
25	Andrew MARSHALL	(ENG)	(13)	59698.00	75	Matthew CRYER	(ENG)	(20)	21626.31
26	Matthew SOUTHGATE	(ENG)	(22)	58560.92	76	Michael LORENZO-VERA	(FRA)	(13)	21336.00
27	Jamie ELSON	(ENG)	(7)	55931.00	77	Baptiste CHAPELLAN	(FRA)	(16)	20664.79
28	Chris LLOYD	(ENG)	(20)	55183.50	78	Ben EVANS	(ENG)	(20)	20279.60
29	Peter GUSTAFSSON	(SWE)	(19)	54829.86	79	Jack DOHERTY	(SCO)	(21)	20276.46
30	Knut BORSHEIM	(NOR)	(13)	53158.50	80	André BOSSERT	(SUI)	(14)	19963.38
31	Julien GUERRIER	(FRA)	(18)	52389.93	81	Agustin DOMINGO	(ESP)	(14)	19724.16
32	Steven TILEY	(ENG)	(18)	51220.68	82	Andrea MAESTRONI	(ITA)	(11)	19643.33
33	Victor RIU	(FRA)	(22)	50505.33	83	Gavin DEAR	(SCO)	(21)	19457.65
34	Bernd RITTHAMMER	(GER)	(21)	48891.10	84	Jamie MCLEARY	(SCO)	(11)	18786.25
35	Espen KOFSTAD	(NOR)	(23)	47996.49	85	Matteo DELPODIO	(ITA)	(20)	17447.16
36	Chris DOAK	(SCO)	(20)	47895.83	86	Joakim LAGERGREN	(SWE)	(13)	16937.30
37	Phillip ARCHER	(ENG)	(20)	47483.26	87	Jason PALMER	(ENG)	(20)	15825.57
38	Nicolas MEITINGER	(GER)	(22)	46835.32	88	Pablo DEL GROSSO	(ARG)	(20)	15411.86
39	Andrew TAMPION	(AUS)	(17)	46180.00	89	Carl SUNESON	(ESP)	(13)	15203.00
40	Martin ERLANDSSON	(SWE)	(17)	43707.64	90	Mads VIBE-HASTRUP	(DEN)	(16)	15018.75
41	François DELAMONTAGNE	(FRA)	(13)	41472.48	91	James HEPWORTH	(ENG)	(16)	14449.33
42	Tyrone FERREIRA	(RSA)	(17)	41234.00	92	Jurrian VAN DER VAART	(NED)	(19)	14314.33
43	Lasse JENSEN	(DEN)	(23)	40687.52	93	Leif WESTERBERG	(SWE)	(17)	14150.50
44	Lloyd KENNEDY	(ENG)	(21)	39142.33	94	Tom WHITEHOUSE	(ENG)	(16)	13283.21
45	Michiel BOTHMA	(RSA)	(18)	39111.07	95	Stuart DAVIS	(ENG)	(8)	13133.50
46	Klas ERIKSSON	(SWE)	(20)	36389.35	96	Sebi GARCIA	(ESP)	(7)	12632.14
47	Daniel BROOKS	(ENG)	(23)	36316.50	97	Wil BESSELING	(NED)	(19)	12578.21
48	Sam HUTSBY	(ENG)	(20)	36162.50	98	Francis VALERA	(ESP)	(15)	12431.00
49	Callum MACAULAY	(SCO)	(20)	34209.33	99	Julien GRILLON	(FRA)	(17)	12283.00
50	Matt FORD	(ENG)	(20)	33995.44	100	Julien CLÉMENT	(SUI)	(16)	12141.25

Martin Kaymer - January and Nov/Dec

Paul Lawrie - March

Charl Schwartzel - April

Rory McIlroy - June

THE 2011 RACE TO DUBAI EUROPEAN TOUR GOLFER OF THE MONTH AWARDS

The Race to Dubai European Tour Golfer of the Month Awards are presented throughout the year followed by an Annual Award. The winners receive an engraved alms dish and a jeroboam of Moët & Chandon champagne

GOLFER OF THE YEAR WINNERS

2010	Martin Kaymer and Graeme McDowell	1997	Colin Montgomerie
2009	Lee Westwood	1996	Colin Montgomerie
2008	Padraig Harrington	1995	Colin Montgomerie
2007	Padraig Harrington	1994	Ernie Els
2006	Paul Casey	1993	Bernhard Langer
2005	Michael Campbell	1992	Sir Nick Faldo
2004	Vijay Singh	1991	Severiano Ballesteros
2003	Ernie Els	1990	Sir Nick Faldo
2002	Ernie Els	1989	Sir Nick Faldo
2001	Retief Goosen	1988	Severiano Ballesteros
2000	Lee Westwood	1987	Ian Woosnam
1999	Colin Montgomerie	1986	Severiano Ballesteros
1998	Lee Westwood	1985	Bernhard Langer

George O'Grady and Luke Donald - February and May

Darren Clarke - July

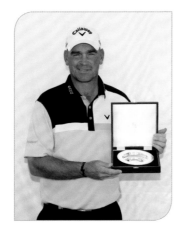

Thomas Björn - August

Michael Hoey - September

Sergio Garcia - October

Paul Casey - January

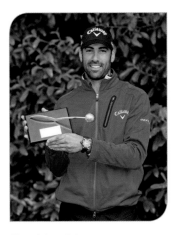

Alvaro Quiros - February

David Horsey - March

Matteo Manassero - April

THE 2011 EUROPEAN TOUR SHOT OF THE MONTH AWARDS

The European Tour Shot of the Month Awards are presented throughout the year followed by an Annual Award

SHOT OF THE YEAR WINNERS

2010	Graeme McDowell	
2009	Rafa Echenique	
2008	Padraig Harrington	
2007	Angel Cabrera	
2006	Paul Casey	
2005	Paul McGinley	
2004	David Howell	
2003	Fredrik Jacobson	

Rory McIlroy and Keith Waters - June, July and December

Luke Donald - May

Thomas Björn - August

Michael Hoey - September

Miguel Angel Jiménez - October

Martin Kaymer - November

European Tour Properties – World Class Venues

Le Golf National, the Host Venue for The 2018 Ryder Cup in France, and Terre Blanche Golf Club in Provence to the south of the country, have become European Tour Destinations and members of the network of world class venues operated under The European Tour Properties banner.

Le Golf National - The Albatros, Hole 18

In 2009, European Tour Properties announced London Golf Club in Kent, England, as the first European Tour Destination. London Golf Club is well known as the outstanding host venue of The European Open in both 2008 and 2009 and for having previously hosted several European Senior Tour events.

Le Golf National, situated on the outskirts of Versailles near Paris, is well established as the home of the Alstom Open de France and, following the historic announcement in May 2011, that France will host The 2018

Ryder Cup, it will become only the second Continental venue – following Club de Golf Valderrama, Spain, in 1997 – to host the biennial event when the 42nd edition between Europe and the United States unfolds there.

The Albatros Championship Course, globally recognised as an impressive 'stadium' course and possessing a perfect strategic fit for The European Tour, sits in the flatland region of Guyancourt which surrounds the historic Chateau of Versailles, once home to Louis XIV, and comprises vast undulating

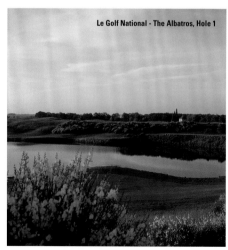

Le Golf National - The Albatros, Hole 1

fairways dotted with large and small water hazards and innumerable links-style bunkers.

Terre Blanche, situated in the hills of Provence and close to the French Riviera, is a world class golf resort with a five-star hotel and spa and an outstanding golf academy. Featuring two 18-hole, par 72 Championship courses – Le Riou and Le Château – designed by former Ryder Cup golfer Dave Thomas, the venue has preserved existing reliefs and melds harmoniously into the surrounding landscape. Le Riou features rolling contours and fairways which wend through pine and oak-lined hills and valleys with inspirational views of Medieval Provençal villages and the Southern Alps. Le Château, the more demanding of the two courses and stretching 6,616 metres (7,235 yards), rewards players for precision and distance and is made all the more challenging by many spectacular water hazards.

David MacLaren, Director of Property and Venue Development of The European Tour, said: "The existence and development of European Tour Properties is founded on strong partnerships and prior to The 2018 Ryder Cup announcement, the Tour had already forged a long-term relationship with Le Golf National where 19 editions of the Alstom Open de France have been played.

"European Tour Destinations will all be world class venues, offering a comprehensive range of facilities and services to members and their guests with their identity closely aligned to The European Tour, and we were delighted to welcome Terre Blanche alongside London Golf Club, Belek Golf Club and Le Golf National. All European Tour Destinations will be uniquely positioned to host tournaments on The European Tour International Schedule in addition to the Senior and

Terre Blanche - Le Riou, Hole 6

Challenge Tours and the Qualifying School."

The European Tour Properties network also comprises a select number of European Tour Courses located across Europe, providing golfers with a range of outstanding playing opportunities. Each and every one is regarded as being among the highest quality venues in their respective countries. This is emphasised by the current portfolio of European Tour Courses which comprises Vanajanlinna Golf and Country Club, Finland; Estonian Golf and Country Club, host venue of the European Qualifier for the Omega Mission Hills World Cup; Fleesensee Golf and Country Club, Germany, host venue for the Qualifying School Stage 1; PGA Catalunya Resort, Spain, host venue of The European Tour Qualifying School Finals; Quinta do Lago, Portugal; and Kungsängen, Sweden. Many of these venues regularly feature in Golf World magazine's Top 100 European Courses.

London Golf Club - International, Hole 5

Meanwhile London Golf Club, which successfully hosted GOLF LIVE in May 2011, also unveiled plans for a new five star hotel and spa. The proposed 130-bedroomed luxury hotel and leisure development will complement the venue's two existing Jack Nicklaus-designed signature courses and will bring to fruition the vision for a world class golf venue just 20 miles south east of central London.

Mitchell Platts

PGA Catalunya Resort

Estonian G&CC

Fleesensee G&CC

Kungsängen

Linna Golf

Quinta do Lago

Honorary Life Membership of The European Tour

Rory McIlroy and Darren Clarke were confirmed as the 39th and 40th recipients of one of the most coveted awards in sport – Honorary Life Membership of The European Tour – when they were presented with their silver money clips by George O'Grady, the Chief Executive of The European Tour and Ireland's Taioseach Enda Kenny, following another sensational summer for Northern Ireland in the Major Championships.

L-R: George O'Grady, Darren Clarke, Rory McIlroy and Enda Kenny

First McIlroy claimed victory in the 111th United States Open at Congressional Country Club, Bethesda, Maryland, and then Clarke captured The 140th Open Championship at Royal St Georges, Sandwich.

"Rory's victory in the US Open was the complete performance and remarkable for someone so young, while Darren's win in his 20th attempt in The Open only a month later was simply thrilling," said O'Grady. "Both are strong supporters of The European Tour and we were delighted, of course, to also acknowledge

a truly magnificent period for golf in Northern Ireland following Graeme McDowell's US Open triumph in 2010."

Charl Schwartzel had earlier in the year, following his win in the Masters Tournament, earned Membership of this exclusive club while at the same time consummating an historic 'Grand Slam' for European Tour Members following the victories in 2010 by McDowell (US Open), Louis Oosthuizen (The Open Championship) and Martin Kaymer (US PGA Championship).

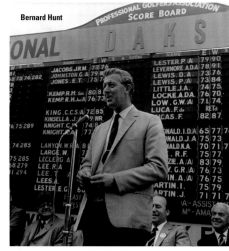

Bernard Hunt

L-R: George O'Grady, Charl Schwartzel, Retief Goosen and Louis Oosthuizen

John Jacobs

McDowell, Oosthuizen and Kaymer had been honoured when, together, they received their silver Honorary Life Membership and money clips from O'Grady at a special presentation in the Jumeirah Golf Estates clubhouse ahead of the 2010 Dubai World Championship presented by DP World.

Six months later, the quartet stood shoulder to shoulder at the glittering Players' Awards Dinner hosted by The European Tour on the eve of the BMW PGA Championship in May 2011, before Schwartzel was presented with his silver money clip.

George O'Grady and Tom Watson

L-R: Martin Kaymer, Graeme McDowell, Louis Oosthuizen and George O'Grady

O'Grady, joined on the stage by Oosthuizen and Retief Goosen – who received Honorary Life Membership in 2001 following the first of his two US Open triumphs – said: "It is a great privilege to honour Charl in this way with the highest award we as a Tour can bestow, and even more appropriate that he receives his Membership card in the distinguished company of two fellow Life Members and Major Champions – Retief and Louis.

"We were all delighted at The European Tour to see him win the Masters Tournament and ensure that all four Major titles were held by members of our Tour. We congratulated Graeme, the first European to win the US Open since Tony

Jacklin 40 years earlier, Martin Kaymer, the second German player to receive Honorary Life Membership after Bernhard Langer and Louis, who followed in the footsteps of his fellow countrymen Bobby Locke, Gary Player, Ernie Els, Retief Goosen and Trevor Immelman by winning a Major.

"So to be able present Charl with his Honorary Life Membership in their

company without question ratifies one of the most significant moments in the history of The European Tour and one which makes us all very proud in terms of our progress since the birth of the Tour itself in 1971."

John Jacobs, the founding father of The European Tour, joined Bernard Hunt and Dai Rees in becoming, in 1978, the first Honorary Life Members of The European

Dai Rees

Tony Jacklin and Seve Ballesteros